American Politics

IN THE TWENTIETH CENTURY

Crowell Source Readers in American History

DAVID BRODY, *General Editor*

The purpose of this series is to provide students of American history
with a means for approaching key problems through the evaluation of
the historical evidence. Each of the volumes in the series concentrates
on several major issues relating to one area of American history. The
editors have chosen documents that focus on those issues in an
immediate way and from a variety of contemporary standpoints.
Each section contains a solid body of evidence for the study of the
topic being covered. Introductory essays that set the issues in their
historical context are included in each volume and each section is
preceded by a headnote that relates each document to the theme of
the section. The objective of this series will be fulfilled if the student
is enabled to think independently about the issues contained in these
volumes. The titles in the series are *American Foreign Relations in the
Twentieth Century*, edited by Manfred Jonas; *American Thought in
the Twentieth Century*, edited by David Van Tassel; *The American
South in the Twentieth Century*, edited by Robert L. Brandfon; *Industrial
America in the Twentieth Century*, edited by David Brody; *Urban
America in the Twentieth Century*, edited by Milton Spiezman;
and *American Politics in the Twentieth Century*, edited by John
Braeman.

American Politics

IN THE TWENTIETH CENTURY

Documents Selected and Edited by

JOHN BRAEMAN

The University of Nebraska

Thomas Y. Crowell Company / *New York* / *Established 1834*

Contents

Introduction

PART I / *The Beginnings of Progressivism*

1 Lincoln Steffens on "The Shame of the Cities"   20
2 Robert M. La Follette and the "Wisconsin Idea"   32
3 David Graham Phillips on "The Treason of the Senate"   45
4 The Progressive Impulse   55

PART II / *Progressivism at High Tide*

5 T.R. and the Square Deal   74
6 Theodore Roosevelt and the New Nationalism   79
7 Woodrow Wilson and the New Freedom   90
8 Wilson and the High Tide of Progressivism   100

PART III / *The 1920's*

9 Warren G. Harding and the Return to Normalcy   108
10 Herbert Hoover: Prophet of the "New Era"   111
11 What Happened to Progressivism in the Twenties?   119
12 Al Smith and the Clash of Cultures   130
13 Herbert Hoover and the Great Depression   131

PART IV / *The New Deal*

14 F.D.R. Reassures the Country   142
15 Thunder on the Right   147

16 Thunder on the Left   149
17 The Second New Deal   157
18 The New Deal at High Tide   166
19 The End of the New Deal   171

PART V / *Post-World War II America*

20 Harry S Truman and the Fair Deal   180
21 McCarthyism   191
22 Dwight D. Eisenhower and Modern Republicanism   194
23 The Eisenhower Years—A Critical Appraisal   196
24 John F. Kennedy and the New Frontier   201
25 Barry Goldwater and the New Conservatism   209
26 Lyndon Johnson and the Great Society   218
27 More Than Legal Equality Is Required   227
28 The Problem Before Us   236

Introduction

AMERICAN politics in the twentieth century has revolved around three major questions—"Who should control the government?" "For what purpose?" and "For whose benefit?" The struggle over the answers to these questions has taken, and is taking, place at all levels of the federal system. But as industrialization and technology diminished the significance of local and state boundaries, attention more and more focused upon the federal government. Nor did the contest take place solely within the political arena. Since both federal and state governments operated under written constitutions delimiting their powers, the courts became in many instances the final arbiter of the constitutionality —and thus indirectly of the wisdom—of a given policy. In the first two outbursts of reform activity that marked the twentieth century—the progressive movement and the New Deal—the judiciary stood as a barrier against legislative experimentation. In the years since World War II, the courts have often taken the lead in areas where the legislatures and Congress were unwilling or unable to act.

The progressive movement of the first two decades of the twentieth century was not an organized movement with a single, unified program. What historians have lumped together under this rubric was several different movements taking place roughly simultaneously and with some, but far from complete, overlapping of personnel and constituencies. Yet beneath the differences there was an underlying unity. The archetypical progressive belonged to the middle class. Today nearly everyone belongs to the middle

1

class; at the turn of the century, the term had a more restricted application. When men spoke of the middle class they had in mind the white Anglo-Saxon Protestant independent business and professional man and the more prosperous farmer.

Despite the prosperity of the time, this middle class felt threatened. One threat was the super-city with its largely alien and lower-class population and its "boss" rule. A second was the rise of the giant corporation and the growing bureaucratization of economic life. Big business did not merely threaten their status, but more directly their independence and even their livelihood. The independent fabricator of steel products who had to deal with the mammoth United States Steel Corporation did not have to read the muckraking journalists to be aware of the trust problem. The final, and perhaps most alarming, threat came from the left. The crisis of the 1890's had a lasting impact. The farmers' revolt, the march of Coxey's Army, and the bitter and bloody strikes appeared to a large part of middle-class America to be grim portents of social revolution. The rapid growth of labor unions and increasing Socialist strength after the turn of the century kept alive the anxieties generated in the 1890's.

In response, the middle class evolved its own distinctive political ethos with the neutral state as the keynote. Convinced that the excesses of the plutocracy were responsible for the threat from the left, the progressives called for the neutral state to step in and maintain an evenhanded justice to prevent the development of European-style class warfare. No man of the time more fully understood, or more eloquently articulated, this mood than Theodore Roosevelt. Therein lay the explanation for the tremendous appeal T.R. and his "Square Deal" had for his generation.

The first prerequisite for the implementation of this middle-class ethos was to make the government responsive to "the people." The movement to break the rule of the "boss" and restore popular government had its roots in the 1890's. Those years witnessed the beginning in the cities of the revolt against bossism that would reach flood tide in the next decade, while in the countryside the Populists made reform of the political machinery to make the government more responsive to the popular will one of their leading demands. In the 1890's, however, too many solid citizens were too frightened by what they regarded as impending social upheaval to support measures which proposed tinkering with the governmental machinery. But with the return of prosperity and the relaxation of the tension that had marked the 1890's, the popular government movement took on renewed impetus. Muckraking articles about corruption at municipal, state, and national levels focused public attention on the betrayal of the people on behalf of "the interests" by their supposed representatives. The result was the wide adoption of a host of institutional gimmicks—the direct primary, the secret ballot, the referendum, initiative, and recall, and popular elections of United States senators—to guarantee popular rule.

Though the reformers of the time had a ready answer—"the people"—to the question "Who should rule?", the answer to the questions "For what purpose?" and "For whose benefit?" proved more difficult and divisive. In many cities, the leaders of the reform forces were upper- and upper-middle-class business and professional men who wished, through adoption of the city manager or commission form of government, city-wide elections instead of by ward, and civil service requirements to curb the excessive political influence of lower- and lower-middle-class elements and promote administrative efficiency and bureaucratic rationalization. Too often, "good government" came to mean no more than keeping taxes low and curbing such un-American vices as drinking, Sabbath-breaking, gambling, and prostitution. But there were municipal reformers of the Tom Johnson stripe who envisaged the revitalized city governments as positive agencies for promoting the health, welfare, and happiness of their citizens. The same division appeared at the state level. There were the genteel reformers like Charles Evans Hughes in New York whose main aim was the promotion of administrative efficiency and moral uplift. On the other hand, Robert M. La Follette put through in Wisconsin a broader and more positive program of reform that he called the "Wisconsin idea."

Nor were the progressives of a single mind on the question of "big business." Those led by Theodore Roosevelt—whom I have called the "modernists"—equated bigness with efficiency, regarded consolidation and combination as inevitable and even de-

sirable, and eschewed indiscriminate trust-busting. They admitted
that abuses had accompanied the rise of big business, but their
slogan was regulation, not destruction. And because of the nation-
wide scope of modern business, they insisted that only the federal
government, not the individual states, could do the job. T.R.
tended to be somewhat vague about what he meant by regulation.
At first, his favorite remedy was publicity—at times he went so
far as to imply that fear of the public opprobrium which would
follow exposure would be sufficient to deter would-be malefactors
—coupled with a judicious application of the Sherman Antitrust
law in individual cases of persistent wrongdoing. Later, in his
maturing progressivism, he appeared to favor establishment of a
powerful administrative body, along the lines of the Federal
Trade Commission, to exercise continuous supervision over businesses engaged in interstate commerce.

On the other hand were those progressives—the "tradition-
alists"—who wished to break up "monopoly" and restore free competition. The intellectual spokesmen for this position, future Supreme Court Justice Louis D. Brandeis, denied that big business
was efficient or inevitable; monopoly was the result of unfair competitive practices. Given the immense economic power wielded
by the giant corporations, attempts at regulation were not merely
futile, but dangerous. The regulatory agencies would end up controlled by those whom they were supposedly regulating. In the
1912 election, Woodrow Wilson took this position, and his program—named by him the "New Freedom"—called for government intervention to break the grip of monopoly, open the
channels of mobility to the little man on the make, and maintain
fair and thus free competition as the primary regulator of the
market place.

Although there were stalwart conservatives who saw no grounds
for government intervention of any kind, the simplistic view of
the politics of this era as a struggle of "the interests" versus "the
people" is misleading. In the first place, many businessmen—the
railroads, for example—welcomed government regulation, though
not always the form that regulation took, to eliminate cut-throat
competition and promote stability. Second, the more sophisticated big businessmen—such as J. P. Morgan partner and Pro-

gressive Party leader George W. Perkins—saw federal regulation
as a safeguard against harassment by a multitude of individual
states and a shield against the ever-present danger of antitrust
suits. Most importantly, businessmen were badly divided within
their own house. Much of what has been termed reform was simply a question of whose ox was gored. Thus, in the fight over railroad regulation, the shippers were aligned against the carriers
and the less-favored localities against the more favored. And
although the middle western "insurgents" in the fight over the
Payne-Aldrich tariff (1909)—the single most important issue in
splitting the Republican party—claimed to be speaking for the
consumer everywhere, the crux of their grievance was that the
measure benefited the heavily protected industries of the North-
east at the expense of their own constituents.

Not only did progressives differ on the problem of big business,
but also on how to deal with the threat from the left. Where
unions were powerful and/or tinged with radicalism, the progressives tended to be anti-union; but probably a majority accepted unions so long as they were peaceful, law-abiding, and not
too strong. At their strongest, however, the unions included a frac-
tion of the total working force, and that mainly among the more
skilled workers. What about the millions outside union ranks?
After the turn of the century, there developed an increasingly
vocal social justice movement—led by an alliance of upper-class
philanthropists and the new professional social workers—calling
for legislation to protect those who because of sex, age, or lack of
bargaining power could not take care of themselves. Here was another line of division within progressivism. In New York, for example, the advocates of social justice gained the support of
"machine" politicians who depended on lower-class votes, while
many "good government" reformers opposed such legislation as
contrary to their ethos of the neutral state.

The years of the Roosevelt administration saw the first harvest
of the progressive ferment at the national level—the revitalization
of the Sherman Antitrust Act; the Elkins anti-rebating law (1903);
the establishment of the Bureau of Corporations (1903); the
Hepburn Act (1906) giving the Interstate Commerce Commission authority to fix maximum railroad rates; and the passage of

an effective meat inspection law and the Pure Food and Drug Act (1906).

Roosevelt hoped to see his reform program rounded out and consolidated under his successor, William Howard Taft. But Taft quickly lost the support of the progressive wing of the Republican Party, first by his refusal to back the move to clip the power of Speaker of the House Joseph G. Cannon, and then, more importantly, by his failure to support the insurgents in the battle over the Payne-Aldrich tariff. The Ballinger-Pinchot controversy over the administration's conservation policy and differences over the postal savings bank bill and railroad legislation made the split irreparable. The disaffected rallied behind T.R. in an attempt to defeat Taft for the Republican nomination in 1912. When the administration steamroller carried the day, Roosevelt, crying fraud and robbery, launched the Progressive Party to continue the battle for his "New Nationalism." The split in the G.O.P. ranks opened the door for the victory of Democratic nominee Woodrow Wilson.

At the start of his administration, Wilson appeared determined to hew to his limited program of the New Freedom, with its Jeffersonian credo of equal rights for all, special privileges for none. He skillfully pushed through Congress his first two major pieces of legislation—the Underwood-Simmons Tariff Act and the Federal Reserve Act—while standing firm against special legislation in behalf of labor or the farmer. But in 1914, he began to move away from the New Freedom and closer to Roosevelt's New Nationalism. The first sign of shift was his abandoning the effort to prohibit unfair competition by statute and his backing instead the establishment of a Federal Trade Commission with a broad-ranging, discretionary authority to deal with business malpractices. And in 1916, because of the exigencies of politics in that election year, he reversed himself on the question of social welfare legislation and gave his blessings to the Federal Farm Loan Act, a model workmen's compensation law for federal employees, and the Keating-Owen Child Labor Act. The Keating-Owen law, which barred child-made goods from interstate commerce, represented the boldest and most far-reaching affirmation of federal authority under the commerce power ever made by Congress—so much so that the Supreme Court, in a five-to-four decision in the case of *Hammer* v. *Dagenhart* (1918), declared the law unconstitutional. In the 1916 campaign, Wilson boasted that his administration had enacted into law nearly all the reforms demanded by the Progressive Party in 1912. This record, combined with the peace issue, brought him his narrow margin of victory.

But 1916 represented the high point of progressivism. The war diverted the nation's energies from further reform. Wilson's hopes of making the 1920 election "a great and solemn referendum" on the League of Nations were frustrated when both parties and both candidates—Democratic nominee James M. Cox as much as Republican standard-bearer Warren G. Harding—straddled the issue. The war-born resentments against the "ins" over high taxes, wartime shortages, rising prices, and increased governmental control over people's daily lives swept the Republicans to an overwhelming victory, and Harding entered the White House as the apostle of America's "return to normalcy." He rejected any government intervention to alleviate the business depression that marred the first years of his presidency—the business cycle would have to right itself. His Secretary of the Treasury, multimillionaire financier and industrialist Andrew W. Mellon, sponsored tax relief for those in the higher-income brackets, insisting that the resultant increased investment bringing more jobs would benefit the lower-income groups. The Fordney-McCumber tariff (1922) was the highest in the nation's history. The breaking of railroad shopmen's strike in 1922 revealed the administration's anti-labor bias. As their solution to the problems facing the nation's farmers, Harding and the two Republican Presidents that followed him encouraged voluntary self-help through cooperatives, but stood firm against any attempt to raise farm prices through government intervention.

Yet the Republican administrations of the 1920's were not simply a return to McKinleyism. The difference was epitomized in the leading spokesman of the "new era," Secretary of Commerce Herbert Hoover. Hoover was no admirer of old-fashioned unrestrained competition, which, in his judgment, was inefficient and wasteful. He was instead an advocate of voluntary cooperation among businessmen through trade associations to promote industry-wide stability and rationalization. He feared expansion and

extension of federal authority as a threat to that individual liberty
which was the genius of America, but he was no doctrinaire advocate of laissez-faire. The federal government had a positive
role to perform, a role that was twofold: first, to maintain equality of opportunity; second, to assist business in becoming more
efficient, gaining new markets and making bigger profits, because
the more business prospered the more the nation as a whole
would benefit.

If nothing succeeds like success, then the policies of the Republican administrations were successful—at least in the short
run. Although there were hidden weaknesses—the decade-long
farm depression, the lag of wages behind profits, the dependence
of the export trade upon continued American loans abroad, and
"sick" industries such as coal and textiles—the country as a whole
enjoyed boom times after 1922. Despite the exposure of the Harding administration scandals, Calvin Coolidge won the election in
1924 handily. The businessman regained his place as America's
culture hero, and the more optimistic spokesmen for the "new
era" foresaw the final conquest of poverty.

In this atmosphere, reform languished. The single most important factor in the weakness of progressivism in the 1920's was the
desertion of the bulk of its former middle-class supporters. The
legislation of the progressive era, coupled with the public service
facade adopted by large corporations in the 1920's, removed or
softened their grievances against big business, while the growth
of unions, the rash of strikes in 1919, and the "red scare" had
heightened their anxiety about the thrust from below. Intensify-
ing this trend was the decline of the old independent middle class
and the rise of a new white-collar class dependent upon, and
identifying with, the large corporation. The bureaucratization of
business provided vast new opportunities for this white-collar
class in the 1920's, thus strengthening its allegiance to the status
quo.

With the loss of its middle-class constituency, reform had to
find a new mass base among the depressed farmers and urban
working class. But the 1920's were a period of transition between
the old progressivism and the new liberalism. The program of
the most ambitious reform movement of the decade, Robert M.

La Follette's Progressive Party of 1924, was more an echo of the battles of the past than a harbinger of the future. There were, however, developments that prepared the ground for the New Deal. The demands by farm groups for federal intervention to raise agricultural prices were a milestone in the acceptance of the doctrine that the government had a duty to assist the economically depressed. Social workers were drawing up comprehensive programs of social insurance that would come to fruition in the New Deal. And an occasional figure like New York Congressman Fiorello La Guardia, with his efforts to build a farmer-labor coalition, foreshadowed the new political configurations of the 1930's.

In a larger sense, however, progressivism had not so much died in the 1920's as changed its direction. At bottom, the movement was an attempt to preserve traditional American middle-class values in a rapidly industrializing and urbanizing world. And the twenties thus witnessed a last convulsive effort to safeguard these traditional values—and the hegemony of the old-stock Americans who held them—from the enemies without and the even more dangerous enemies within. The keystones of this attempt were national prohibition and immigration restriction. The credo of the Ku Klux Klan was but the more extreme expression of sentiments held by millions of old-stock Americans.

The presidential election of 1928 was not simply a political contest but a clash of different cultures. Al Smith's eagerness to assure the voters of his soundness on economic questions unwittingly served to accentuate the cleavage over more basic values. Everything about Smith was anathema to the defenders of traditional Americanism—his Roman Catholicism, his "wetness," his New York manner and accent. But these were the very things that made him the hero of the northern big-city masses. Although Smith was overwhelmingly defeated by Herbert Hoover, Democratic gains in the big cities marked the beginning of a political realignment that the Depression and New Deal would solidify.

When the Depression struck, President Hoover refused to sit back like his predecessors and wait for the business cycle to right itself. The federal government had a positive function to perform, and that was to assist business to overcome the crisis through voluntary cooperation. Hoover's tragedy was his intellectual rigidity, his sticking adamantly to his limited program long after voluntary business cooperation had proved a failure. The pressure of events forced him to adopt a larger measure of governmental intervention than he had foreseen. The most notable examples were the establishment in January, 1932, of the Reconstruction Finance Corporation to make loans to railroads, banks, and other financial institutions, and the Emergency Relief and Construction Act of July, 1932, authorizing the R.F.C. to make loans to the states to finance unemployment relief and public works. But Hoover's deep-seated hostility to big government and commitment to balancing the budget led him to resist the growing demands for more vigorous federal action.

With Hoover the popular scapegoat for the Depression, Democratic nominee Franklin D. Roosevelt won a sweeping victory in the 1932 elections. F.D.R. did not enter the White House with a ready-made program at hand. Rather, the New Deal emerged as a series of largely *ad hoc* measures, often conflicting and even contradictory. Roosevelt had a set of basic principles in which he believed—he believed in democracy; he was a humanitarian who believed in the duty of the government to assist the unfortunate and underprivileged; and he was committed to preserving the capitalist system. Yet he was not doctrinaire when it came to questions of means. As a master political strategist, he acted as broker in picking and choosing among, conciliating, and compromising the conflicting pressures that flowed in upon the White House. There were wide differences over policy even among his closest advisors. Rexford G. Tugwell wanted over-all governmental planning in which the federal government would make the important economic decisions such as the allocation of resources, wages, and profits in terms of the larger national interest; Raymond Moley called for a friendly partnership between business and government, with business the more important partner; while the so-called Brandeisians favored the restoration of competition.

F.D.R.'s first task was to restore public confidence, and that was the keynote of his first inaugural address. Over the next two years Congress passed in rapid succession one measure after another to get the economy moving again and relieve distress—the Glass-

Steagall Banking Act of 1933, reforming the banking system; the Truth-in-Securities Act (1933) and the establishment of the Securities Exchange Commission (1934); an expanded public works program under the Public Works Administration and the Civil Works Administration; the Federal Emergency Relief Act, appropriating $500,000,000 for emergency relief of the unemployed; the Civilian Conservation Corps (1933); the Home Owners Loan Corporation (1933), created to refinance existing home mortgages, and the Federal Housing Authority (1934), to insure mortgages for new construction; monetary inflation through devaluation of the dollar in terms of gold and the Silver Purchase Act (1934); the Tennessee Valley Authority (1933); farm mortgage relief; and the Agricultural Adjustment Act (1933), to raise farm prices to parity levels by reducing the surplus.

The most ambitious attempt to promote recovery in this first phase of the New Deal was the National Industrial Recovery Act (1933). As a sop to organized labor and its champions, Section 7(a) guaranteed workers the right to bargain collectively and form unions of their own choosing. But the heart of the act was its provision for "industrial self-government" under federal supervision. There was to be a code for each industry—to be prepared by representatives from each business in the industry, labor, the consumer, and the government—having the force of law when approved by the National Recovery Administration. Unhappily, the workings of the act satisfied no one. In most industries, the representatives of the largest firms dominated the writing of the codes. Smaller businessmen resented the domination by big business, while big businessmen were aggrieved at the labor provisions of the law. Unionists found that Section 7(a) did not in practice fulfill their hopes, and consumers grumbled about higher prices. The Supreme Court resolved the problem by unanimously declaring the law unconstitutional in the Schechter case (1935).

By 1934, the political honeymoon that had marked the first phase of the New Deal was over. Having recovered from their panic, conservatives—organized in the American Liberty League—assailed the New Deal as creeping socialism. On the left were Upton Sinclair's EPIC (End Poverty in California) movement, Huey Long's "Share Our Wealth" movement, Father Coughlin's

radio attacks on the international bankers, and the growing
popularity of the Townsend Plan for old-age pensions for all unemployed persons over sixty. In response, Roosevelt moved to the
left in 1935 and 1936, years that saw the passage of a flood of
legislation aimed at recovery and reform: the Emergency Relief
Appropriation Act of 1935, with a record appropriation of nearly
five billion dollars for relief and public works for fiscal year
1935–1936, and the establishment of the Works Progress Administration under Harry Hopkins; the National Youth Administration
(1935); the Wagner National Labor Relations Act (1935); the
Social Security Act (1935); increased inheritance taxes and higher
income taxes in the upper brackets; the Banking Act of 1935,
strengthening the authority of the Federal Reserve Board over
the nation's banking system; the establishment of the Rural Electrification Administration (1935) to bring electricity to the
countryside; and the Public Utility Holding Company Act (1935),
requiring the break-up of the giant utilities empires of the 1920's.

In the 1936 campaign, the attacks of the Liberty League played
into Roosevelt's hands. Making his campaign one against the
"economic royalists," Roosevelt won an overwhelming victory.
The movement of reform appeared to be only beginning, but at
its seeming high point of strength, the New Deal began to run
out of steam. The first setback was the defeat of what hostile
newspapers called F.D.R.'s "court-packing bill." Angered by the
Supreme Court's repeated striking down of New Deal legislation,
Roosevelt asked in February, 1937, for authority to appoint an
additional Supreme Court Justice—up to a maximum of six—
whenever a sitting judge failed to retire within six months after
reaching age seventy. Conservatives were outraged, but even
many previously loyal supporters of the administration balked.
The opposition was bolstered by the Court's famous "switch in
time that saved nine" in upholding the Wagner and Social
Security Acts at the height of the struggle.

The rejection of the court plan and later the defeat of his
governmental reorganization proposal were serious blows to
F.D.R.'s prestige. The sharp economic recession that began late
in 1937 aggravated the situation, and the failure of Roosevelt's
attempted purge of Democratic dissidents in the 1938 congres-

sional primaries hastened the breakdown of party discipline. The increasingly bold opposition of Democratic conservatives, mostly Southerners, combined with the Republican gains of the 1938 elections, placed Congress under the control of a bipartisan conservative coalition. At the same time, foreign-policy questions increasingly divided the New Deal coalition. To gain conservative support for his foreign policy, Roosevelt more and more toned down his program of domestic reform to the extent that the only major piece of reform legislation passed after the 1936 election was the Fair Labor Standards Act (1938). Going far beyond the Keating-Owen Child Labor Act of 1916, the new law not only barred child-made goods from interstate commerce but also required a minimum wage of twenty-five cents an hour—to go up to forty cents in 1945—and a maximum work week of forty-four hours—to go down to forty hours in 1940—for *all* workers engaged in interstate commerce. And to show how much opinion —even judicial opinion—had changed since 1918, the Supreme Court, in a unanimous decision, explicitly overruled *Hammer* v. *Dagenhart* (1918) and upheld the new law in *United States* v. *Darby Lumber Co.* (1941).

The New Deal permanently changed the face of American politics. Although the United States still lagged behind most other major industrialized countries, the welfare state was here to stay. Thanks to the Wagner Act and the generally sympathetic attitude of the administration, labor unions grew rapidly to become a major countervailing force vis-à-vis business. Moreover, the New Deal extended and strengthened public control over business. At the same time, Roosevelt had saved capitalism from the capitalists. American capitalism was in far stronger shape at the end of his presidency than when he entered the White House. And finally, the New Deal had transformed the Democrats into the normal majority party. The Democratic coalition was composed of the "solid South," a large segment of middle-western farmers grateful for past favors and hopeful for continued governmental price supports, and the urban masses in the big cities. Democratic strength in the big cities was the result not simply of the New Deal's social and economic legislation but also of the party's recognition of ethnic minorities in patronage and office-holding. While the Republican Party—and the old-stock middle class that constituted its backbone—was reduced to minority status, the newer Americans came into their own under F.D.R. and achieved first-class political citizenship. The only sizable group not included was the Negroes. Although most Negroes in the 1930's switched from the Republican to the Democratic Party because they were poor and the Democrats were the party of the poor, Roosevelt treaded softly in the civil rights sphere lest he lose the support of the Southern wing of his party.

When the United States entered World War II in 1941, F.D.R. announced that "Dr. Win-the-War" would replace "Dr. New Deal" for the duration. After Roosevelt's death in May, 1945, his successor Harry S Truman took up the cudgels for a broad program of reform to carry forward the aims of the New Deal— extension of Social Security, an increase in the minimum wage, national health insurance, federal assistance for slum clearance, additional T.V.A.'s, a full employment bill, and continuance of wartime economic controls to ease the transition to peacetime. But his proposals were largely blocked by the bipartisan conservative majority in Congress. In 1946, the Republicans won majorities in both houses of Congress, and the new Congress even passed over Truman's veto the Taft-Hartley bill (1947) to curb the power of organized labor.

By the 1948 elections, the Democratic coalition appeared to be disintegrating. On the left, those dissatisfied with the administration's "get tough with Russia" policy rallied behind Henry A. Wallace and his Progressive Party. On the right, Southerners outraged by the Democratic Party's strong civil-rights plank supported J. Strom Thurmond of South Carolina and his Dixiecrat— or more formally, States' Rights Democratic—Party. But Truman, attacking the "do-nothing" Republican Congress and playing upon popular anxieties that the Republicans would attempt to roll back the gains of the New Deal era, won an upset victory over G.O.P nominee Thomas E. Dewey.

Yet Truman was only partially successful in overcoming congressional opposition to his "Fair Deal" program. Although he succeeded in obtaining a hike in the minimum wage, increased Social Security benefits and coverage, and the Housing Act of

1949, providing large sums for slum clearance and low-income housing, Congress turned down his requests for a Missouri Valley Authority, for repeal of the Taft-Hartley law, for adoption of the Brannan plan to maintain a "farm income standard," and for national health insurance.

Before the end of his second term, the chief executive found himself increasingly on the defensive. Republican charges of corruption embarrassed the administration, but its most serious weakness was an outgrowth of the Cold War. The Korean War heightened popular antagonism toward the Soviet Union, while the Rosenberg and Alger Hiss cases roused exaggerated fears about Communist subversion and infiltration at home. Sensing partisan advantage, the Republicans belabored the Truman administration for being "soft on Communism." In the early 1950's, Republican Senator Joseph R. McCarthy of Wisconsin ran amuck with lurid tales of Communist infiltration in the government and cries of twenty years of treason.

The 1952 and 1956 election triumphs of Dwight D. Eisenhower were more a testimony to his personal appeal than to the popularity of the Republican Party. The pro-business atmosphere of his administration was epitomized in the remark by Secretary of Defense Charles E. Wilson, the former president of General Motors, during the Senate committee hearings on his appointment, that he believed "what was good for our country was good for General Motors, and vice versa." Eisenhower stood forth as the champion of "modern Republicanism"—by which he meant acceptance of the reforms of the New Deal era, but restraint in the introduction of any new programs that would expand federal authority over private enterprise or unbalance the budget. This policy of consolidation proved highly popular with the majority of American voters after more than twenty years of depression, reform, and war.

In 1960, John F. Kennedy defeated Vice President Richard M. Nixon to become the first Roman Catholic in the White House— an indication of increased religious tolerance in the political sphere since the early part of the century. Despite his brave rhetoric of leading the country forward to conquer "New Frontiers," his major proposals—such as federal aid to education and health insurance for the aged under Social Security—were stymied by a hostile Congress. His successor Lyndon B. Johnson, taking advantage of the feelings of national guilt over the Kennedy assassination and utilizing to the full his skill in handling Congress, succeeded in pushing through the Civil Rights and Economic Opportunity Acts of 1964.

In the 1964 campaign, Republican nominee Barry Goldwater roused widespread anxieties that his triumph would mean turning the clock back and wiping out the gains achieved since 1933 and even that he might involve the country in a nuclear war. The result was an overwhelming Democratic victory. With large Democratic majorities in both houses of Congress, Johnson pushed forward with his "Great Society" program. The Eighty-ninth Congress compiled the most impressive record of reform legislation adopted since F.D.R.'s first administration—including Medicare, federal aid to education, the Voting Rights Act of 1965, and the Appalachia bill. But Republican gains in the 1966 congressional elections, the increasing cost of the Vietnam war, and a white "backlash" against Negro demands made the Ninetieth Congress more resistant to the administration's "war on poverty" proposals.

In the late 1960's, the questions that preoccupied Americans at the turn of the century remain with us. The question "Who should control the government?" is still in the process of being answered. Notwithstanding the tremendous shift of population to the cities and their suburbs, the rural and small-town-dominated state legislatures dragged their feet on redistricting. And since the malapportioned state legislatures drew the congressional district lines, the national House of Representatives had become increasingly unrepresentative. In response to the growing outcry, the Supreme Court in a series of cases beginning with *Baker* v. *Carr* (1962) laid down its one man, one vote rule. Despite the desperate efforts by die-hard supporters of rural and small-town dominance—led by Republican Senate leader Everett McKinley Dirksen of Illinois—to overturn the Court's ruling, reapportionment has moved swiftly ahead. But the chief beneficiaries have been not so much the core cities as their suburbs. The result has been a shift in political power to the new suburban middle class. This class—often of newer-stock background whose parents had voted Democratic—is largely satisfied with the status quo and hostile to attempts to rock the boat, from right or left. Its growing political importance has contributed to the rise of a new type of politics emphasizing image over substance, and a new type of politician whose television personality is more important than his program. The Kennedys were the first great practitioners of the art—but there are now a host of eager imitators.

The questions "For what purpose ought the government to act?" and "For whose benefit?" are also still in the process of being answered. The publication in 1963 of Michael Harrington's *The Other America: Poverty in the United States* stimulated a new awareness of the plight of America's poor and new proposals to relieve their distress. The resulting war on poverty has become inextricably intertwined with the question of the position of the Negro in American society. The years following World War II saw the first concerted drive since Reconstruction to assure the Negro first-class citizenship. Gunnar Myrdal's highly influential *An American Dilemma: The Negro Problem and Modern Democracy* (1944) had shown the inconsistency between the democratic ideals espoused by the United States in its fight against the Axis powers and the treatment of its Negro minority. At the same time, there was increasing militancy within the ranks of the Negroes themselves. The first breakthrough on the civil rights front came under the Truman administration, when the special Advisory Committee on Civil Rights recommended a permanent Fair Employment Practices Commission, federal anti-lynching and anti-poll-tax laws, abolition of the white primaries, and prohibition of segregation on public interstate transportation. It was the endorsement of most of the Committee's recommendations in the 1948 Democratic platform that precipitated the Dixiecrat revolt.

Despite Truman's victory, the Southern Democrats in the Senate—with the covert backing of many Northern Republicans—were able to block, by use of the filibuster, the passage of any civil rights legislation. In the absence of congressional action, Truman did what he could by executive orders—banning segregation in the armed forces and strengthening the civil rights section of the Justice Department. Given the impasse in the political arena, the Supreme Court took the lead in the civil rights battle. In *Brown* v. *Board of Education* (1954), Chief Justice Earl Warren, speaking for a unanimous court, outlawed segregated public education. While President Eisenhower was no enthusiast in the civil rights sphere, the pressure of events forced him to send federal troops into Little Rock, Arkansas, in September, 1957, to enforce federal court-ordered school desegregation and to support the moderate—or to be more accurate, modest—proposals to insure Negro voting rights embodied in the Civil Rights Acts of 1957 and 1960.

The next major legislation was enacted under Lyndon Johnson. The Civil Rights Act of 1964 prohibited race discrimination by either employers or unions and by hotels, restaurants, theaters, and other places of public accommodation, while the Voting Rights Act of 1965 authorized federal examiners to register Negro applicants throughout large parts of the South. Although with the adoption of these measures the battle for legal equality for the Negro had been largely won, legal equality was of scant benefit to the millions of Negroes trapped in poverty in the ghettos of the Northern cities and the rural South. In his address at Howard University on June 4, 1965, Johnson called for massive governmental assistance to help the Negro overcome the handicaps imposed by a century of discrimination and before that by slavery.

The response of Congress and the public at large remains to be seen. But the bloody riots that have rocked American cities from 1964 on underline the seriousness of the question for the future of the United States. And the question that faces the country is no less than whether the American tradition of orderly progress through law can survive. A new lawlessness—hiding behind the rhetoric of supposed high moral purpose—threatens the very foundation of American society.

PART I

The Beginning of Progressivism

PROGRESSIVISM as a political movement found expression first at the municipal level. The target was the corrupt alliance of the public service corporations, the political boss, and organized vice that held so many cities in its grip at the turn of the century. Nothing did more to focus public attention and indignation upon municipal evils than Lincoln Steffens' muckraking articles in *McClure's Magazine* during 1902–1903, which were published in book form in 1904 under the title *The Shame of the Cities* (Selection 1).

A similar fight took place at the state level. The most successful and imaginative of the state reformers was Robert M. La Follette, who made Wisconsin the model for progressives throughout the country (Selection 2).

Since modern business and technology were more and more diminishing the importance of state lines, progressivism inevitably went national. David Graham Phillips' sensational series in *Cosmopolitan Magazine* revealed in the United States Senate many of the same evils the reformers had found in the cities and state (Selection 3).

The first aim of the progressives was to restore popular government—to return control of their government to the people. But the institutional reforms adopted to achieve this goal were only means to a larger end—to subject big business to stricter government control in the public interest and to remedy the worst abuses and insecurities of modern industrial society (Selection 4).

1 / LINCOLN STEFFENS ON
"THE SHAME OF THE CITIES"

More than any other person, Lincoln Steffens started the wave of muckraking journalism with his six articles on municipal corruption and reform in St. Louis, Minneapolis, Pittsburgh, Philadelphia, Chicago, and New York, which appeared in McClure's Magazine *starting October, 1902. The following is from Steffens' introduction when the articles were brought together in book form under the title* The Shame of the Cities *(1904).*

. . . [These articles] were written with a purpose, they were published serially with a purpose, and they are reprinted now together to further that same purpose, which was and is—to sound for the civic pride of an apparently shameless citizenship.

There must be such a thing, we reasoned. All our big boasting could not be empty vanity, nor our pious pretensions hollow sham. American achievements in science, art, and business mean sound abilities at bottom, and our hypocrisy a race sense of fundamental ethics. Even in government we have given proofs of potential greatness, and our political failures are not complete; they are simply ridiculous. But they are ours. Not alone the triumphs and the statesmen, the defeats and the grafters also represent us, and just as truly. Why not see it so and say it?

Because, I heard, the American people won't "stand for" it. You may blame the politicians, or, indeed, any one class, but not all classes, not the people. Or you may put it on the ignorant foreign immigrant, or any one nationality, but not on all nationalities, not on the American people. But no one class is at fault, nor any one breed, nor any particular interest or group of interests.

SOURCE: Lincoln Steffens, *The Shame of the Cities* (New York: McClure Company, 1904), pp. 3–26.

The misgovernment of the American people is misgovernment by the American people.

When I set out on my travels, an honest New Yorker told me honestly that I would find that the Irish, the Catholic Irish, were at the bottom of it all everywhere. The first city I went to was St. Louis, a German city. The next was Minneapolis, a Scandinavian city, with a leadership of New Englanders. Then came Pittsburg, Scotch Presbyterian, and that was what my New York friend was. "Ah, but they are all foreign populations," I heard. The next city was Philadelphia, the purest American community of all, and the most hopeless. And after that came Chicago and New York, both mongrel-bred, but the one a triumph of reform, the other the best example of good government that I had seen. The "foreign element" excuse is one of the hypocritical lies that save us from the clear sight of ourselves.

Another such conceit of our egotism is that which deplores our politics and lauds our business. This is the wail of the typical American citizen. Now, the typical American citizen is the business man. The typical business man is a bad citizen; he is busy. If he is a "big business man" and very busy, he does not neglect, he is busy with politics, oh, very busy and very businesslike. I found him buying boodlers in St. Louis, defending grafters in Minneapolis, originating corruption in Pittsburg, sharing with bosses in Philadelphia, deploring reform in Chicago, and beating good government with corruption funds in New York. He is a self-righteous fraud, this big business man. He is the chief source of corruption, and it were a boon if he would neglect politics. But he is not the business man that neglects politics; that worthy is the good citizen, the typical business man. He too is busy, he is the one that has no use and therefore no time for politics. When his neglect has permitted bad government to go so far that he can be stirred to action, he is unhappy, and he looks around for a cure that shall be quick, so that he may hurry back to the shop. Naturally, too, when he talks politics, he talks shop. His patent remedy is quack; it is business.

"Give us a business man," he says ("like me," he means). "Let him introduce business methods into politics and government; then I shall be let alone to attend to my business."

There is hardly an office from United States Senator down to
Alderman in any part of the country to which the business man
has not been elected; yet politics remains corrupt, government
pretty bad, and the selfish citizen has to hold himself in readiness
like the old volunteer firemen to rush forth at any hour, in any
weather, to prevent the fire; and he goes out sometimes and he
puts out the fire (after the damage is done) and he goes back
to the shop sighing for the business man in politics. The business
man has failed in politics as he has in citizenship. Why?

Because politics is business. That's what's the matter with it.
That's what's the matter with everything—art, literature, religion,
journalism, law, medicine—they're all business, and all—as you
see them. Make politics a sport, as they do in England, or a pro-
fession, as they do in Germany, and we'll have—well, something
else than we have now—if we want it, which is another question.
But don't try to reform politics with the banker, the lawyer, and
the dry-goods merchant, for these are business men and there are
two great hindrances to their achievement of reform: one is that
they are different from, but no better than, the politicians; the
other is that politics is not "their line." There are exceptions both
ways. Many politicians have gone out into business and done
well (Tammany ex-mayors, and nearly all the old bosses of Philadelphia are prominent financiers in their cities), and business
men have gone into politics and done well (Mark Hanna, for example). They haven't reformed their adopted trades, however,
though they have sometimes sharpened them most pointedly. The
politician is a business man with a specialty. When a business
man of some other line learns the business of politics, he is a
politician, and there is not much left in him. Consider the United
States Senate and believe me.

The commercial spirit is the spirit of profit, not patriotism; of
credit, not honor; of individual gain, not national prosperity; of
trade and dickering, not principle. "My business is sacred," says
the business man in his heart. "Whatever prospers my business, is
good; it must be. Whatever hinders it, is wrong; it must be. A
bribe is bad, that is, it is a bad thing to take; but it is not so bad
to give one, not if it is necessary to my business." "Business is

business" is not a political sentiment, but our politician has caught it. He takes essentially the same view of the bribe, only he saves his self-respect by piling all his contempt upon the bribe-giver, and he has the great advantage of candor. "It is wrong, maybe," he says, "but if a rich merchant can afford to do business with me for the sake of a convenience or to increase his already great wealth, I can afford, for the sake of a living, to meet him half way. I make no pretensions to virtue, not even on Sunday." And as for giving bad government or good, how about the merchant who gives bad goods or good goods, according to the demand?

But there is hope, not alone despair, in the commercialism of our politics. If our political leaders are to be always a lot of political merchants, they will supply any demand we may create. All we have to do is to establish a steady demand for good government. The bosses have us split up into parties. To him parties are nothing but means to his corrupt ends. He "bolts" his party, but we must not; the bribe-giver changes his party, from one election to another, from one country to another, from one city to another, but the honest voter must not. Why? Because if the honest voter cared no more for his party than the politician and the grafter, then the honest vote would govern, and that would be bad—for graft. It is idiotic, this devotion to a machine that is used to take our sovereignty from us. If we would leave parties to the politicians, and would vote not for the party, not even for men, but for the city, and the State, and the nation, we should rule parties, and cities, and States, and nation. If we would vote in mass on the more promising ticket, or, if the two are equally bad, would throw out the party that is in, and wait till the next election and then throw out the other party that is in—then, I say, the commercial politician would feel a demand for good government and he would supply it. That process would take a generation or more to complete, for the politicians now really do not know what good government is. But it has taken as long to develop bad government, and the politicians know what that is. If it would not "go," they would offer something else, and, if the demand were steady, they, being so commercial, would "deliver the goods."

But do the people want good government? Tammany says they

don't. Are the people honest? Are the people better than Tammany? Are they better than the merchant and the politician? Isn't our corrupt government, after all, representative?

President Roosevelt has been sneered at for going about the country preaching, as a cure for our American evils, good conduct in the individual, simple honesty, courage, and efficiency. "Platitudes!" the sophisticated say. Platitudes? If my observations have been true, the literal adoption of Mr. Roosevelt's reform scheme would result in a revolution, more radical and terrible to existing institutions, from the Congress to the Church, from the bank to the ward organization, than socialism or even than anarchy. Why, that would change all of us—not alone our neighbors, not alone the grafters, but you and me.

No, the contemned methods of our despised politics are the master methods of our braggart business, and the corruption that shocks us in public affairs we practice ourselves in our private concerns. There is no essential difference between the pull that gets your wife into society or for your book a favorable review, and that which gets a heeler into office, a thief out of jail, and a rich man's son on the board of directors of a corporation; none between the corruption of a labor union, a bank, and a political machine; none between a dummy director of a trust and the caucus-bound member of a legislature; none between a labor boss like Sam Parks, a boss of banks like John D. Rockefeller, a boss of railroads like J. P. Morgan, and a political boss like Matthew S. Quay. The boss is not a political, he is an American institution, the product of a freed people that have not the spirit to be free.

And it's all a moral weakness; a weakness right where we think we are strongest. Oh, we are good—on Sunday, and we are "fearfully patriotic" on the Fourth of July. But the bribe we pay to the janitor to prefer our interests to the landlord's, is the little brother of the bribe passed to the alderman to sell a city street, and the father of the air-brake stock assigned to the president of a railroad to have this life-saving invention adopted on his road. And as for graft, railroad passes, saloon and bawdy-house blackmail, and watered stock, all these belong to the same family. We are pathetically proud of our democratic institutions and our republican form of government, of our grand Constitution and our just laws.

We are a free and sovereign people, we govern ourselves and the government is ours. But that is the point. We are responsible, not our leaders, since we follow them. We *let* them divert our loyalty from the United States to some "party"; we *let* them boss the party and turn our municipal democracies into autocracies and our republican nation into a plutocracy. We cheat our government and we let our leaders loot it, and we let them wheedle and bribe our sovereignty from us. True, they pass for us strict laws, but we are content to let them pass also bad laws, giving away public property in exchange; and our good, and often impossible, laws we allow to be used for oppression and blackmail. And what can we say? We break our own laws and rob our own government, the lady at the custom-house, the lyncher with his rope, and the captain of industry with his bribe and his rebate. The spirit of graft and of lawlessness is the American spirit.

. . . . .

The people are not innocent. That is the only "news" in all the journalism of these articles, and no doubt that was not new to many observers. It was to me. When I set out to describe the corrupt systems of certain typical cities, I meant to show simply how the people were deceived and betrayed. But in the very first study —St. Louis—the startling truth lay bare that corruption was not merely political; it was financial, commercial, social; the ramifications of boodle were so complex, various, and far-reaching, that one mind could hardly grasp them, and not even Joseph W. Folk, the tireless prosecutor, could follow them all. . . .

The first St. Louis article was called "Tweed Days in St. Louis," and though the "better citizen" received attention the Tweeds were the center of interest. In "The Shame of Minneapolis," the truth was put into the title; it was the Shame of Minneapolis; not of the Ames administration, not of the Tweeds, but of the city and its citizens. And yet Minneapolis was not nearly so bad as St. Louis; police graft is never so universal as boodle. It is more shocking, but it is so filthy that it cannot involve so large a part of society. So I returned to St. Louis, and I went over the whole ground again, with the people in mind, not alone the caught and convicted boodlers. And this time the true meaning of "Tweed Days in St. Louis" was made plain. The article was called "The

Shamelessness of St. Louis," and that was the burden of the story. In Pittsburg also the people was the subject, and though the civic spirit there was better, the extent of the corruption throughout the social organization of the community was indicated. But it was not till I got to Philadelphia that the possibilities of popular corruption were worked out to the limit of humiliating confession. That was the place for such a study. There is nothing like it in the country, except possibly, in Cincinnati. Philadelphia certainly is not merely corrupt, but corrupted, and this was made clear. Philadelphia was charged up to—the American citizen.

It was impossible in the space of a magazine article to cover in any one city all the phases of municipal government, so I chose cities that typified most strikingly some particular phase or phases. Thus as St. Louis exemplified boodle; Minneapolis, police graft; Pittsburg, a political and industrial machine; and Philadelphia, general civic corruption; so Chicago was an illustration of reform, and New York of good government. All these things occur in most of these places. There are, and long have been, reformers in St. Louis, and there is to-day police graft there. Minneapolis has had boodling and council reform, and boodling is breaking out there again. Pittsburg has general corruption, and Philadelphia a very perfect political machine. Chicago has police graft and a low order of administrative and general corruption which permeates business, labor, and society generally. As for New York, the metropolis might exemplify almost anything that occurs anywhere in American cities, but no city has had for many years such a good administration as was that of Mayor Seth Low.

That which I have made each city stand for, is that which it had most highly developed. It would be absurd to seek for organized reform in St. Louis, for example, with Chicago next door; or for graft in Chicago with Minneapolis so near. After Minneapolis, a description of administrative corruption in Chicago would have seemed like a repetition. Perhaps it was not just to treat only the conspicuous element in each situation. But why should I be just? I was not judging; I arrogated to myself no such function. I was not writing about Chicago for Chicago, but for the other cities, so I picked out what light each had for the instruction of the others. But, if I was never complete, I never exaggerated. Every one of those articles was an understatement, especially where the conditions were bad, and the proof thereof is that while each article seemed to astonish other cities, it disappointed the city which was its subject.

. . . . . .

This is all very unscientific, but then, I am not a scientist. I am a journalist. I did not gather with indifference all the facts and arrange them patiently for permanent preservation and laboratory analysis. I did not want to preserve, I wanted to destroy the facts. My purpose was no more scientific than the spirit of my investigation and reports; it was, as I said above, to see if the shameful facts, spread out in all their shame, would not burn through our civic shamelessness and set fire to American pride. That was the journalism of it. I wanted to move and to convince. That is why I was not interested in all the facts, sought none that was new, and rejected half those that were old. I often was asked to expose something suspected. I couldn't: and why should I? Exposure of the unknown was not my purpose. The people: what they will put up with, how they are fooled, how cheaply they are bought, how dearly sold, how easily intimidated, and how led, for good or for evil—that was the inquiry, and so the significant facts were those only which everybody in each city knew, and of these, only those which everybody in every other town would recognize, from their common knowledge of such things, to be probable. But these, understated, were charged always to the guilty persons when individuals were to blame, and finally brought home to the people themselves, who, having the power, have also the responsibility, they and those they respect, and those that guide them.

This was against all the warnings and rules of demagogy. What was the result?

After Joseph W. Folk had explored and exposed, with convictions, the boodling of St. Louis, the rings carried an election. "Tweed Days in St. Louis" is said to have formed some public sentiment against the boodlers, but the local newspapers had more to do with that than *McClure's Magazine*. After the Minneapolis grand jury had exposed and the courts had tried and the common juries had convicted the grafters there, an election showed that public opinion was formed. But that one election was regarded as final. When I went there the men who had led the reform movement were "all through." After they had read "The Shame of Minneapolis," however, they went back to work, and they have perfected a plan to keep the citizens informed and to continue the fight for good government. They saw, these unambitious, busy citizens, that it was "up to them," and they resumed the unwelcome duties of their citizenship. Of resentment there was very little. At a meeting of leading citizens there were honest speeches suggesting that something should be said to "clear the name of Minneapolis," but one man rose and said very pleasantly, but firmly, that the article was true; it was pretty hard on them, but it was true and they all knew it. That ended that.

When I returned to St. Louis and rewrote the facts, and, in rewriting, made them just as insulting as the truth would permit, my friends there expressed dismay over the manuscript. The article would hurt Mr. Folk; it would hurt the cause; it would arouse popular wrath.

"That was what I hoped it would do," I said.

"But the indignation would break upon Folk and reform, not on the boodlers," they said.

"Wasn't it obvious," I asked, "that this very title, 'Shamelessness,' was aimed at pride; that it implied a faith that there was self-respect to be touched and shame to be moved?"

That was too subtle. So I answered that if they had no faith in the town, I had, and anyway, if I was wrong and the people should resent, not the crime, but the exposure of it, then they would punish, not Mr. Folk, who had nothing to do with the article, but the magazine and me. Newspaper men warned me that they would not "stand for" the article, but would attack it. I answered that I would let the St. Louisans decide between us. It was true, it was just; the people of St. Louis had shown no shame. Here was a good chance to see whether they had any. I was a fool, they said. "All right," I replied. "All kings had fools in the olden days, and the fools were allowed to tell them the truth. I would play the fool to the American people."

The article, published, was attacked by the newspapers; friends of Mr. Folk repudiated it; Mr. Folk himself spoke up for the people. Leading citizens raised money for a mass meeting to "set the city right before the world." The mayor of the city, a most excellent man, who had helped me, denounced the article. The boodle party platform appealed for votes on the strength of the attacks in "Eastern magazines." The people themselves contradicted me; after the publication, two hundred thousand buttons for "Folk and Reform" were worn on the streets of St. Louis.

But those buttons were for "Folk and Reform." They did go to prove that the article was wrong, that there was pride in St. Louis, but they proved also that that pride had been touched. Up to that time nobody knew exactly how St. Louis felt about it all. There had been one election, another was pending, and the boodlers, caught or to be caught, were in control. The citizens had made no move to dislodge them. Mr. Folk's splendid labors were a spectacle without a chorus, and, though I had met men who told me the people were with Folk, I had met also the grafters, who cursed only Folk and were building all their hopes on the assumption that "after Folk's term" all would be well again. Between these two local views no outsider could choose. How could I read a strange people's hearts? I took the outside view, stated the facts both ways—the right verdicts of the juries and the confident plans of the boodlers—and the result was, indeed, a shameless state of affairs for which St. Louis, the people of St. Louis, were to blame.

And they saw it so, both in the city and in the State, and they ceased to be spectators. That article simply got down to the self-respect of this people. And who was hurt? Not St. Louis. From that moment the city has been determined and active, and boodle seems to be doomed. Not Mr. Folk. After that, his nomination for Governor of the State was declared for by the people, who formed Folk clubs all over the State to force him upon his party and theirs, and thus insure the pursuit of the boodlers in St. Louis and in Missouri too. Nor was the magazine hurt, or myself. The next time I went to St. Louis, the very men who had raised money for the mass meeting to denounce the article went out of their way to say to me that I had been right, the article was true, and they asked me to "do it again." And there may be a chance to do it again. Mr. Folk lifted the lid off Missouri for a moment after that, and the State also appeared ripe for the gathering. Moreover, the boodlers of State and city have joined to beat the people and keep them down. The decisive election is not till the fall of 1904, and the boodlers count much on the fickleness of public opinion. But I believe that Missouri and St. Louis together will prove then, once for all, that the people can rule—when they are aroused.

The Pittsburg article had no effect in Pittsburg, nor had that on Philadelphia any results in Philadelphia. Nor was any expected there. Pittsburg, as I said in the article, knew itself, and may pull out of its disgrace, but Philadelphia is contented and seems hopeless. The accounts of them, however, and indeed, as I have said, all of the series, were written, not for the cities described, but for all our cities; and the most immediate response came from places not mentioned, but where similar evils existed or similar action was needed. Thus Chicago, intent on its troubles, found useless to it the study of its reform, which seems to have been suggestive elsewhere, and Philadelphia, "Corrupt and Contented," was taken home in other cities and seems to have made the most lasting impression everywhere.

But of course the tangible results are few. The real triumph of the year's work was the complete demonstration it has given, in a thousand little ways, that our shamelessness is superficial, that beneath it lies a pride which, being real, may save us yet. And it is real. The grafters who said you may put the blame anywhere but on the people, where it belongs, and that Americans can be moved only by flattery—they lied. They lied about themselves. They, too, are American citizens; they too, are of the people; and some of them also were reached by shame. The great truth I tried to make plain was that which Mr. Folk insists so constantly upon: that bribery is no ordinary felony, but treason, that the "corruption which breaks out here and there and now and then" is not an occasional offense, but a common practice, and that the effect of it is literally to change the form of our government from one that is representative of the people to an oligarchy, representative of special interests. Some politicians have seen that this is so, and it bothers them. I think I prize more highly than any other of my experiences the half-dozen times when grafting politicians I had "roasted," as they put it, called on me afterwards to say, in the words of one who spoke with a wonderful solemnity:

"You are right. I never thought of it that way, but it's right. I don't know whether you can do anything, but you're right, dead right. And I'm all wrong. We're all, all wrong. I don't see how we can stop it now; I don't see how I can change. I can't, I guess. No, I can't, not now. But, say, I may be able to help you, and I will if I can. You can have anything I've got."

So you see, they are not such bad fellows, these practical politicians. I wish I could tell more about them: how they have helped me; how candidly and unselfishly they have assisted me to facts and an understanding of the facts, which, as I warned them, as they knew well, were to be used against them. If I could—and I will some day—I should show that one of the surest hopes we have is the politician himself. Ask him for good politics; punish him when he gives bad, and reward him when he gives good; make politics pay. Now, he says, you don't know and you don't care, and that you must be flattered and fooled—and there, I say, he is wrong. I did not flatter anybody; I told the truth as near as I could get it, and instead of resentment there was encouragement. After "The Shame of Minneapolis," and "The Shamelessness of St. Louis," not only did citizens of these cities approve, but citizens of other cities, individuals, groups, and organizations, sent in invitations, hundreds of them, "to come and show us up; we're worse than they are."

We Americans may have failed. We may be mercenary and selfish. Democracy with us may be impossible and corruption inevitable, but these articles, if they have proved nothing else, have demonstrated beyond doubt that we can stand the truth; that there is pride in the character of American citizenship; and that this pride may be a power in the land. So this little volume, a record of shame and yet of self-respect, a disgraceful confession, yet a declaration of honor, is dedicated, in all good faith, to the accused—to all the citizens of all the cities in the United States.

2 / ROBERT M. LA FOLLETTE AND
THE "WISCONSIN IDEA"

*Governor of Wisconsin from 1901 to 1906, then
United States Senator until his death in 1925, Robert M.
La Follette relates in his autobiography the purposes
and achievements of the progressive movement in
the Badger State.*

. . . At the opening of the legislature of 1903, I felt that the time had arrived to advance vigorously with the railroad regulation issue. There were good reasons for doing this. We had the support of the public. We had discussed the subject pretty thoroughly in the preceding campaign, so that the people were prepared to back us up in our plans. . . .

The regulation bill did not pass at that session, nor did we expect it to pass. But the contest accomplished the purposes we had chiefly in mind. It stirred the people of the state as they had never been stirred before, and laid the foundations for an irresistible campaign in 1904. It also gave the lobby so much to do —as we had anticipated—that it could not spend any time in resisting our measures for railroad taxation. It also forced some members of the legislature who were really opposed to us, and who intended to vote against the regulation bill, to vote with us on the taxation bill as a bid for the favor of the people of their districts.

So, at last, after all these years of struggle, we wrote our rail-

SOURCE: Robert M. La Follette, *La Follette's Autobiography* (Madison: University of Wisconsin Press, 1963), pp. 120, 123–128, 132–134, 137, 143, 145–146, 149–158. There has been some alteration in the sequence of paragraphs for the sake of clarity. Reprinted with permission of the copyright owners, The Regents of the University of Wisconsin.

road tax legislation into the statutes of Wisconsin. As an immediate result, railroad taxes were increased more than $600,000 annually. . . .

Indeed, we so reorganized and equalized our whole system of taxation that the state to-day is on a sounder, more businesslike foundation than ever before. We brought in so much property hitherto not taxed or unequally taxed that, while the expenses of the state have greatly increased, still the burden of taxation on the people has actually decreased. While corporations in 1900 paid taxes of $2,059,139 a year, in 1910 they paid $4,221,504 a year, or more than double. Wisconsin to-day leads all the states of the union in the proportion of its taxes collected from corporations. It derives 70 per cent. of its total state taxes from that source, while the next nearest state, Ohio, derives 52 per cent.

In 1903 we passed an inheritance tax law which yielded us $26,403 in the following year and has increased steadily since.

In 1905 I recommended a graduated income tax which has since been adopted by the state. It is the most comprehensive income tax system yet adopted in this country. Those who receive incomes of over $500 must make a return to the tax assessor. The tax at 1 per cent. begins on incomes above $800 in the case of unmarried people and above $1,200 in the case of married persons, increasing one half of 1 per cent. or thereabout for each additional $1,000, until $12,000 is reached, when the tax becomes 5.5 per cent. On incomes above $12,000 a year the tax is 6 per cent.

All of these new sources of income have enabled us to increase greatly the service of the state to the people without noticeably increasing the burden upon the people. Especially have we built up our educational system. In 1900 the state was expending $550,000 a year on its university; in 1910 it appropriated over $1,700,000, and there has been a similar increase for our normal and graded schools and charitable institutions.

. . . . .

We had now passed one of the two great measures so long struggled for—the railroad taxation bill. The other, that providing for direct primaries, seemed almost within reach.

I prepared that part of my message which dealt with direct nominations of candidates for office as though on trial for my life.

I felt that the legislature simply *must* be made to see its duty and that we *must* pass the direct primary at that session. I feared that if it failed again, after six years of agitation, we might begin to lose ground with the public. There comes a time when public interest cannot be sustained in further discussion of a subject no matter how important. The people will give an administration their support two or three times and then they begin to expect results.

The primary bill as introduced easily passed the assembly, and after a long and hard fight we finally got it through the senate by accepting a provision submitting the act on a referendum to the voters of the state in the election of 1904. The machine senators let it go through with this provision because, first, it left the caucus and convention system in force for nearly two years longer. They felt that they would thus have another chance to secure our defeat and get control of the state. It also gave them a chance to defeat the measure, if they could, at the polls. They believed, I am confident, that the people themselves would fail to adopt it; they still thought that it had back of it only "agitators" and "demagogues." It was necessarily a lengthy measure, with some forty or more sections, and they figured that to present the details of a complex bill was a task too great for us in a campaign involving other important issues. Under the referendum as now adopted in many states publication of such measures is provided for at public expense, months in advance of the election, and there is wide distribution of literature on the subject. But there was no such provision in Wisconsin at that time and they relied on the difficulties and expense we would have in reaching all the voters, and on their own ability to checkmate us.

But, as usual, the bosses were mistaken in their estimate of the intelligence of the people. When the time came the Democratic party as well as the Republican party declared for it, and although a desperate fight was made upon the measure at the polls, nevertheless it carried in the election of 1904 by a majority of over 50,000.

Except for one omission I think it is the most perfect law for the nomination of candidates by direct vote ever enacted. It failed to make provision for the second choice, which permits voters to indicate on the ballot not only their first choice of candidates for each office, but a second choice as well, thereby positively assuring a nomination by the group of the party which is actually in the vast majority.

We struggled for a second choice amendment to our Wisconsin primary law for nearly seven years, and finally obtained it in the session of the legislature of last year (1911). . . .

We needed one more thing in connection with the primary law, and that was a stringent Corrupt Practices Act to prevent the corrupt use of money in primaries and in elections. We tried hard to get such a law in 1903. We failed at that time, but Wisconsin now [1913] has an admirable measure. . . .

Reformers often stop fighting before the battle is really won: before the new territory is completely occupied. I felt that the campaign of 1904 was the very crux of our whole movement. We had passed our railroad taxation and direct primary measures in 1903; but the railroad taxation law would be a barren victory until it was supplemented by a commission to control railroad rates; and the direct nomination of candidates would fail unless we carried the election and secured the adoption of the primary bill at the referendum that fall. Without the direct primary law it would be an easy matter for the old machine to regain control of the legislature and not only prevent further progressive legislation, but undo part, if not all, of the work already accomplished.

I felt absolutely sure that another term, with another legislature, would securely ground and bulwark self-government in Wisconsin. I knew that the opposition understood this too, and that they would make the most desperate fight in that campaign that they had ever made. . . .

I am free to confess that it had been my great ambition to be governor of Wisconsin, not just to be governor (for that seemed to me in itself but an empty honor), but to be in reality the chief executive of the state; to be a strong factor in securing legislation that should build into the life of the people a new order of things —laws that should be a recognition of human rights, that should make safe the vital principles of representative government. To aid in achieving such results was the realization of my highest ambition. I had gone through two sessions of the legislature, through three hard campaigns prior to that time; I had given to the work some of the best years of my life, and here I was at the end of my second term as governor with almost nothing of a lasting nature accomplished. I was determined, therefore, to make this a campaign that should result in the election of a legislature that would finally execute the will of the people. It was an unheard of thing for the governor of the state to "interfere" in the nomination of candidates for the legislature; but I knew perfectly well that those members of the legislature who had served the political machine instead of their constituents would, many of them, seek renomination and reelection to the legislature, when they would again repudiate their party pledges. And so, with the calling of the caucuses, I went out into senate and assembly districts, announced public meetings and executed the new policy upon which I had resolved. I did not engage in personalities; I did not attack individuals as such, but I took the journals of the two houses of the legislature on to the public platform, and presented fairly and clearly the character of the different measures of public importance, and then read from the journal the record vote of the candidate seeking reelection upon those measures. I selected districts in which those men who had wronged the public were seeking renomination, and almost without exception in those districts where I held meetings I secured the defeat of the candidates who sought renomination. . . .

I was elected by about 50,000, and the direct primary law, for which we had campaigned vigorously, carried by about the same majority. We also elected a safe majority of both houses of the legislature. . . . At the outset of the legislature of 1905, therefore, we took the greatest pains in drawing our railroad bill. . . .

It was a very strong regulatory bill. It provided for a commission with power not only to fix rates but to control service and to make a complete physical valuation of all the railroad property in the state. It was more sweeping than any legislation enacted by any state up to that time. . . .

As soon as the legislature passed our regulation law I appointed the three commissioners. I had contended all along for an appointive rather than an elective commission. I felt that the state should have the best experts in the country in these positions, whether residents of Wisconsin or not, for much would depend upon the way in which our new law was administered. . . .

The commission proceeded with wisdom. Though under great pressure at first, it refused to consider complaints until it had laid a broad foundation of scientific knowledge. Expert engineers and contractors were employed and many months were spent in making a physical valuation of all railroad property in the state. This is the logical first step if you are going to fix rates. It then became necessary to determine the actual cost of maintenance and operation—a very difficult matter in our case—because the railroads of Wisconsin are parts of great systems.

When all this immense work was done, the commission had the wisdom and foresight to submit its findings to the railroad officials, who went over them and approved them. This prevented disputes in the future upon fundamental facts.

Having all this data, the commissioners began to entertain complaints, and to fix rates upon a basis which they knew positively was fair to the public and fair to the railroads. They so reduced transportation charges as to effect a saving of over $2,000,000 per year to the people of the state, and they have only made a beginning. Generally the rates of public utility corporations have been reduced, but in some cases the investigation showed that the rates were too low already and the commission raised them. The result is that individuals may be found in communities where rates have been increased or have not been promptly or radically reduced who declare that the Railroad Commission has not met expectations by "going after" the corporations.

All through our fight for railroad control the lobbyists and the railroad newspapers made the most mournful prophecies of disaster: they predicted that capital would fly from the state, that new construction would stop, that equipment would deteriorate, and so on and so on. What are the facts?

The object of our legislation was not to "smash" corporations, but to drive them out of politics, and then to treat them exactly the same as other people are treated. Equality under the law was our guiding star. It is the special discriminations and unjust rates that are being corrected; the privileges, unfair advantages, and political corruption that have been abolished. Where these do not exist the object has been to foster and encourage business activity. Consequently, no state in the union to-day offers better security for the savings of its people than Wisconsin. The honest investor, or business man, or farmer, or laborer, who simply wants equal opportunity with others and security for what he honestly earns, is protected and encouraged by the laws. The mere speculator, or monopolist, or promoter, who wants to take advantage of others under protection of law, is held down or driven out. The result is that instead of falling behind, the state has actually gone forward more rapidly than the rest of the country. This may be shown by incontrovertible facts and figures in practically every direction where there has been progressive legislation affecting business.

The Railroad Commission keeps accurate account of all the business of every railroad and public utility in the state. It has jurisdiction over property whose total value amounts to $450,-000,000. The books are kept exactly as the commission orders them to be kept. These accounts show that while during the first five years of its existence the commission reduced rates by more than $2,000,000 a year, the *net earnings* of the railroads of Wisconsin increased relatively just a little more than the net earnings for all railways in the United States. The increase in Wisconsin was 18.45 per cent., and in the United States it was 18.41 per cent.

How did this come about? Simply from the fact that the decrease in rates for freight and passengers was followed by an enormous increase in the amount of freight and number of passengers carried. So it happened that, notwithstanding the *reduction in rates*, there was an actual increase of nearly 20 per cent. in the revenue, while the increase of revenue of all the railroads in the United States was only 16 per cent.

This remarkable increase took place notwithstanding the fact that, mainly on account of the greatly improved service which the commission required the railroads to perform, the expense of railroad operation in Wisconsin increased 33 per cent. more than the average rate of increase in the entire United States.

Much of what the railroads lost in the reduction of open rates that everybody shares they recovered by being compelled to abolish free passes and secret cut rates that went only to insiders and grafters. The special examiners whom I appointed in 1903 uncovered $5,992,731.58 as Wisconsin's share of rebates paid by twelve roads during the six years 1898 to 1903. By stopping rebates alone the railroads have gained at least $1,000,000 a year toward offsetting $2,000,000 they lost by reduction of rates. They must also have gained largely by the stoppage of political contributions and expenses. The railroads to-day are gaining far more by treating everybody on an equality than they could have gained if their old methods of politics and secret favoritism had continued.

It is not claimed that railroads are both *making* and *keeping* more money in Wisconsin than they did before the progressive legislation began. Indeed, they are *making more but keeping a smaller proportion of it.* They are now paying taxes the same as other people on exactly what their property is worth. This they began to do in 1904. Under the old system of unequal taxation, in 1903, when the railroads practically assessed themselves, they paid taxes in the state amounting to $1,711,900. Under the new system, in 1910, when the State Tax Commission assessed them exactly like farms and other property, they paid $3,142,886. This was an increase of 83 per cent. in the amount of their taxes. But during the years 1903 to 1909 the taxes of all railroads in the United States increased only 41 per cent. That is, railroad taxation in Wisconsin has been increased by the progressive legislation in six years nearly twice as much as the increase for all of the United States. If this increase in taxation is a hardship on the railroads, it is simply because equal taxation is always a hardship on those who had not been formerly paying their equal share of taxes.

Nor did progressive legislation stop new construction: During the years 1903 to 1909 the railroads invested in new construction in Wisconsin an amount estimated by the Railroad Commission at $39,000,000, an increase of 15 per cent. over 1903. This is not a fictitious increase in capitalization. It is *actual cash paid out* for new road and equipment. A cash investment by railroads of $6,500,000 a year for six years of progressive legislation refutes their prophecies of disaster.

Other public utilities besides railroads were not brought under the control of the Railroad Commission until 1907, and it was not until 1909 that the commission was able to get their accounts into such shape as to be reliable. But, for the year 1910, compared with 1909, notwithstanding reductions in rates and improvements in service, the water utilities increased their net earnings 7.1 per cent., the telephone utilities 7.1 per cent., gas utilities 7.4 per cent., and electric utilities 25 per cent. These utilities have even exceeded the railroads in the rate at which they have made cash investments for new construction. While the increase in railroad construction has averaged 2.5 per cent. a year for six years, the water utilities in 1910 increased their new construction of property 2.5 per cent. over what it had been in 1909; the telephone utilities 5.4 per cent., gas utilities 1.6 per cent., and electric utilities 35.5 per cent. For the year 1911 compared with 1910 the water utilities increased their net earnings 4.3 per cent., the telephone utilities 15.9 per cent., gas utilities 5.7 per cent., and electric utilities 24.2 per cent. The water utilities in 1911 increased their property by new construction 4 per cent. over that of 1910; the telephone utilities 5.7 per cent., gas utilities 6.1 per cent., and electric utilities, 22.1 per cent.

Wisconsin is certainly not driving capital out of the state when the electrical business in the single year 1910, after two years of regulation by the state, made *bona fide* new investments 35 per cent. greater than it had done in 1909. All of this has been accomplished notwithstanding the fact that the Railroad Commission has reduced the rates charged by public utilities $250,000 a year, and has required improvements in the quality of service amounting to $125,000 a year—a total saving to the consumers of gas, water, and electricity of $375,000 a year.

A single example will show how these different results have been brought about. In April, 1910, after two years of careful investigation, the Railroad Commission, after improving the quality of service, reduced the maximum price of electricity in the city of Madison from 16 cents to 14 cents per kilowatt-hour, and adjusted the other rates on a lower basis. The result was that the sales of electricity increased 16 per cent., the net earnings increased 24 per cent., the company increased its investment 12 per cent., and the savings to consumers, comparing old rates with new rates, was $18,308 a year. At the end of another fifteen months, in July, 1911, after such an increase in profits following the reduction in rates, the company accepted without protest another reduction to 12 cents. No additional investigation was necessary, because the books of the company had been kept in the way prescribed by the commission so as to show every item of expense, income, and investment. Supervision by the state commission has thus proven of great benefit to the private corporation itself.

How has it been possible that both the people of Wisconsin and the investors in public utilities have been so greatly benefited by this regulation? *Simply because the regulation is scientific.* The Railroad Commission has found out through its engineers, accountants, and statisticians what it actually costs to build and operate the road and utilities. Watered stock and balloon bonds get no consideration. On the other hand, since the commission knows the costs, it knows exactly the point below which rates cannot be reduced. It even raises rates when they are below the cost, including reasonable profit.

The people are benefited because they are not now paying profits on inflated capital. The investors are benefited because the commission has all the facts needed to prevent a reduction of rates below a fair profit on their true value. . . .

In other ways our progressive legislation has materially benefited all the people of the state. For example, beginning in 1903, I secured in every water-power franchise the insertion of a provision that the rates charged should be regulated by arbitration. Since that time the water powers of the state serving as public utilities have been placed under the control of the Railroad Commission, and a great corporation, supervised by the Railroad Commission, with its profits limited to 6 per cent. on actual cost, has been created and has improved the headwaters of the Wisconsin River in order to secure a steady flow through the year. Several enormous power dams have been constructed, and through these means the state has gone far toward utilizing its 1,000,000 available horsepower, while protecting the state against water-power monopoly.

Wisconsin began in 1905 to build up a state forest reserve on the headwaters of its principal rivers. It now ranks next to New

York and Pennsylvania in its areas of forests belonging to the state, and has adopted a permanent policy of adding annually to the reserve. . . .

I have always had respect for the man who labors with his hands. My own life began that way. Manual labor, industry, the doing of a good day's work, was the thing that gave a man standing and credit in the country neighborhood where I grew up. We all worked hard at home, and the best people I ever knew worked with their hands. I have always had a feeling of kinship for the fellow who carries the load—the man on the under side. . . .

As soon as I became governor we began pressing for new labor legislation which should place Wisconsin on a level with the most progressive state or nation; and it can be truthfully said, since the passage last year of a law creating an Industrial Commission, that Wisconsin now easily leads the states of the union in its body of labor legislation. Child labor has been reduced and the children kept in the schools. Excessive hours for women workers have been abolished. The doctrine of comparative negligence has been adopted for railways, and the long hours of trainmen have been done away with. The most carefully drawn of all workmen's compensation laws has been adopted, and the employers of the state have organized, under a new insurance law, an employer's mutual insurance association, similar to those which in Germany have greatly reduced accidents and compensated the workmen. Many other laws have been added and old ones strengthened, and finally our new Industrial Commission, modeled after the Railroad Commission, has been placed in charge of all the labor laws, with *full power to enforce* the laws and protect the life, health, safety and welfare of employees. This commission has employed one of the leading experts of the United States to cooperate with employers in devising ways and means of safety and sanitation. . . . The Industrial Commission is a new departure of the first importance—the first of its kind in the country. By this measure the state assumes to control and regulate the most difficult questions of sanitation, safety, health and moral well-being which affect the workers of the state. It is one of the most important innovations we have made, one charged with the greatest possibilities of improving the lives of working men and women, and one which should be watched and studied by every one who is interested in forward movements. . . .

The public service of the state has been democratized by a civil service law opening it to men and women on an equal footing independent of everything excepting qualification and fitness for office. I think the passing of this law was the only case of the kind where the employees then holding office were not blanketed into the service, but were required to take the regular competitive examinations in order to retain their jobs. The law has worked to the great advantage of the service and to the general improvement of political standards. There is no longer any political pull in Wisconsin.

I give here, also, some further facts to show that Wisconsin, instead of being retarded by progressive legislation, is advancing more rapidly than the country taken as a whole.

Since 1904, when we recodified our whole system for the examination of state banks, there has not been a single failure among the 573 state banks in Wisconsin, with $27,000,000 of capital, surplus and undivided profits. The only bank failures in the state have been those of three national banks through embezzlement.

During the years 1903 to 1911 the capital, surplus and undivided profits of all state and national banks in Wisconsin increased 72 per cent., whereas for the United States they increased only 48 per cent. Individual deposits for the same years in Wisconsin banks increased 82 per cent., while in the United States as a whole they increased but 74 per cent.

The clearing-house exchanges for Milwaukee increased 117.5 per cent. from 1900 to 1910, whereas for the United States the increase was 106 per cent. Milwaukee's increase was greater than Chicago's.

Judged by commercial failures, Wisconsin has prospered better in proportion than the country. The total liabilities in commercial failures for the entire United States in the four years 1906 to 1909 increased 33 per cent. over the total amount for the preceding four years 1902 to 1905. But the liabilities in Wisconsin for the same years *fell off* 5.3 per cent. In other words, comparing the four years that followed the progressive victory of 1905 with the four years that preceded it, the business failures in Wisconsin *fell off* one twentieth, but for the whole United States they *increased one third.*

These are a few of the conclusive proofs that progressive legislation in Wisconsin has not been destructive, as its enemies predicted. Instead of driving capital out of the state it has attracted capital more than other states. It has made investments safe for all, instead of speculative for a few. It has been conservative and constructive as well as progressive. Only one of the progressive laws—a law passed in 1911, declaring flowing water public property—has been overturned by the supreme court of the state, and not one has been carried into the federal courts.

No account of the long and successful struggle in Wisconsin would be fair and complete that did not record the splendid services of the men who led the fight for progressive principles. I regret that I cannot here give to each the individual recognition that is merited. That must wait for a more detailed history of the Wisconsin movement. It was a day-and-night service with them; they left their offices and business interests and devoted years to the great constructive work which has made Wisconsin the safest guide in dealing with the political, economic and social problems of our time.

This closes the account of my services in Wisconsin—a time full of struggle, and yet a time that I like to look back upon. It has been a fight supremely worth making, and I want it to be judged, as it will be ultimately, by results actually attained. If it can be shown that Wisconsin is a happier and better state to live in, that its institutions are more democratic, that the opportunities of all its people are more equal, that social justice more nearly prevails, that human life is safer and sweeter—then I shall rest content in the feeling that the Progressive movement has been successful. And I believe all these things can really be shown, and that there is no reason now why the movement should not expand until it covers the entire nation. While much has been accomplished, there is still a world of problems yet to be solved; we have just begun; there is hard fighting, and a chance for the highest patriotism, still ahead of us. The fundamental problem as to which shall rule, men or property, is still unsettled; it will require the highest qualities of heroism, the profoundest devotion to duty in this and the coming generation, to reconstruct our institutions to meet the requirements of a new age. . . .

3 / DAVID GRAHAM PHILLIPS ON
"THE TREASON OF THE SENATE"

The popular novelist David Graham Phillips
applied the muckraking technique to the
United States Senate in a series of sensational
articles in Cosmopolitan Magazine *starting March, 1906.*
The following is his scathing portrait of the man
whom he called "the Head of It All,"
Republican Senator Nelson W. Aldrich of Rhode Island.

Politics does not determine prosperity. But in this day of concentrations, politics does determine *the distribution of prosperity.* Because the people have neglected politics, have not educated themselves out of credulity to flimsily plausible political lies and liars, because they will not realize that *it is not enough to work, it is also necessary to think,* they remain poor, or deprived of their fair share of the products, though they have produced an incredible prosperity. The people have been careless and unwise enough in electing every kind of public administrator. When it comes to the election of the Senate, how describe their stupidity, how measure its melancholy consequences? The Senate is the most powerful part of our public administration. It has vast power in the making of laws. It has still vaster power through its ability to forbid the making of laws and in its control over the appointment of the judges who say what the laws mean. It is, in fact, *the final arbiter of the sharing of prosperity.* The laws it

SOURCE: David Graham Phillips, "The Treason of the Senate," *Cosmopolitan Magazine*, XL, 5 (March, 1906), 488; XL, 6 (April, 1906), 628–638.

permits or compels, the laws it refuses to permit, the interpreters of laws it permits to be appointed—these factors determine whether the great forces which modern concentration has produced shall operate to distribute prosperity equally or with shameful inequality and cruel and destructive injustice. The United States Senate is a larger factor than your labor or your intelligence, you average American, in determining your income. And the Senate is a traitor to you.

The treason of the Senate! Treason is a strong word, but not too strong, rather too weak, to characterize the situation in which the Senate is the eager, resourceful, indefatigable agent of interests as hostile to the American people as any invading army could be, and vastly more dangerous; interests that manipulate the prosperity produced by all, so that it heaps up riches for the few; interests whose growth and power can only mean the degradation of the people, of the educated into sycophants, of the masses toward serfdom.

A man cannot serve two masters. The senators are not elected by the people; they are elected by the "interests." A servant obeys him who can punish and dismiss. Except in extreme and rare and negligible instances, can the people either elect or dismiss a senator? The senator, in the dilemma which the careless ignorance of the people thrusts upon him, chooses to be comfortable, placed and honored, and a traitor to oath and people rather than to be true to his oath and poor and ejected into private life. . . .

For the organizer of this treason we must look at Nelson W. Aldrich, senior senator from Rhode Island. Rhode Island is the smallest of our states in area and thirty-fourth in population—twelve hundred and fifty square miles, less than half a million people, barely seventy thousand voters with the rolls padded by the Aldrich machine. But size and numbers are nothing; it contains as many sturdy Americans proportionately as any other state. Its bad distinction of supplying the enemy with a bold leader is due to its ancient and aristocratic constitution, changed once, away back before the middle of the last century, but still an archaic document for class rule. The apportionment of legislators is such that one-eleventh of the population, and they the most ignorant and most venal, elect a majority of the legislature

—which means that they elect the two United States senators. Each city and township counts as a political unit; thus, the five cities that together have two-thirds of the population are in an overwhelming minority before twenty almost vacant rural townships—their total population is not thirty-seven thousand—where the ignorance is even illiterate, where the superstition is mediæval, where tradition and custom have made the vote an article of legitimate merchandising.

The combination of bribery and party prejudice is potent everywhere; but there come crises when these fail "the interests" for the moment. No storm of popular rage, however, could unseat the senators from Rhode Island. The people of Rhode Island might, as a people and voting almost unanimously, elect a governor; but not a legislature. Bribery is a weapon forbidden those who stand for right and justice—who "fights the devil with fire" gives him choice of weapons, and must lose to him, though seeming to win. A few thousand dollars put in the experienced hands of the heelers, and the senatorial general agent of "the interests" is secure for another six years.

The Aldrich machine controls the legislature, the election boards, the courts—the entire machinery of the "republican form of government." In 1904, when Aldrich needed a legislature to reëlect him for his fifth consecutive term, it is estimated that carrying the state cost about two hundred thousand dollars—a small sum, easily to be got back by a few minutes of industrious pocket-picking in Wall Street; but a very large sum for Rhode Island politics, and a happy augury of a future day, remote, perhaps, but inevitable, when the people shall rule in Rhode Island. Despite the bribery, despite the swindling on registration lists and all the chicane which the statute book of the state makes easy for "the interests," Aldrich elected his governor by a scant eight hundred on the face of the returns. His legislature was, of course, got without the least difficulty—the majority for "the interests" is on joint ballot seventy-five out of a total of one hundred and seventeen. The only reason Aldrich disturbed himself about the governorship was that, through the anger of the people and the carelessness of the machine, a people's governor had been elected in 1903 and was up for reëlection; this people's governor, while without any power whatever under the Constitution, still could make disagreeable demands on the legislature, demands which did not sound well in the ears of the country and roused the people everywhere to just what was the source of the most respectable politician's security. So, Aldrich, contrary to his habit in recent years, took personal charge of the campaign and tried to show the people of Rhode Island that they were helpless and might as well quiet down, accept their destiny and spare his henchmen the expense and labor of wholesale bribery and fraud.

But, as a rule, Aldrich no longer concerns himself with Rhode Island's petty local affairs. "Not until about a year or so before it comes time for him to be elected again, does he get active," says his chief henchman, Gen. Charles R. Brayton, the state's boss. "He doesn't pay much attention to details." Why should he? Politically, the state is securely "the interests'" and his; financially, "the interests" and he have incorporated and assured to themselves in perpetuity about all the graft—the Rhode Island Securities Company, capitalized at and paying excellent dividends upon thirty-nine million dollars, representing an actual value of less than nine million dollars, owns, thanks to the munificence of the legislature, the state's street and trolley lines, gas and electric franchises, etc., etc. It began in a street railway company of Providence in which Aldrich, president of the Providence council and afterwards member of the legislature, acquired an interest. The sugar trust's Searles put in a million and a half shortly after the sugar trust got its license to loot through Aldrich at Washington; the legislature passed the necessary laws and gave the necessary franchises; Senator Steve Elkins and his crowd were invited in; more legislation; more franchises, more stocks and bonds, the right to loot the people of the state in perpetuity. Yes, Aldrich is rich, enormously rich, and his mind is wholly free for the schemes he plots and executes at Washington. And, like all the other senators who own large blocks of stocks and bonds in the great drainage companies fastened upon America's prosperity, his service is not the less diligent or adroit because he himself draws huge dividends from the people. . . .

In 1901 his daughter married the only son and destined successor of John D. Rockefeller. Thus, the chief exploiter of the

American people is closely allied by marriage with the chief schemer in the service of their exploiters. This fact no American should ever lose sight of. It is a political fact; it is an economic fact. It places the final and strongest seal upon the bonds uniting Aldrich and "the interests."

When Aldrich entered the Senate, twenty-five years ago, at the splendid full age of forty, the world was just beginning to feel the effects of the principles of concentration and combination, which were inexorably and permanently established with the discoveries in steam and electricity that make the whole human race more and more like one community of interdependent neighbors. It was a moment of opportunity, an unprecedented chance for Congress, especially its deliberate and supposedly sagacious senators, to "promote the general welfare" by giving those principles free and just play in securing the benefits of expanding prosperity to all, by seeing that the profits from the coöperation of all the people went *to* the people. Aldrich and the traitor Senate saw the opportunity. But they saw in it only a chance to enable a class to despoil the masses.

Before he reached the Senate, Aldrich had had fifteen years of training in how to legislate the proceeds of the labor of the many into the pockets of the few. He entered it as the representative of local interests engaged in robbing by means of slyly worded tariff schedules that changed protection against the foreigner into plunder of the native. His demonstrated excellent talents for sly, slippery work in legislative chambers and committee rooms and his security in his seat against popular revulsions and outbursts together marked him for the position of chief agent of the predatory band which was rapidly forming to take care of the prosperity of the American people.

Various senators represent various divisions and subdivisions of this colossus. But Aldrich, rich through franchise grabbing, the intimate of Wall Street's great robber barons, the father-in-law of the only son of *the* Rockefeller—Aldrich represents the colossus. Your first impression of many and conflicting interests has disappeared. You now see a single interest, with a single agent-in-chief to execute its single purpose—getting rich at the expense of the labor and the independence of the American people. And the largest head among the many heads of this monster is that of Rockefeller, father of the only son-in-law of Aldrich and his intimate in all the relations of life!

There are many passages in the Constitution in which a Senate, true to its oath and mindful of the welfare of the people and of the nation, could find mandates to stop wholesale robbery, and similar practices.

And yet, what has the Senate done—the Senate, with its high-flown pretenses of reverence for the Constitution? It has so legislated and so refrained from legislating that more than half of all the wealth created by the American people belongs to less than one per cent. of them; that the income of the average American family has sunk to less than six hundred dollars a year; that of our more than twenty-seven million children of school age, less than twelve millions go to school, and more than two millions work in mines, shops, and factories.

And the leader, the boss of the Senate for the past twenty years has been—Aldrich!

In vain would "the interests" have stolen franchises, in vain would they have corrupted the public officials of states and cities, if they had not got absolute and unshakable control of the Senate. But, with the Senate theirs, how secure, how easy and how rich the loot!

Source of His Power

The sole source of Aldrich's power over the senators is "the interests"—the sole source, but quite sufficient to make him permanent and undisputed boss. Many of the senators . . . are . . . the direct agents of the various states or sectional subdivisions of "the interests," and these senators constitute about two-thirds of the entire Senate. Of the remainder several know that if they should oppose "the interests" they would lose their seats; several others are silent because they feel that to speak out would be useless; a few do speak out, but are careful not to infringe upon the rigid rule of "senatorial courtesy," which thus effectually protects the unblushing corruptionists, the obsequious servants of corruption, and likewise the many traitors to party as well as the people, from having disagreeable truths dinged into their ears. Tillman will "pitchfork" a president, but not a senator, and not the Senate in any but the most useless, futile way—this, though none knows better than he how the rights and the property of the people are trafficked in by his colleagues of both parties, with a few exceptions. There are a few other honest men from the South and from the West, as many of the few honest Republicans as honest Democrats. Yet party allegiance and "senatorial courtesy" make them abettors of treason, allies of Aldrich and Gorman.

"Senatorial courtesy!" We shall have to return to it, as it is the hypocritical mask behind which the few senators who pose as real representatives of the people hide in silence and inaction.

The greatest single hold of "the interests" is the fact that they are the "campaign contributors"—the men who supply the money for "keeping the party together," and for "getting out the vote." Did you ever think where the millions for watchers, spellbinders, halls, processions, posters, pamphlets, that are spent in national, state and local campaigns come from? Who pays the big election expenses of your congressman, of the men you send to the legislature to elect senators? Do you imagine those who foot those huge bills are fools? Don't you know that they make sure of getting their money back, with interest, compound upon compound? Your candidates get most of the money for their campaigns from the party committees; and the central party committee is the national committee with which congressional and state and local committees are affiliated. The bulk of the money for the "political trust" comes from "the interests." "The interests" will give only to the "political trust." And that means Aldrich and his Democratic (!) lieutenant, Gorman of Maryland, leader of the minority in the Senate. Aldrich, then, is the head of the "political trust" and Gorman is his right-hand man. When you speak of the Republican party, of the Democratic party, of the "good of the party," of the "best interests of the party," of "wise party policy," you mean what Aldrich and Gorman, acting for their clients, deem wise and proper and "Republican" or "Democratic."

To relate the treason in detail would mean taking up bill after

bill and going through it, line by line, word by word, and
showing how this interpolation there or that excision yonder
meant millions on millions more to this or that interest, millions
on millions less for the people as merchants, wage or salary
earners, consumers; how the killing of this measure meant immunity to looters all along the line; how the alteration of the
wording of that other "trifling" resolution gave a quarter of a
cent a pound on every one of hundreds of millions of pounds of
some necessary of life to a certain small group of men; how this
innocent looking little measure safeguarded the railway barons
in looting the whole American people by excessive charges and
rebates. Few among the masses have the patience to listen to
these dull matters—and, so, "the interests" and their agents
have prosperity and honor instead of justice and jail.

No railway legislation that was not either helpful to or harmless against "the interests"; no legislation on the subject of corporations that would interfere with "the interests," which use the
corporate form to simplify and systematize their stealing; no
legislation on the tariff question unless it secured to "the interests"
full and free license to loot; no investigations of wholesale robbery
or of any of the evils resulting from it—there you have in a few
words the whole story of the Senate's treason under Aldrich's
leadership, and of why property is concentrating in the hands of
the few and the little children of the masses are being sent to
toil in the darkness of mines, in the dreariness and unhealthful-
ness of factories instead of being sent to school; and why the
great middle class—the old-fashioned Americans, the people with
the incomes of from two thousand to fifteen thousand a year—
is being swiftly crushed into dependence and the repulsive
miseries of "genteel poverty." The heavy and ever heavier taxes
of "the interests" are swelling rents, swelling the prices of food,
clothing, fuel, all the necessities and all the necessary comforts.
And the Senate both forbids the lifting of those taxes and levies
fresh taxes for its master. . . .

Like the Aldrich-emasculated anti-trust legislation, like the
Aldrich-manipulated laws for the regulation of the railways, [the
Dingley tariff of 1897] is, in its main schedules—those dealing
with the fundamental necessaries of civilized life used by all the

people—a stupendous robbery, taking cognizance of the huge developments of American resources to arrange that all but a scanty share of them shall become profit for the plunderers. And since 1897 the up-piling of huge fortunes, the reduction of the American people toward wage and salary slavery has gone forward with amazing rapidity. The thieves use each year's rich haul to make larger nets for larger hauls the next.

The abounding prosperity, the immense amount of work to do, has caused the paying of salaries and wages that, as the reports of the commercial agencies show, are *in money* almost as high as they were fifteen years ago and about where they were *in purchasing power* thirty years ago. But the cost of living is going up, up, faster than incomes; and the number of tenant farmers, of renters, of paupers, of unemployed has increased as never before, even in straightened times. In place of the old proportion in the lot of the American people, there is gross disproportion. How Aldrich must laugh as he watches the American people meekly submitting to this plundering through tariff and railway rates and hugely overcapitalized corporations! And what, think you, must be his opinion of the man who in all seriousness attributes the astounding contrasts between the mountainous fortunes of the few and the ant-hill hoardings of the many to the superior intelligence of the few? Yet, Aldrich's contempt for the mentality of the masses is not unjustified, is it?

A JUGGLER OF LEGISLATION

How does Aldrich work? Obviously, not much steering is necessary, when the time comes to vote. "The interests" have a majority and to spare. The only questions are such as permitting a senator to vote and at times to speak against "the interests" when the particular measure is mortally offensive to the people of his particular state or section. Those daily sham battles in the Senate! Those paradings of sham virtue! Is it not strange that the other senators, instead of merely busying themselves at writing letters or combing their whiskers, do not break into shouts of laughter?

Aldrich's real work—getting the wishes of his principals, directly or through their lawyers, and putting these wishes into

proper form if they are orders for legislation or into the proper
channels if they are orders to kill or emasculate legislation—this
work is all done, of course, behind the scenes. When Aldrich is
getting orders, there is of course never any witness. The second
part of his task—execution—is in part a matter of whispering with
his chief lieutenants, in part a matter of consultation in the secure
secrecy of the Senate committee rooms. Aldrich is in person chairman of the chief Senate committee—finance. There he labors, assisted by Gorman, his right bower, who takes his place as chairman when the Democrats are in power; by Spooner, his left
bower and public mouthpiece; by Allison, that Nestor of craft;
by the Pennsylvania Railroad's Penrose; by Tom Platt of New
York, corruptionist and lifelong agent of corruptionists; by Joe
Bailey of Texas, and several other sympathetic or silent spirits.
Together they concoct and sugar-coat the bitter doses for the
people—the loot measures and the suffocating of the measures in
restraint of loot. In the unofficial but powerful steering committee
—which receives from him the will of "the interests" and trans-
lates it into "party policy"—he works through Allison as chairman—but Allison's position is recognized as purely honorary.

And, also, Aldrich sits in the powerful interstate-commerce
committee; there, he has his "pal," the brazen Elkins of West
Virginia, as chairman. He is not on the committee on appropriations; but Allison is, is its chairman, and Cullom of Illinois is
there. . . . In the commerce committee, he has Frye of Maine,
to look after such matters as the projected, often postponed, but
never abandoned, loot through ship subsidy; in the Pacific Railroad committee he has the valiant soldier, the honest lumber and
railway multi-millionaire, the embalmed-beef hero, Alger, as
chairman; in the post-office and post-roads committee, which
looks after the railways' postal graft, a clean steal from the
Treasury of upward of ten millions a year—some put it as high
as thirty millions—he has Penrose as chairman. In that highly
important committee, the one on rules, he himself sits; but mouthpiece Spooner is naturally chairman. Their associates are Elkins
and Lodge—another pair that need to be better known to the
American people. Bailey is the chief "Democratic" member. . . .

These committees carry on their colorless routine and also their

real work—promoting thievish legislation, preventing decent legislation, devising ways and means of making rottenest dishonesty
look like honesty and patriotism—these committees carry on their
work in secrecy. . . .

Aldrich is rich and powerful. Treachery has brought him
wealth and rank, if not honor, of a certain sort. He must laugh at
us, grown-up fools, permitting a handful to bind the might of our
eighty millions and to set us all to work for them.

4 / THE PROGRESSIVE IMPULSE

*Noted writer, Kansas progressive, and Theodore Roosevelt
admirer William Allen White appraises the
achievements of the progressive movement as of 1912.*

They were sitting in the dining room of a club in Chicago three
years ago, the night after the nomination of William H. Taft for
president. One man was from California, one from Michigan,
one from New Jersey—all devoted followers of the Rough Rider.
They didn't like the way things were going. They regarded the
platform adopted by the convention as a straddle; they saw
Sherman, a reactionary, looming up for the vice-presidency, and
they were sickened by the stink of money that was permeating
the proceedings. The California man was inclined to think that
perhaps Roosevelt's friends had made a mistake in permitting
him to keep out of the race. The New Jersey man believed that
things were headed wrong and was willing to make any sacrifice
of Roosevelt's name and fame in history to turn the tide of reaction that seemed to be flowing in. When up spake the Michigan
man.

SOURCE: William Allen White, "Three Years of Progress," *Saturday
Evening Post*, CLXXXIV, 35 (February 24, 1912), 3–5, 38–40. Copyright
1912 The Curtis Publishing Company. Reprinted by permission from *The
Saturday Evening Post*.

"No," quoth he, "not on your life! If the people of this country can't buck this thing themselves, if they can't run this country as they would like it run, they will deserve all the misgovernment they get rubbed into them. It's merely a question of who is boss here—whether property is going to own the people or the people are going to own property. I'm for the Rough Rider bigger'n a wolf, but the time has come when we have got to do business without him. We must hustle for ourselves. Four years more of spoon-fed reform will ruin us. If the people desire to progress— and they do or I'm all wrong—they must get out and fight for it; stand on their two legs and go after it tooth and nail. I'm glad to see Theodore Roosevelt go—we've got to fight it out in this country ourselves sooner or later without him, and the sooner the quicker."

What It Means to Get a Finger in the Pie of Politics

And so Theodore the First, sometimes called the Brash, "sailed away for a year and a day to the land where the palmtree grows," along with other tropical flora; and the spoon-fed people stood up on their legs and began that contest which Mr. Paul D. Cravath, certainly a qualified witness, has seen fit to call "the contest between the people, through their Government, and organized wealth, through the corporations." For three years the contest has been waged with some asperity. In every city, in every state and in the Federal Government, some form of that struggle has been manifest. In caucuses; in primaries; in conventions; at the elections; in legislatures; in Congress; in the White House; in the minor courts, state and Federal; and in the Supreme Court itself, the political contest for the ownership of the United States has been raging. The battle has not been drawn; the "people, through their Government," have won—not finally, of course; but they have made substantial gains.

It is doubtful if any other three peaceful years in American history have seen more substantial changes in the attitude of the people toward things fundamental than the past three years have shown. These changes have appeared in the state governments of some of the commonwealths of New England and in the

Pacific Coast region, in the rich sagebrush principalities of the Rockies and in the industrial and agricultural states of the Mississippi Valley. Whatever is moving the people is, of course, but a continuation of the impulse that carried them so far during the first years of the century; and naturally during the past three years they have used the experience that the earlier years of the contest under President Roosevelt gave them—and they have had the accumulated momentum of those years. The important thing, however, is that there has been no let-up in the struggle begun ten years ago. The wave of reform has not ebbed.

Moreover, the political purpose remains stronger than the economic motive. The movement is institutional at base. It began with the primary, which was designed to break the alliance between business and politics; and, now that the primary is operating in three-fourths of the states, it is used as a lever for giving the individual more direct control of the other institutions of government.

To this end the people are creating new institutions—nothing but a rebuff from the United States Supreme Court can stop the spread of that institution called the initiative and referendum. It is now in force in two hundred and nine cities in twenty-five states and is a part of the fundamental law for state purposes in eleven commonwealths. These eleven are Maine, Missouri, South Dakota, Arkansas, Oklahoma, California, Colorado, Arizona, Montana, Nevada and Oregon. The legislatures that adjourned this spring submitted it to the people of eight other states—Washington, Idaho, Wyoming, North Dakota, Nebraska, Florida, Wisconsin and Indiana—where it is incorporated in the new constitutions. In Ohio it was granted to all cities. The urban population forms a major part of the people of that state; and, moreover, a working majority of the delegates to the constitutional convention are pledged publicly in writing to put the initiative and referendum in the new Ohio constitution. In three other states the initiative and referendum passed both houses of the legislature —Kansas, Massachusetts and Illinois—but lacked a constitutional majority in one house. In Minnesota and Michigan it passed one house of the legislature by the required majority and lacked but a few votes in the other house.

New Political Ideas and Forms of Government

Here are, all told, twenty-five American states where the fundamental relation of the people to the state government is being changed. If, during the next decade, direct legislation gains as rapidly as it has gained since 1908, three-fourths of the American states will be made over. The initiative and referendum today are exactly where the primary was in 1906. The recall has been adopted by the people of Oregon, California and Arizona; it has been submitted to the people for a vote in 1912 as a constitutional amendment in Nebraska, Wisconsin, Indiana, North Dakota and Washington, and by initiation it will go before the people of Colorado. It is a live political issue, for in the cities also it is spreading. It will be found in about one-third of the cities that have adopted the initiative and referendum as parts of their charters.

The legislatures of the states were busy last winter with municipal grants of these weapons of fundamental democracy. We find the right to adopt the recall was granted to cities in Idaho, Montana, North and South Dakota, Washington, Wisconsin, Wyoming and California; and the right to adopt the initiative and referendum was granted to cities adopting the commission form of government in Illinois, Louisiana, Virginia and Michigan.

Coincident with the feeling that the powers of government should be extended to the individual voters, there seems to be a well-defined tendency toward widening the suffrage. Four states last year submitted the question of equal suffrage for women to the voters as constitutional amendments—California, Kansas, Oregon and Wisconsin. California adopted the amendment. This is the largest number of states that ever had this proposition before the people in any one year. Heretofore the suffrage movement has been successful only in the Far West, where men exceeded the women in numbers. The states having woman suffrage are Washington, Idaho, Wyoming, Colorado, California and Utah. If the people of Wisconsin, for instance, should adopt woman suffrage in the election of 1912, the question would cease to be sectional and become part of the national democratic movement; for Iowa, Michigan and Massachusetts are regarded as good fighting ground.

Another evidence of the closer relation growing up between the people and their servants is the growth of what is known as the Oregon plan for the election of United States senators. It is the direct development of the primary. After the party candidates for United States senators are nominated at the primary in the summer, the names of the successful candidates of all the parties are put upon the ballot at the general election in November for an advisory vote. To make that advisory vote binding, every legislative candidate is given an opportunity to sign at option one of two statements; First, that he will vote for the United States senator designated by the advisory vote of the people of his state; second, that he will not vote for the candidate chosen by the people. Naturally most of the legislative candidates agree in writing to obey the people, and the advisory vote becomes binding. Thus, in 1909 the Republican legislature in Oregon elected a Democrat, and in 1911 a Democratic legislature in Nevada elected a Republican, and a Democratic legislature in Nebraska elected a Democrat—all because the people so voted in an advisory vote. In 1911 three United States senators were so elected. In 1913, as the result of the work of the legislatures of 1911, a dozen senators will be elected by the Oregon plan of a direct advisory vote.

The Latest Creation in Democracy

In addition to the three states named above, Idaho, California, Colorado, Arizona, Kansas, Minnesota, Ohio, Montana and New Jersey will elect senators by a direct advisory vote that will be all but mandatory. The Iowa legislature indorsed this plan; but a reactionary governor thought Iowa people were not so capable of choosing senators by a direct vote as the people of Kansas, Nebraska and Minnesota—and he vetoed the bill. However, with twelve states electing senators by a practically direct vote and with the fourteen states of the South, wherein there is but one party, electing United States senators at the primary, it is easy

to see that if the constitutional amendment to the Federal Constitution legalizing a common custom should happen to lag it
will make little difference.

In a few years more, if the tendency is not checked, most of
the states will have the direct vote for senators under the Oregon
plan, and those that do not have it will probably be of a type
whose electorate is so sluggish that it will make little difference
how they choose their senatorial representatives. The people of
a state deserve about what they get in the way of representation.
If they are not willing to sacrifice their time and their money for
the common good they will get the type of senator that represents
a selfish, sordid people.

The amendment, by avoidance, of the Federal Constitution in
the election of United States senators by a direct vote is not the
limit of the cheerful audacity of these reformers. The Constitution
provides that the president and vice-president shall be chosen
by the electoral college. It has suited the purposes of politicians
in practically all of the American states to ignore this constitutional provision by placing the names of the president and vice-
president on the ballots at the general elections; and now the
reformers are going one step farther and are seeking to place the
candidates for party nomination for president and vice-president
upon the primary ballot. This permits the Republicans to choose
at the primary in their states between Mr. Taft and Mr. La
Follette, and the Democrats to express their choice by direct
primary vote as between Mr. Woodrow Wilson, Mr. Harmon,
Mr. Folk and Mr. Clark. In six states this idea has been legalized:
in Oregon—where the people initiated the law—California, Nebraska, Wisconsin, North Dakota and New Jersey. In a number of
other states—notably Kansas, Ohio and Michigan—the idea will
be adopted probably without warrant of law.

The presidential primary may be called the very latest creation
in fundamental democracy. It is as untried as the primary was ten
years ago and stands about where the initiative and referendum
stood five years ago. It is only about two laps behind the recall;
but the idea appeals to the common-sense of the people, for the
reason that if they are wise enough to vote for president they are
wise enough to choose presidential candidates. And it is likely

the conventions which nominate presidential candidates in 1920 will be composed of spectacled, high-browed gentlemen of sedentary temperament, who will register the choice of the people on an adding machine while the delegates devote themselves to the nice points of verbiage in the platform. By that time, perhaps even the platform planks will be submitted to the people by a primary initiative system such as Texas now has, in which case the national political conventions may be run by correspondence or by long-distance telephone.

What a crowd of candidates for post-offices, and for United States district marshals and attorneys and revenue collectors, will be put out of commission by the change! The conventions will not be so dramatic as they are now, but they will be representative—which, after all, is a more or less important point. Prophecies are dangerous, but analogies are harmless. And we may look back a little over a century and surmise how Alexander Hamilton and the dear old Fathers would have smiled superciliously if they had been told that their well-laid plans to put the choosing of a president in a few hands would be laid low by a party system which gave every voter in all the land a direct vote in the election of a president! The electoral college, however, went into atrophy before the demands of the people for a closer grip upon national affairs, and the national party convention may follow the electoral college into disuse during the present decade —for all over the country the convention system is passing. It is passing because the people have found that the system offers to a few men great power to work their selfish ends in national politics. In working those ends these few men open a clear way for the forces amenable only to property to enter American politics and corrupt it.

It is against the perversion of American politics to selfish ends that the whole strength of the so-called Progressive or reform movement is directed. No one cares for the primary because it is the primary; or the initiative and referendum because of the name, or the Oregon plan for electing senators because it belittles the legislature; or the presidential nomination law because it would destroy the national convention's prestige. It is because money gets into conventions and legislatures and turns the will of the people into a byword that these institutional changes in our form of government have risen during the past ten years. All that the people demand is self-government. And it is interesting to note that, coincident with the growth of the primary system and its logical development in fundamental democracy, in nearly every state of the North and West a corrupt-practices law has been passed.

THE TEN BACKWARD STATES

Three years ago more than half the states north of the Ohio River and west of the Alleghanies had laws requiring publicity of campaign expenses after the election. These laws in general have been amended or replaced by other laws going a step farther. It is now generally provided that there shall be publicity of campaign expenses before the primary or before the election, or both; so that the voters may know how much money a party committee or a candidate is spending, where it comes from and where it is going. In several states, notably Oregon and Wisconsin, the amount of money that may be spent by a candidate is limited. The legislatures of 1910–11 in the various states overhauled their corrupt-practices acts and amended them to provide for publicity of campaign expenses, both as to source and disbursement, before the election. This was done in Idaho, Indiana, Maryland, New Hampshire, Ohio, South Dakota, Wisconsin, New Jersey, Wyoming and California. Colorado is to vote in November upon a corrupt-practices law initiated by the people. In New York, North Dakota and Maine stringent acts or amendments have been added to the present law.

Democracy is almost cynically frank; it acknowledges that without rigid restrictions it will be as easy to beat the game of self-government through fundamental democracy as it was to beat self-government through representatives. Three years ago a state's rank in the Progressive column might have been estimated by the breadth of its primary law and the rigor of its anti-pass law; today these laws are nearly universal, and a state's stand is best measured by the kind of a corrupt-practices law it enjoys. Before leaving the political activities of the forward movement in the country it may be worth while to set down the states that do not have the primary law, in some of its forms, covering practically all important offices and generally providing for the nomination of United States senators. These backward states are Connecticut, Vermont, Rhode Island, Pennsylvania, Indiana, Delaware, North Carolina, West Virginia, Utah and Montana—hardly a respectable minority; and even Montana provides that the party convention nominees for United States senators shall be put on the ballot in November for a direct advisory vote, which the legislature, in advance of its election, pledges itself to follow. In some cases, as in Oregon, South Dakota, Maine and Colorado, the primary came after the initiative and referendum; but generally direct legislation and the recall follow the primary as a natural development of a self-governing people.

Democracy seems to feel a need to mend economic conditions; for, all over the country, in all the courts, in Congress and in the White House, we are tinkering away at this job—cheerfully withal, even though we know what a task it is. Speaking broadly and ignoring a wide neutral zone, in the state legislature the economic activities of those states in the forward movement are divided into efforts of two kinds—to curb the encroachment of those who have and to ameliorate the conditions of those who have not. Perhaps this is robbing Peter to pay Paul; but there is a feeling among the people that certain artificial conditions that make some men rich and keep others poor must be changed, and that by taking away special privileges in one direction we may establish justice in another; that in some way unearned increment shall be distributed in wages.

So, all over the nation, and particularly in that group of states which have adopted the primary and its accessories, we find the legislatures devoting themselves to the two branches of the problem as they are revealed—first, in the control and regulation of public utilities, and second, in securing for labor compensation for trade accidents. The endeavor is definitely to take from capital employed in the manufacture and sale of public utilities —transportation, water, light, fuel, power and communication— everything but a decent rate of interest, with reasonable managerial salaries, and to make capital bear the sickness and accident expenses due to any trade as a change against the trade—to be passed on to the consumer of the manufactured article if it seems necessary, but to be taken off the back of labor in any event.

During the past three years a sort of tacit agreement seems to have been reached between the people and the railroads that much of the regulation of railroads, as to rates at least, may be safely left to the Interstate Commerce Commission and to the railroad commissions of the states appealing to that central body for aid. The legislation of 1910–11 has shown a distinct tendency away from state regulation of railroads and toward the centralization of regulation in the Interstate Commerce Commission. In the place of stringent state railroad legislation, about which there is some dispute, we find the state legislatures in the more intelligent and progressive of the states devoting themselves to local utilities—to the electric company, the interurban railroad, the gas company, the telephone company, the waterworks and the town street cars—touching the large transportation problem only in dealing with express companies, whose business is more or less local, and with telegraph companies in connection with their local rates and service and taxes.

The public-utility commission is the old railroad commission enlarged. This public-utility commission, with powers over practically all public utilities as above designated, is found now in Kansas, Maryland, Connecticut, Michigan, Ohio, New Jersey, California, Washington, New York, Wisconsin, Massachusetts, South Dakota, Oregon and Nebraska; and North Dakota has given cities the right of initial action in fixing rates and securing service from local utilities. The control of the issue of stocks and bonds—to prevent overcapitalization—is given to public-utilities commissions in Kansas, Maryland, Michigan, Nebraska, Ohio, New Jersey, California, Wisconsin and Massachusetts; and, as a corollary of the right to control the issue of stocks and bonds, the commissions are empowered to make physical valuations of the properties of public utilities in Kansas, Maryland, Michigan, Ohio, Oregon, South Dakota, Washington, Wisconsin, California and New Jersey. Except in New York, Wisconsin, Massachusetts and Nebraska, these powers over local public utilities have been given to the commissions by the state during the past three years; and even in the states just named, within the year the powers of the commissions have been extended either by judical confirmation or legislative action.

This creation of a public-utility commission was an issue in Iowa, Missouri, Colorado, Wyoming, Minnesota and Montana, and will be prominently before the legislatures of these states in 1912 and 1913; for the rights of the states to control purely local utilities will hardly be denied by the courts. And as civilization broadens these utilities will touch more and more intimately the lives of all the people. The sale of these commodities does not require great skill in trading; their management calls for no more extraordinary talent than is developed by a colonel in a regular army regiment. It is not fair that great profits should be taken by capitalists and promoters in conducting these enterprises. What is more to the point, the people, through their cities and states, are beginning to take the matter in hand; and, unless the tendencies that have begun within the three years last past and have overspread a dozen of the great American commonwealths are checked, within half a decade exorbitant profits on watered stock in local public utilities will begin to see their declining days.

Of course control by the state or nation in the realm of public utilities is no new thing. For nearly a generation public control of railroads has been common, and the extension of control to other utilities is merely broadening the application of an old idea; but the introduction of working-men's compensation laws and the removal from the shoulders of labor of liability for accidents and disease arising in a trade, and putting that liability upon capital—these are new things in our politics.

FAIRER LIABILITY LAWS

Until within the last half-decade labor bore the burden of the wear and tear of men; capital bore the burden of the wear and tear of machinery. In Europe for a generation capital has borne both burdens; but here in America the employer of labor was allowed to defend himself against the claim of his employee by claiming contributory negligence or the negligence of a fellow servant, or by setting up the claim that when the laborer went to work in the factory or upon the railroad or in the mine, or what-not, he knew the risks of the employment and took them with his eyes open and could not claim damages for accidents occurring in the ordinary run of the business. Today sentiment in America is changing rapidly upon the question of the assumed risk, and it is changing also as to the broader question of the responsibility of capital for the wear and tear of men in any trade, whether the wear and tear comes from accidents peculiar to the trade or from diseases peculiar to the trade.

This change of sentiment is evidenced by enactment in ten states widely separated as to conditions and sectional viewpoint. These states have recently secured laws providing for definite compensations for different accidents to workingmen. At the same time, these states have removed the defenses that capital heretofore has set up that have made it difficult for employees to recover damages for the common run of accidents in any trade. These states are California, Kansas, Washington, New Jersey, Massachusetts; Ohio—where an insurance fund is provided; New York—where the state court of appeals set aside the working-men's compensation law as unconstitutional; New Hampshire; Oregon—where the people initiated the law after the legislature refused to pass it; and Illinois. Nebraska and Iowa have appointed commissions to draw up laws conforming to their constitutions and submit them to the next session of their respective legisla-tures. In addition to this, Indiana, Maine, Montana and South Dakota have removed the old defenses that placed the liability for accidents upon labor and have left to juries the amount of damages to be assessed.

Here are sixteen states wherein, during three years, public sentiment has expressed itself definitely in legislation against the barbarous doctrine of the assumed risk. The sentiment is too widely diffused among the people to be a mere local cataclysm of sentiment. When, for instance, Ohio, Indiana and Wisconsin think alike upon a subject there is no reason to believe that their neighbors, Minnesota, Michigan and West Virginia, will lag far behind their sister states in expressing in laws the same sentiment.

And it is highly grotesque for wise gentlemen with mechanical views of the law to sit in judgment upon the matter and say that the Constitution will check the legislation of this sentiment. The Constitution is a good and great document, but when public sentiment in this country has become thoroughly set the Constitution never affords a serious impediment to the legal expression of this sentiment; or when majorities are for a proposition courts may always be depended upon to find excellent law to support the majorities in interpreting the Constitution. The Constitution is merely a coffer-dam to prevent the legalization of temporary clamor.

In the case of the liability of capital for the accidents of the trades public sentiment in this country is becoming fairly well crystallized.

In the matter of the conditions of labor public sentiment is changing rapidly all over the country. A dozen states made laws last winter limiting the hours of service of women and children. These states are Illinois, Indiana, California, Michigan, New Hampshire, Missouri, Montana, Nebraska, New York, Ohio, Wisconsin and Washington. Oregon, the first state to secure a law that passed muster in the United States Supreme Court, got her law by the initiative and has materially strengthened it since. Laws regulating the hours of service in certain trades—as for instance railroading—are so common that the fact that seven states have recently come up with the majority in enacting such laws is worth scarcely a comment. These states are Kansas, Indiana, Iowa, Montana, Nebraska, Ohio and North Carolina. Massachusetts—which is the most progressive of American commonwealths in the matter of economic legislation and is moving forward in the matter of political and institutional development— has supplemented her savings-bank substitute for old-age pensions by a law providing for a retirement allowance for employees. This law provides for a fund to which both employer and employee contribute. It is invested under control and supervision of the state and it becomes a pension for the employee after a certain number of years of service, when he is ready to retire.

KANSAS PENSION ACTS

Kansas passed two laws providing for pensioning citizens: the first, providing that school-teachers, under a mutually collected fund in first-class cities, may be pensioned; and the second, providing that the county commissioners may pension indigent persons instead of sending them to the poorhouse. Legislation of this kind, though at present sporadic, is occurring too frequently in different sections of the country for the entire comfort of those persons who believe that the wave of reform has spent itself, and that soon we shall go back to the good old days when labor was a commodity like hoop-poles, and every man had a right to do as he pleased with his own money, his own employees and his own business. Public control of capital invested in necessary industries is slowly but steadily extending. And, with the fundamental institutional changes that are remaking the states—the primary, direct legislation, the recall, the direct election of senators and the direct nomination of presidents, all hedged about by rigid corrupt-practices acts—the power of capital in American political affairs is not likely to enjoy a renaissance for a long and possibly a weary time.

Of course the political and economic activities hereinbefore enumerated are not the only national movements evidenced by state legislation. The establishment of a state tax commission, with powers to demand a full valuation of all property, is one of the important tendencies of the time. Two states, Missouri and Oregon, will vote for the adoption of what is known as the single tax. The enactment in a dozen states of laws putting many state employees upon the merit system, and putting all state institutions—except the educational and penal—under one board, is characteristic of the political spirit of the times. As the convention system is abolished, the need for political jobs for political camp-followers falls off; and the ideal state government, wherein every man pays his equitable share of the taxes and every dollar's worth of taxes brings a dollar's worth of service, is more and more nearly approached as the professional politician is further and further eliminated in state affairs.

The tax commission and the central bipartisan board of control of the state institutions are putting state affairs nearer to a scientific standard of management than they ever were; and it is a significant fact that these institutions have made most effective headway in the primary states; for the primary brings state officers and members of the legislature into office without entangling trades and promises—to be paid for out of the public treasury by supernumerary officers. Whatever else may be charged to the new movement in politics, as far as it touches state affairs, it has not been convicted of loading the tax rolls with useless offices; for under the new rule the public officials are responsible not to the politicians but directly to the voters and taxpayers. When a new office is created it must be such an office as the people approve, even if the politicians sniff at it.

The rise in importance of the state university and agricultural college in a state runs parallel with its advance in those political and economic changes that are remaking our American state institutions. The leading commonwealths in the progressive movement are Wisconsin, California, Oregon, Nebraska, Kansas, Washington, Illinois, Ohio, Iowa, New Jersey, Minnesota, the two Dakotas, Michigan, Maine, Massachusetts and New Hampshire. With the exception of Massachusetts, New Jersey and New Hampshire, each of these states spends more money for higher education than for any other single item in its state budget. And the influence of Harvard upon Massachusetts and of Princeton upon New Jersey, of course, must not be discounted.

The rule seems to work well backward; and one may account for the conservatism of the South, which today is the most reactionary section of the country, by the fact that during the past generation the South had other problems and could not afford to spend lavish sums for higher education. The hope of the South is in the fact that during the last decade the Southern state universities and industrial schools have been striding into their proper places in the social schemes of their respective states.

THE OVERTHROW OF CANNON

So much for the work of the states as states. The work of the states as the United States is worthy of consideration. In the main the Federal activities of the people are along lines exactly parallel to their activities in the states; and the three years' progress they have made in the Federal Government is just as satisfactory, when one remembers the size of the political body that is to be moved, as the progress in the several commonwealths. In the Federal Government, as in the states, we find the activities of the people both political and economic. The overthrow of Cannon and Cannonism, which made the House of Representatives more truly representative, was purely political—in the sense that its economic significance was negligible, except indirectly; but the greater freedom with which the House has moved since the changed rules have broken the autocratic power of the Committee on Rules, and since the power of the Speaker to name house committees has been taken from him, has justified the bitterness of that contest.

In the Senate the chief contest upon the purely political side of the activities of progress was in the two affirmative votes taken for the direct election of United States senators. The second important political contest in the Senate was the prolonged struggle to unseat Senator Lorimer. A third political contest of importance was developed in the refusal of the Senate to elect any president pro tem. rather than to elect a pronounced reactionary who would direct the course of the Senate, as far as he was able, along reactionary lines. The victory of the Progressives in these three contests is the direct result of the primaries in the states. The Republican senators who accomplished these three results, with but one exception, came from primary states. That one exception, Dixon, of Montana, came from a state that requires a direct advisory vote on senators. In the fight in the House of Representatives on Cannonism the Insurgents, with few exceptions, also came from districts which nominated their candidates for Congress by a direct vote; and the indorsement of those congressmen by the primary and the defeat of a score of their reactionary colleagues at the primaries seems to give direct evidence of the political power of the movement that has grown for the past ten years.

In thirty-six states congressmen are now nominated by a direct primary vote, and the last Congress has convened that will deliberately defy the people as the members of the Sixtieth Congress defied it. Within three years the United States has seen the entire spirit of Congress change; the control upon big basic matters has passed from the great property interests to the people. It is true that Mr. Roosevelt time and again compelled Congress to stand for human rights against the unfair demands of property; but then Congress moved under the lash and grudgingly. Now, with no great leader, but under the force of sheer public sentiment unmistakably expressed in the primaries, Congress takes its stand without a whimper. The gain is evolutional; the contrast is revolutionary!

New Fields of Federal Activity

The passage of the [Mann-Elkins] law broadening the powers of the Government in the control of the railroads, along the lines of control that the most progressive states have adopted with respect to their local utilities, marks the most important step taken by the Government for a generation. The bill is not all that its best friends hope for, but it is far in advance of the Hepburn law and points a way to the control of other interstate corporations—the so-called trusts—that may prove a solution of our greatest economic problem. That solution would seem to be the conservation of the benefits of monopoly, by regulation and control, under the strictest Federal supervision. The postal savings-bank law—another compromise—is an entering wedge, and probably marks the beginning of a number of lines of Federal activity, for banking leads to insurance; and it must not be forgotten that Wisconsin has established a state insurance company and now furnishes life insurance at cost to the people of Wisconsin.

Now all this progress is the result of a healthy, insistent demonstration of sane, unselfish public sentiment. In the states and in the nation, through the legislatures and through Congress, and through the courts, the people of the United States have demonstrated that they not only know what they desire but they can make their wants felt calmly and without clamor, yet with great force and emphasis. What the people seriously desire and ask for, this they get; and courts are as ready as legislatures to follow public sentiment—across the Constitution, if necessary. It is only raw clamor that goes to pot in this country. Wise progress never before has had such a successful triennium in America as has just passed. The Taft Administration has been anything but a period of waiting. It has been a period of effective action; and the action has been promoted by the rank and file of citizenship. Mr. Roosevelt, Mr. La Follette, Mr. Taft, Mr. Wilson, Mr. Bryan, Mr. Harmon, and a score of colonels, captains, sergeants and privates, have done their part—not all an equal part, but their part as they saw it. Either or all of the officers might have died or deserted and still the fight would have been waged without abatement and with success—for it has been a fight of the folks. The faith is amply justified of those who believed that the people would stand up and fight their own battles, even without the leader who roused them. Those who believed the country had been fattening on spoon-fed reform must see their folly. Those who have been predicting that the wave of agitation would recede may as well come aboard the ark. The American mind is beginning to apply itself to problems of concrete justice. It is an active mind—that American mind; and what it has done in a material way during the last century will be paralleled in a spiritual way in this century. We have come far in ten years. Those who think they can lock the spokes of progress by defeating this or the other radical leader should realize that radical leaders do not make a radical people. Radicalism in the people develops radical leaders. This is the one big fact that the departure of Mr. Roosevelt from the White House, the eclipse of President Taft, and the rise of La Follette, Wilson, and the Progressive Insurgent group in Congress, prove beyond any reasonable doubt.

PART II

Progressivism at High Tide

PROGRESSIVISM came of age nationally with the accession of Theodore Roosevelt to the presidency in September, 1901. Hardly a radical, Roosevelt saw himself as an enlightened conservative who would save the United States from European-style class warfare by reforming the worst abuses of industrial capitalism (Selection 5). During his first years in the White House, political exigencies forced him to tread softly. But his growing alarm over the dangers of inaction led him to embrace a far-reaching reform program which he called the "New Nationalism." The fullest exposition of his mature progressivism was his speech at Osawatomie, Kansas, October 31, 1910 (Selection 6).

The growing split within the Republican Party between its standpat and progressive wings became an irreparable breach under his successor, William H. Taft. When Taft succeeded in winning renomination, T.R. bolted and launched the Progressive Party. This division in the G.O.P. ranks provided an opportunity for the victory of Democratic candidate Woodrow Wilson.

During the 1912 campaign, Wilson had sharply distinguished his program—which he called the "New Freedom"—from Roosevelt's New Nationalism (Selection 7). But by 1916 he would boast that he had carried out most of the planks of the 1912 Progressive Party platform (Selection 8).

5 / T.R. AND THE SQUARE DEAL

In these excerpts from two of his letters,
Theodore Roosevelt expresses alarm over the way
the excesses of "predatory wealth" were threatening the
social fabric and describes the meaning of his Square Deal.

The first excerpt is from Roosevelt's letter to Secretary of War
William Howard Taft, March 15, 1906:

I do not at all like the social conditions at present. The dull,
purblind folly of the very rich men; their greed and arrogance,
and the way in which they have unduly prospered by the help
of the ablest lawyers, and too often through the weakness or
shortsightedness of the judges or by their unfortunate possession
of meticulous minds; these facts, and the corruption in business
and politics, have tended to produce a very unhealthy condition
of excitement and irritation in the popular mind, which shows
itself in part in the enormous increase in the socialistic propaganda. Nothing effective, because nothing at once honest and
intelligent, is being done to combat the great amount of evil
which, mixed with a little good, a little truth, is contained in the
outpourings of the *Cosmopolitan,* of *McClure's,* of *Collier's,* of
Tom Lawson, of David Graham Phillips, of Upton Sinclair. Some
of these are socialists; some of them merely sensationalists; but
they are all building up a revolutionary feeling which will most
probably take the form of a political campaign.

SOURCE: Elting Elmore Morison, *et al.* (eds.), *The Letters of Theodore
Roosevelt* (Cambridge: Harvard University Press, 1951–1954), V, 183–184,
and VI, 884, 887–890. Copyright, 1952, by the President and Fellows of
Harvard College.

The second excerpt is from his letter of January 2, 1908, to At-
torney General Charles J. Bonaparte, congratulating him on his
administration of the Department of Justice:

You have shown by what you have actually accomplished that
the law is enforced against the wealthiest corporation, and the
richest and most powerful manager or manipulator of that corporation, just as resolutely and fearlessly as against the humblest
citizen. The Department of Justice is now in very fact the Department of Justice, and justice is meted out with an even hand
to great and small, rich and poor, weak and strong. Those who
have denounced you and the action of the Department of Justice
are either misled, or else are the very wrongdoers, and the agents
of the very wrongdoers, who have for so many years gone scot-
free and flouted the laws with impunity. Above all, you are to be
congratulated upon the bitterness felt and exprest towards you by
the representatives and agents of the great law-defying corporations of immense wealth, who, until within the last half dozen
years, have treated themselves and have expected others to treat
them as being beyond and above all possible check from law.
It was time to say something, for the representatives of predatory wealth, of wealth accumulated on a giant scale by iniquity,
by wrongdoing in many forms, by plain swindling, by oppressing
wageworkers, by manipulating securities, by unfair and unwhole-
some competition, and by stockjobbing, in short by conduct abhorrent to every man of ordinarily decent conscience, have during the last few months made it evident that they are banded
together to work for a reaction, to endeavor to overthrow and dis-
credit all who honestly administer the law, and to secure a return
to the days when every unscrupulous wrongdoer could do what
he wisht unchecked, provided he had enough money. They attack
you because they know your honesty and fearlessness, and dread
them. The enormous sums of money these men have at their
control enable them to carry on an effective campaign. They find
their tools in a portion of the public press including especially
certain of the great New York newspapers. They find their agents

in some men in public life—now and then occupying, or having occupied, positions as high as Senator or Governor—in some men in the pulpit, and most melancholy of all, in a few men on the bench. By gifts to colleges and universities they are occasionally able to subsidize in their own interest some head of an educational body, who, save only a judge, should of all men be most careful to keep his skirts clear from the taint of such corruption. . . .

The keynote of all these attacks upon the effort to secure honesty in business and in politics, is exprest in a recent speech in which the speaker stated that prosperity had been checked by the effort for the "moral regeneration of the business world," an effort which he denounced as "unnatural, unwarranted and injurious" and for which he stated the panic was the penalty. The morality of such a plea is precisely as great as if made on behalf of the men caught in a gambling establishment when that gambling establishment is raided by the police. If such words mean anything they mean that those sentiments they represent stand against the effort to bring about a moral regeneration of business which will prevent a repetition of the insurance, banking and street railroad scandals in New York; repetition of the Chicago and Alton deal; a repetition of the combination between certain professional politicians, certain professional labor leaders and certain big financiers from the disgrace of which San Francisco has just been rescued; a repetition of the successful efforts by the Standard Oil people to crush out every competitor, to overawe the common carriers, and to establish a monopoly which treats the public with the contempt which the public deserves so long as it permits men like the public men of whom I speak to represent it in politics, men like the heads of colleges to whom I refer to educate its youth. The outcry against stopping dishonest practices among the very wealthy is precisely similar to the outcry raised against every effort for cleanliness and decency in city government because, forsooth, it will "hurt business." The same outcry is made against the Department of Justice for prosecuting the heads of colossal corporations that is made against the men who in San Francisco are prosecuting with impartial severity the wrongdoers among businessmen, public officials, and labor lead-

ers alike. The principle is the same in the two cases. Just as the
blackmailer and the bribe-giver stand on the same evil eminence
of infamy, so the man who makes an enormous fortune by cor-
rupting Legislatures and municipalities and fleecing his stock-
holders and the public stands on a level with the creature who
fattens on the blood money of the gambling house, the saloon
and the brothel. Moreover both kinds of corruption in the last
analysis are far more intimately connected than would at first
sight appear; the wrongdoing is at bottom the same. Corrupt business and corrupt politics act and react, with ever increasing de-
basement, one on the other; the rebate-taker, the franchise-
trafficker, the manipulator of securities, the purveyor and pro-
tector of vice, the blackmailing ward boss, the ballot-box-stuffer,
the demagogue, the mob leader, the hired bully and man-killer,
all alike work at the same web of corruption, and all alike should
be abhorred by honest men.

The "business" which is hurt by the movement for honesty is
the kind of business which, in the long run, it pays the country
to have hurt. It is the kind of business which has tended to make
the very name "high finance" a term of scandal to which all honest American men of business should join in putting an end. One
of the special pleaders for business dishonesty, in a recent speech,
in denouncing the Administration for enforcing the law against
the huge and corrupt corporations which have defied the law,
also denounced it for endeavoring to secure a far-reaching law
making employers liable for injuries to their employees. It is
meet and fit that the apologists for corrupt wealth should oppose
every effort to relieve weak and helpless people from crushing
misfortune brought upon them by injury in the business from
which they gain a bare livelihood and their employers fortunes.
It is hypocritical baseness to speak of a girl who works in a factory where the dangerous machinery is unprotected as having the
"right" freely to contract to expose herself to dangers to life and
limb. She has no alternative but to suffer want or else to expose
herself to such dangers, and when she loses a hand or is otherwise
maimed or disfigured for life it is a moral wrong that the burden
of the risk necessarily incidental to the business should be placed
with crushing weight upon her weak shoulders and the man who

has profited by her work escape scot-free. This is what our opponents advocate, and it is proper that they should advocate it, for it rounds out their advocacy of those most dangerous members of the criminal class, the criminals of vast wealth, the men who can afford best to pay for such championship in the press and on the stump. . . .

We have no quarrel with the individuals, whether public men, lawyers or editors, to whom I refer. These men derive their sole power from the great, sinister offenders who stand behind them. They are but puppets who move as the strings are pulled by those who control the enormous masses of corporate wealth which if itself left uncontrolled threatens dire evil to the Republic. It is not the puppets, but the strong, cunning men and the mighty forces working for evil behind, and to a certain extent thru, the puppets, with whom we have to deal. We seek to control law-defying wealth, in the first place to prevent its doing evil, and in the next place to avoid the vindictive and dreadful radicalism which if left uncontrolled it is certain in the end to arouse. Sweeping attacks upon all property, upon all men of means, without regard to whether they do well or ill, would sound the death knell of the Republic; and such attacks become inevitable if decent citizens permit rich men whose lives are corrupt and evil to domineer in swollen pride, unchecked and unhindered, over the destinies of this country. We act in no vindictive spirit, and we are no respecters of persons. If a labor union does what is wrong we oppose it as fearlessly as we oppose a corporation that does wrong; and we stand with equal stoutness for the rights of the man of wealth and for the rights of the wageworkers; just as much so for one as for the other. We seek to stop wrongdoing; and we desire to punish the wrongdoer only so far as is necessary in order to achieve this end. We are the staunch upholders of every honest man, whether businessman or wageworker.

I do not for a moment believe that our actions have brought on business distress; so far as this is due to local and not world-wide causes, and to the actions of any particular individuals, it is due to the speculative folly and flagrant dishonesty of a few men of great wealth, who now seek to shield themselves from the effects of their own wrongdoings by ascribing its results to the actions of those who have sought to put a stop to the wrongdoing. But if it were true that to cut out rottenness from the body politic meant a momentary check to an unhealthy-seeming prosperity, I should not for one moment hesitate to put the knife to the cancer. On behalf of all our people, on behalf no less of the honest man of means than of the honest man who earns each day's livelihood by that day's sweat of his brow, it is necessary to insist upon honesty in business and politics alike, in all walks of life, in big things and in little things; upon just and fair dealing as between man and man. . . .

6 / THEODORE ROOSEVELT AND THE NEW NATIONALISM

In his speech at Osawatomie, Kansas, October 31, 1910, T.R. most fully expounded his mature progressivism.

In every wise struggle for human betterment one of the main objects, and often the only object, has been to achieve in large measure equality of opportunity. In the struggle for this great end, nations rise from barbarism to civilization, and through it people press forward from one stage of enlightenment to the next. One of the chief factors in progress is the destruction of special privilege. The essence of any struggle for healthy liberty has always been, and must always be, to take from some one man or class of men the right to enjoy power, or wealth, or position, or immunity, which has not been earned by service to his or their fellows. . . .

At many stages in the advance of humanity, this conflict between the men who possess more than they have earned and the men who have earned more than they possess is the central condition of progress. In our day it appears as the struggle of free

SOURCE: Theodore Roosevelt, *The New Nationalism* (New York: The Outlook Company, 1911), pp. 9–18, 20–33.

men to gain and hold the right of self-government as against the special interests, who twist the methods of free government into machinery for defeating the popular will. At every stage, and under all circumstances, the essence of the struggle is to equalize opportunity, destroy privilege, and give to the life and citizenship of every individual the highest possible value both to himself and to the commonwealth. . . .

Practical equality of opportunity for all citizens, when we achieve it, will have two great results. First, every man will have a fair chance to make of himself all that in him lies; to reach the highest point to which his capacities, unassisted by special privilege of his own and unhampered by the special privilege of others, can carry him, and to get for himself and his family substantially what he has earned. Second, equality of opportunity means that the commonwealth will get from every citizen the highest service of which he is capable. No man who carries the burden of the special privileges of another can give to the commonwealth that service to which it is fairly entitled.

I stand for the square deal. But when I say that I am for the square deal, I mean not merely that I stand for fair play under the present rules of the game, but that I stand for having those rules changed so as to work for a more substantial equality of opportunity and of reward for equally good service. One word of warning, which, I think, is hardly necessary in Kansas. When I say I want a square deal for the poor man, I do not mean that I want a square deal for the man who remains poor because he has not the energy to work for himself. If a man who has had a chance will not make good, then he has got to quit. . . .

Now, this means that our government, national and state, must be freed from the sinister influence or control of special interests. . . . The great special business interests too often control and corrupt the men and methods of government for their own profit. We must drive the special interests out of politics. That is one of our tasks to-day. Every special interest is entitled to justice—full, fair, and complete,—and, now, mind you, if there were any attempt by mob violence to plunder and work harm to the special interest, whatever it may be, that I most dislike, and the wealthy man, whomsoever he may be, for whom I have the greatest contempt, I would fight for him, and you would if you were worth your salt. He should have justice. For every special interest is entitled to justice, but not one is entitled to a vote in Congress, to a voice on the bench, or to representation in any public office. The Constitution guarantees protection to property, and we must make that promise good. But it does not give the right of suffrage to any corporation.

The true friend of property, the true conservative, is he who insists that property shall be the servant and not the master of the commonwealth; who insists that the creature of man's making shall be the servant and not the master of the man who made it. The citizens of the United States must effectively control the mighty commercial forces which they have themselves called into being.

There can be no effective control of corporations while their political activity remains. To put an end to it will be neither a short nor an easy task, but it can be done.

We must have complete and effective publicity of corporate affairs, so that the people may know beyond peradventure whether the corporations obey the law and whether their management entitles them to the confidence of the public. It is necessary that laws should be passed to prohibit the use of corporate funds directly or indirectly for political purposes; it is still more necessary that such laws should be thoroughly enforced. Corporate expenditures for political purposes, and especially such expenditures by public service corporations, have supplied one of the principal sources of corruption in our political affairs.

It has become entirely clear that we must have government supervision of the capitalization, not only of public service corporations, including, particularly, railways, but of all corporations doing an interstate business. I do not wish to see the nation forced into the ownership of the railways if it can possibly be avoided, and the only alternative is thoroughgoing and effective regulation, which shall be based on a full knowledge of all the facts, including a physical valuation of property. This physical valuation is not needed, or, at least, is very rarely needed, for fixing rates; but it is needed as the basis of honest capitalization.

We have come to recognize that franchises should never be

granted except for a limited time, and never without proper provision for compensation to the public. It is my personal belief that the same kind and degree of control and supervision which should be exercised over public service corporations should be extended also to combinations which control necessaries of life, such as meat, oil, and coal, or which deal in them on an important scale. I have no doubt that the ordinary man who has control of them is much like ourselves. I have no doubt he would like to do well, but I want to have enough supervision to help him realize that desire to do well.

I believe that the officers, and, especially, the directors, of corporations should be held personally responsible when any corporation breaks the law.

Combinations in industry are the result of an imperative economic law which cannot be repealed by political legislation. The effort at prohibiting all combination has substantially failed. The way out lies, not in attempting to prevent such combinations, but in completely controlling them in the interest of the public welfare. For that purpose the Federal Bureau of Corporations is an agency of first importance. Its powers, and, therefore, its efficiency, as well as that of the Interstate Commerce Commission, should be largely increased. We have a right to expect from the Bureau of Corporations and from the Interstate Commerce Commission a very high grade of public service. We should be as sure of the proper conduct of the interstate railways and the proper management of interstate business as we are now sure of the conduct and management of the national banks, and we should have as effective supervision in one case as in the other. The Hepburn Act, and the amendment to the Act in the shape in which it finally passed Congress at the last session, represent a long step in advance, and we must go yet further.

There is a widespread belief among our people that, under the methods of making tariffs which have hitherto obtained, the special interests are too influential. Probably this is true of both the big special interests and the little special interests. These methods have put a premium on selfishness, and, naturally, the selfish big interests have gotten more than their smaller, though equally selfish, brothers. The duty of Congress is to provide a method by which the interest of the whole people shall be all that receives consideration. To this end there must be an expert tariff commission, wholly removed from the possibility of political pressure or of improper business influence. Such a commission can find the real difference between cost of production, which is mainly the difference of labor cost here and abroad. As fast as its recommendations are made, I believe in revising one schedule at a time. A general revision of the tariff almost inevitably leads to log-rolling and the subordination of the general public interest to local and special interests.

The absence of effective state, and, especially, national, restraint upon unfair money getting has tended to create a small class of enormously wealthy and economically powerful men, whose chief object is to hold and increase their power. The prime need is to change the conditions which enable these men to accumulate power which it is not for the general welfare that they should hold or exercise. We grudge no man a fortune which represents his own power and sagacity, when exercised with entire regard to the welfare of his fellows. . . . It is not even enough that it should have been gained without doing damage to the community. We should permit it to be gained only so long as the gaining represents benefit to the community. This, I know, implies a policy of a far more active governmental interference with social and economic conditions in this country than we have yet had, but I think we have got to face the fact that such an increase in governmental control is now necessary.

No man should receive a dollar unless that dollar has been fairly earned. Every dollar received should represent a dollar's worth of service rendered—not gambling in stocks, but service rendered. The really big fortune, the swollen fortune, by the mere fact of its size acquires qualities which differentiate it in kind as well as in degree from what is possessed by men of relatively small means. Therefore, I believe in a graduated income tax on big fortunes, and in another tax which is far more easily collected and far more effective—a graduated inheritance tax on big fortunes, properly safeguarded against evasion and increasing rapidly in amount with the size of the estate. . . .

I recognize the right and duty of this generation to develop and use the natural resources of our land; but I do not recognize the right to waste them, or to rob, by wasteful use, the generations that come after us. I ask nothing of the nation except that it so behave as each farmer here behaves with reference to his own children. That farmer is a poor creature who skins the land and leaves it worthless to his children. The farmer is a good farmer who, having enabled the land to support himself and to provide for the education of his children, leaves it to them a little better than he found it himself. I believe the same thing of a nation.

Moreover, I believe that the natural resources must be used for the benefit of all our people, and not monopolized for the benefit of the few, and here again is another case in which I am accused of taking a revolutionary attitude. People forget now that one hundred years ago there were public men of good character who advocated the nation selling its public lands in great quantities, so that the nation could get the most money out of it, and giving it to the men who could cultivate it for their own uses. We took the proper democratic ground that the land should be granted in small sections to the men who were actually to till it and live on it. Now, with the water power, with the forests, with the mines, we are brought face to face with the fact that there are many people who will go with us in conserving the resources only if they are to be allowed to exploit them for their benefit. That is one of the fundamental reasons why the special interests should be driven out of politics. Of all the questions which can come before this nation, short of the actual preservation of its existence in a great war, there is none which compares in importance with the great central task of leaving this land even a better land for our descendants than it is for us, and training them into a better race to inhabit the land and pass it on. Conservation is a great moral issue, for it involves the patriotic duty of insuring the safety and continuance of the nation. Let me add that the health and vitality of our people are at least as well worth conserving as their forests, waters, lands, and minerals, and in this great work the national government must bear a most important part. . . .

Nothing is more true than that excess of every kind is followed by reaction; a fact which should be pondered by reformer and

reactionary alike. We are face to face with new conceptions of
the relations of property to human welfare, chiefly because certain advocates of the rights of property as against the rights of
men have been pushing their claims too far. The man who
wrongly holds that every human right is secondary to his profit
must now give way to the advocate of human welfare, who rightly
maintains that every man hold his property subject to the general
right of the community to regulate its use to whatever degree the
public welfare may require it.

But I think we may go still further. The right to regulate the
use of wealth in the public interest is universally admitted. Let
us admit also the right to regulate the terms and conditions of
labor, which is the chief element of wealth, directly in the interest of the common good. The fundamental thing to do for
every man is to give him a chance to reach a place in which he
will make the greatest possible contribution to the public welfare.
Understand what I say there. Give him a chance, not push him
up if he will not be pushed. Help any man who stumbles; if he
lies down, it is a poor job to try to carry him; but if he is a
worthy man, try your best to see that he gets a chance to show
the worth that is in him. No man can be a good citizen unless
he has a wage more than sufficient to cover the bare cost of living,
and hours of labor short enough so that after his day's work is
done he will have time and energy to bear his share in the management of the community, to help in carrying the general load.
We keep countless men from being good citizens by the conditions of life with which we surround them. We need comprehensive workmen's compensation acts, both state and national laws
to regulate child labor and work for women, and, especially, we
need in our common schools not merely education in book learning, but also practical training for daily life and work. We need
to enforce better sanitary conditions for our workers and to extend the use of safety appliances for our workers in industry and
commerce, both within and between the states. Also, friends, in
the interest of the workingman himself we need to set our faces
like flint against mob violence just as against corporate greed;
against violence and injustice and lawlessness by wage workers
just as much as against lawless cunning and greed and selfish

arrogance of employers. If I could ask but one thing of my fellow countrymen, my request would be that, whenever they go in for reform, they remember the two sides, and that they always exact justice from one side as much as from the other. I have small use for the public servant who can always see and denounce the corruption of the capitalist, but who cannot persuade himself, especially before election, to say a word about lawless mob violence. And I have equally small use for a man, be he a judge on the bench, or editor of a great paper, or wealthy and influential private citizen, who can see clearly enough and denounce the lawlessness of mob violence, but whose eyes are closed so that he is blind when the question is one of corruption in business on a gigantic scale. Also remember what I said about excess in reformer and reactionary alike. If the reactionary man, who thinks of nothing but the rights of property, could have his way, he would bring about a revolution; and one of my chief fears in connection with progress comes because I do not want to see our people, for lack of proper leadership, compelled to follow men whose intentions are excellent, but whose eyes are a little too wild to make it really safe to trust them. Here in Kansas there is one paper which habitually denounces me as the tool of Wall Street, and at the same time frantically repudiates the statement that I am a Socialist on the ground that that is an unwarranted slander of the Socialists.

National efficiency has many factors. It is a necessary result of the principle of conservation widely applied. In the end it will determine our failure or success as a nation. National efficiency has to do, not only with natural resources and with men, but it is equally concerned with institutions. The state must be made efficient for the work which concerns only the people of the state; and the nation for that which concerns all the people. There must remain no neutral ground to serve as a refuge for lawbreakers, and especially for lawbreakers of great wealth, who can hire the vulpine legal cunning which will teach them how to avoid both jurisdictions. It is a misfortune when the national legislature fails to do its duty in providing a national remedy, so that the only national activity is the purely negative activity of the judiciary in forbidding the state to exercise power in the premises.

I do not ask for overcentralization; but I do ask that we work in a spirit of broad and far-reaching nationalism when we work for what concerns our people as a whole. We are all Americans. Our common interests are as broad as the continent. I speak to you here in Kansas exactly as I would speak in New York or Georgia, for the most vital problems are those which affect us all alike. The national government belongs to the whole American people, and where the whole American people are interested, that interest can be guarded effectively only by the national government. The betterment which we seek must be accomplished, I believe, mainly through the national government.

The American people are right in demanding that New Nationalism, without which we cannot hope to deal with new problems. The New Nationalism puts the national need before sectional or personal advantage. It is impatient of the utter confusion that results from local legislatures attempting to treat national issues as local issues. It is still more impatient of the impotence which springs from overdivision of governmental powers, the impotence which makes it possible for local selfishness or for legal cunning, hired by wealthy special interests, to bring national activities to a deadlock. This New Nationalism regards the executive power as the steward of the public welfare. It demands of the judiciary that it shall be interested primarily in human welfare rather than in property, just as it demands that the representative body shall represent all the people rather than any one class or section of the people.

I believe in shaping the ends of government to protect property as well as human welfare. Normally, and in the long run, the ends are the same; but whenever the alternative must be faced, I am for men and not for property. . . . I am far from underestimating the importance of dividends; but I rank dividends below human character. Again, I do not have any sympathy with the reformer who says he does not care for dividends. Of course, economic welfare is necessary, for a man must pull his own weight and be able to support his family. I know well that the reformers must not bring upon the people economic ruin, or the reforms themselves will go down in the ruin. But we must be ready to face temporary disaster, whether or not brought on by those who will war against us to the knife. Those who oppose all reform will do well to remember that ruin in its worst form is inevitable if our national life brings us nothing better than swollen fortunes for the few and the triumph in both politics and business of a sordid and selfish materialism.

If our political institutions were perfect, they would absolutely prevent the political domination of money in any part of our affairs. We need to make our political representatives more quickly and sensitively responsive to the people whose servants they are. More direct action by the people in their own affairs under proper safeguards is vitally necessary. The direct primary is a step in this direction, if it is associated with a corrupt practices act effective to prevent the advantage of the man willing recklessly and unscrupulously to spend money over his more honest competitor. It is particularly important that all moneys received or expended for campaign purposes should be publicly accounted for, not only after election, but before election as well. Political action must be made simpler, easier, and freer from confusion for every citizen. I believe that the prompt removal of unfaithful or incompetent public servants should be made easy and sure in whatever way experience shall show to be most expedient in any given class of cases.

One of the fundamental necessities in a representative government such as ours is to make certain that the men to whom the people delegate their power shall serve the people by whom they are elected, and not the special interests. I believe that every national officer, elected or appointed, should be forbidden to perform any service or receive any compensation, directly or indirectly, from interstate corporations; and a similar provision could not fail to be useful within the states.

The object of government is the welfare of the people. The material progress and prosperity of a nation are desirable chiefly so far as they lead to the moral and material welfare of all good citizens. Just in proportion as the average man and woman are honest, capable of sound judgment and high ideals, active in public affairs—but, first of all, sound in their home life, and the father and mother of healthy children whom they bring up well —just so far, and no farther, we may count our civilization a success. We must have—I believe we have already—a genuine and permanent moral awakening, without which no wisdom of legislation or administration really means anything; and, on the other hand, we must try to secure the social and economic legislation without which any improvement due to purely moral agitation is necessarily evanescent. . . . No matter how honest and decent we are in our private lives, if we do not have the right kind of law and the right kind of administration of the law, we cannot go forward as a nation. That is imperative; but it must be an addition to, and not a substitution for, the qualities that make us good citizens. In the last analysis, the most important elements in any man's career must be the sum of those qualities which, in the aggregate, we speak of as character. If he has not got it, then no law that the wit of man can devise, no administration of the law by the boldest and strongest executive, will avail to help him. We must have the right kind of character—character that makes a man, first of all, a good man in the home, a good father, a good husband—that makes a man a good neighbor. You must have that, and, then, in addition, you must have the kind of law and the kind of administration of the law which will give to those qualities in the private citizen the best possible chance for development. The prime problem of our nation is to get the right type of good citizenship, and, to get it, we must have progress, and our public men must be genuinely progressive.

7 / WOODROW WILSON AND THE NEW FREEDOM

After the 1912 elections, William Bayard Hale brought together extracts from Wilson's campaign speeches along with some material from other Wilson addresses under the title The New Freedom. *The work was first serialized in* The World's Work *from January to July, 1913, and was published in book form the same year.*

Gentlemen say, they have been saying for a long time, and, therefore, I assume that they believe, that trusts are inevitable. They don't say that big business is inevitable. They don't say merely that the elaboration of business upon a great co-operative scale is characteristic of our time and has come about by the natural operation of modern civilization. We would admit that. But they say that the particular kind of combinations that are now controlling our economic development came into existence naturally and were inevitable; and that, therefore, we have to accept them as unavoidable and administer our development through them. . . .

I admit the popularity of the theory that the trusts have come about through the natural development of business conditions in the United States, and that it is a mistake to try to oppose the processes by which they have been built up, because those processes belong to the very nature of business in our time, and that therefore the only thing we can do, and the only thing we ought to attempt to do, is to accept them as inevitable arrangements and make the best out of it that we can by regulation.

SOURCE: Woodrow Wilson, *The New Freedom* (Garden City, N.Y.: Doubleday, Page & Company, 1913), pp. 163–170, 172–179, 184–190, 200–202, 222. Reprinted by permission of The Estate of Edith Bolling Wilson.

I answer, nevertheless, that this attitude rests upon a confusion of thought. Big business is no doubt to a large extent necessary and natural. The development of business upon a great scale, upon a great scale of co-operation, is inevitable, and, let me add, is probably desirable. But that is a very different matter from the development of trusts, because the trusts have not grown. They have been artificially created; they have been put together, not by natural processes, but by the will, the deliberate planning will, of men who were more powerful than their neighbors in the business world, and who wished to make their power secure against competition. . . .

Did you ever look into the way a trust was made? It is very natural, in one sense, in the same sense in which human greed is natural. If I haven't efficiency enough to beat my rivals, then the thing I am inclined to do is to get together with my rivals and say: "Don't let's cut each other's throats; let's combine and determine prices for ourselves; determine the output, and thereby determine the prices: and dominate and control the market." That is very natural. That has been done ever since freebooting was established. That has been done ever since power was used to establish control. The reason that the masters of combination have sought to shut out competition is that the basis of control under competition is brains and efficiency. I admit that any large corporation built up by the legitimate processes of business, by economy, by efficiency, is natural; and I am not afraid of it, no matter how big it grows. It can stay big only by doing its work more thoroughly than anybody else. And there is a point of bigness—as every business man in this country knows, though some of them will not admit it—where you pass the limit of efficiency and get into the region of clumsiness and unwieldiness. You can make your combine so extensive that you can't digest it into a single system; you can get so many parts that you can't assemble them as you would an effective piece of machinery. The point of efficiency is overstepped in the natural process of development oftentimes, and it has been overstepped many times in the artificial and deliberate formation of trusts.

A trust is formed in this way: a few gentlemen "promote" it—that is to say, they get it up, being given enormous fees for their kindness, which fees are loaded on to the undertaking in the form of securities of one kind or another. The argument of the promoters is, not that every one who comes into the combination can carry on his business more efficiently than he did before; the argument is: we will assign to you as your share in the pool twice, three times, four times, or five times what you could have sold your business for to an individual competitor who would have to run it on an economic and competitive basis. We can afford to buy it at such a figure because we are shutting out competition. We can afford to make the stock of the combination half a dozen times what it naturally would be and pay dividends on it, because there will be nobody to dispute the prices we shall fix.

Talk of that as sound business? Talk of that as inevitable? It is based upon nothing except power. It is not based upon efficiency. It is no wonder that the big trusts are not prospering in proportion to such competitors as they still have in such parts of their business as competitors have access to; they are prospering freely only in those fields to which competition has no access. Read the statistics of the Steel Trust, if you don't believe it. Read the statistics of any trust. They are constantly nervous about competition, and they are constantly buying up new competitors in order to narrow the field. The United States Steel Corporation is gaining in its supremacy in the American market only with regard to the cruder manufactures of iron and steel, but wherever, as in the field of more advanced manufactures of iron and steel, it has important competitors, its portion of the product is not increasing, but is decreasing, and its competitors, where they have a foothold, are often more efficient than it is.

Why? Why, with unlimited capital and innumerable mines and plants everywhere in the United States, can't they beat the other fellows in the market? Partly because they are carrying too much. Partly because they are unwieldy. Their organization is imperfect. They bought up inefficient plants along with efficient, and they have got to carry what they have paid for, even if they have to shut some of the plants up in order to make any interest on their investments; or, rather, not interest on their investments, because that is an incorrect word—on their alleged capitalization. Here we have a lot of giants staggering along under an almost intolerable weight of artificial burdens, which they have put on their own backs, and constantly looking about lest some little pigmy with a round stone in a sling may come out and slay them.

For my part, I want the pigmy to have a chance to come out. And I foresee a time when the pigmies will be so much more athletic, so much more astute, so much more active, than the giants, that it will be a case of Jack the giant-killer. Just let some of the youngsters I know have a chance and they'll give these gentlemen points. Lend them a little money. They can't get any now. See to it that when they have got a local market they can't be squeezed out of it. Give them a chance to capture that market and then see them capture another one and another one, until these men who are carrying an intolerable load of artificial securities find that they have got to get down to hard pan to keep their foothold at all. I am willing to let Jack come into the field with the giant, and if Jack has the brains that some Jacks that I know in America have, then I should like to see the giant get the better of him, with the load that he, the giant, has to carry—the load of water. For I'll undertake to put a water-logged giant out of business any time, if you will give me a fair field and as much credit as I am entitled to, and let the law do what from time immemorial law has been expected to do—see fair play. . . .

I take my stand absolutely, where every progressive ought to take his stand, on the proposition that private monopoly is indefensible and intolerable. And there I will fight my battle. And I know how to fight it. Everybody who has ever read the newspapers knows the means by which these men built up their power and created these monopolies. Any decently equipped lawyer can suggest to you statutes by which the whole business can be stopped. What these gentlemen do not want is this: they do not want to be compelled to meet all comers on equal terms. I am perfectly willing that they should beat any competitor by fair means; but I know the foul means they have adopted, and I know that they can be stopped by law. If they think that coming into the market upon the basis of mere efficiency, upon the mere basis of knowing how to manufacture goods better than anybody else and to sell them cheaper than anybody else, they can carry the immense amount of water that they have put into their enterprises in order to buy up rivals, then they are perfectly welcome to try it. But there must be no squeezing out of the beginner, no crippling his credit; no discrimination against retailers who buy from a rival; no threats against concerns who sell supplies to a rival; no holding back of raw material from him; no secret arrangements against him. All the fair competition you choose, but no unfair competition of any kind. And then when unfair competition is eliminated, let us see these gentlemen carry their tanks of water on their backs. All that I ask and all I shall fight for is that they shall come into the field against merit and brains everywhere. If they can beat other American brains, then they have got the best brains.

But if you want to know how far brains go, as things now are, suppose you try to match your better wares against these gentlemen, and see them undersell you before your market is any bigger than the locality and make it absolutely impossible for you to get a fast foothold. If you want to know how brains count, originate some invention which will improve the kind of machinery they are using, and then see if you can borrow enough money to manufacture it. You may be offered something for your patent by the corporation—which will perhaps lock it up in a safe and go on using the old machinery; but you will not be allowed to manufacture. I know men who have tried it, and they could not get the money, because the great money lenders of this country are in the arrangement with the great manufacturers of this country, and they do not propose to see their control of the market interfered with by outsiders. And who are outsiders? Why, all the rest of the people of the United States are outsiders.

They are rapidly making us outsiders with respect even of the things that come from the bosom of the earth, and which belong to us in a peculiar sense. Certain monopolies in this country have gained almost complete control of the raw material, chiefly in the mines, out of which the great body of manufactures are carried on, and they now discriminate, when they will, in the sale of that raw material between those who are rivals of the monopoly and those who submit to the monopoly. We must soon come to the point where we shall say to the men who own these essentials of industry that they have got to part with these essentials by sale to all citizens of the United States with the same readiness and upon the same terms. Or else we shall tie up the resources of this country under private control in such fashion as will make our independent development absolutely impossible.

There is another injustice that monopoly engages in. The trust that deals in the cruder products which are to be transformed into the more elaborate manufactures often will not sell these crude products except upon the terms of monopoly—that is to say, the people that deal with them must buy exclusively from them. And so again you have the lines of development tied up and the connections of development knotted and fastened so that you cannot wrench them apart.

Again, the manufacturing monopolies are so interlaced in their personal relationships with the great shipping interests of this country, and with the great railroads, that they can often largely determine the rates of shipment. . . .

I have been told by a great many men that the idea I have, that by restoring competition you can restore industrial freedom, is based upon a failure to observe the actual happenings of the last decades in this country; because, they say, it is just free competition that has made it possible for the big to crush the little.

I reply, it is not free competition that has done that; it is illicit competition. It is competition of the kind that the law ought to stop, and can stop—this crushing of the little man.

You know, of course, how the little man is crushed by the trusts. He gets a local market. The big concerns come in and undersell him in his local market, and that is the only market he has; if he cannot make a profit there, he is killed. They can make a profit all through the rest of the Union, while they are underselling him in his locality, and recouping themselves by what they can earn elsewhere. Thus their competitors can be put out of business, one by one, wherever they dare to show a head. Inasmuch as they rise up only one by one, these big concerns can see to it that new competitors never come into the larger field. You have to begin somewhere. You can't begin in space. You can't begin in an airship. You have got to begin in some community. Your market has got to be your neighbors first and those who know you there. But unless you have unlimited capital (which of course you wouldn't have when you were beginning) or unlimited credit (which these gentlemen can see to it that you shan't get), they can kill you out in your local market any time they try, on the same basis exactly as that on which they beat organized labor; for they can sell at a loss in your market because they are selling at a profit everywhere else, and they can recoup the losses by which they beat you by the profits which they make in fields where they have beaten other fellows and put them out. If ever a competitor who by good luck has plenty of money does break into the wider market, then the trust has to buy him out, paying three or four times what the business is worth. Following such a purchase it has got to pay the interest on the price it has paid for the business, and it has got to tax the whole people of the United States, in order to pay the interest on what it borrowed to do that, or on the stocks and bonds it issued to do it with. Therefore the big trusts, the big combinations, are the most wasteful, the most uneconomical, and, after they pass a certain size, the most inefficient, way of conducting the industries of this country. . . .

[T]here has come about an extraordinary and very sinister concentration in the control of business in the country. . . . [M]ore important still [is] that the control of credit also has become dangerously centralized. It is the mere truth to say that the financial resources of the country are not at the command of those who do not submit to the direction and domination of small groups of capitalists who wish to keep the economic development of the country under their own eye and guidance. The great monopoly in this country is the monopoly of big credits. So long as that exists, our old variety and freedom and individual energy of development are out of the question. A great industrial nation is controlled by its system of credit. Our system of credit is privately concentrated. The growth of the nation, therefore, and all our activities are in the hands of a few men who, even if their action be honest and intended for the public interest, are necessarily concentrated upon the great undertakings in which their own money is involved and who necessarily, by very reason of their own limitations, chill and check and destroy genuine economic freedom. This is the greatest question of all, and to this statesmen must address themselves with an earnest determination to serve the long future and the true liberties of men.

This money trust, or, as it should be more properly called, this credit trust, of which Congress has begun an investigation, is no myth; it is no imaginary thing. . . .

The dominating danger in this land is not the existence of great individual combinations—that is dangerous enough in all conscience—but the combination of the combinations—of the railways, the manufacturing enterprises, the great mining projects, the great enterprises for the development of the natural waterpowers of the country, threaded together in the personnel of a series of boards of directors into a "community of interest" more formidable than any conceivable single combination that dare appear in the open.

The organization of business has become more centralized, vastly more centralized, than the political organization of the country itself. Corporations have come to cover greater areas than states; have come to live under a greater variety of laws than the citizen himself, have excelled states in their budgets and loomed bigger than whole commonwealths in their influence over the lives and fortunes of entire communities of men. Centralized business has built up vast structures of organization and equipment which overtop all states and seem to have no match or competitor except the federal government itself.

What we have got to do—and it is a colossal task not to be undertaken with a light head or without judgment—what we have got to do is to disentangle this colossal "community of interest." No matter how we may purpose dealing with a single combination in restraint of trade, you will agree with me in this, that no single, avowed, combination is big enough for the United States to be afraid of; but when all the combinations are combined and this final combination is not disclosed by any process of incorporation or law, but is merely an identity of personnel, or of interest, then there is something that even the government of the nation itself might come to fear—something for the law to pull apart, and gently, but firmly and persistently, dissect. . . .

The facts of the situation amount to this: that a comparatively small number of men control the raw material of this country; that a comparatively small number of men control the water-powers that can be made useful for the economical production of the energy to drive our machinery; that that same number of men largely control the railroads; that by agreements handed around among themselves they control prices, and that that same group of men control the larger credits of the country.

When we undertake the strategy which is going to be necessary to overcome and destroy this far-reaching system of monopoly, we are rescuing the business of this country, we are not injuring it; and when we separate the interests from each other and dismember these communities of connection, we have in mind a greater community of interest, a vaster community of interest, the community of interest that binds the virtues of all men together, that community of mankind which is broad and catholic enough to take under the sweep of its comprehension all sorts and conditions of men; that vision which sees that no society is renewed from the top but that every society is renewed from the bottom. Limit opportunity, restrict the field of originative achievement, and you have cut out the heart and root of all prosperity.

The only thing that can ever make a free country is to keep a free and hopeful heart under every jacket in it. Honest American industry has always thriven, when it has thriven at all, on freedom; it has never thriven on monopoly. It is a great deal better to shift for yourselves than to be taken care of by a great combination of capital. I, for my part, do not want to be taken care of. I would rather starve a free man than be fed a mere thing at the caprice of those who are organizing American industry as they please to organize it. I know, and every man in his heart knows, that the only way to enrich America is to make it possible for any man who has the brains to get into the game. . . .

Shall we try to get the grip of monopoly away from our lives, or shall we not? Shall we withhold our hand and say monopoly is inevitable, that all that we can do is to regulate it? Shall we say that all that we can do is to put government in competition with monopoly and try its strength against it? Shall we admit that the creature of our own hands is stronger than we are? We have been dreading all along the time when the combined power of high finance would be greater than the power of the government. Have we come to a time when the President of the United States or any man who wishes to be the President must doff his cap in the presence of this high finance, and say, "You are our inevitable master, but we will see how we can make the best of it?"

We are at the parting of the ways. We have, not one or two or three, but many, established and formidable monopolies in the United States. We have, not one or two, but many, fields of endeavor into which it is difficult, if not impossible, for the independent man to enter. We have restricted credit, we have restricted opportunity, we have controlled development, and we have come to be one of the worst ruled, one of the most completely controlled and dominated, governments in the civilized world—no longer a government of free opinion, no longer a government by conviction and the vote of the majority, but a government by the opinion and the duress of small groups of dominant men.

If the government is to tell big business men how to run their business, then don't you see that big business men have to get closer to the government even than they are now? Don't you see that they must capture the government, in order not to be restrained too much by it? . . .

Our purpose is the restoration of freedom. We purpose to prevent private monopoly by law, to see to it that the methods by which monopolies have been built up are legally made impossible. We design that the limitations on private enterprise shall be removed, so that the next generation of youngsters, as they come along, will not have to become protégés of benevolent trusts, but will be free to go about making their own lives what they will; so that we shall taste again the full cup, not of charity, but of liberty—the only wine that ever refreshed and renewed the spirit of a people.

8 / WILSON AND THE HIGH TIDE

OF PROGRESSIVISM

In his speech accepting renomination, September 2, 1916,
Wilson reviews the accomplishments of his
first administration.

I cannot accept the leadership and responsibility which the National Democratic Convention has again, in such generous fashion, asked me to accept without first expressing my profound gratitude to the party for the trust it reposes in me after four years of fiery trial in the midst of affairs of unprecedented difficulty, and the keen sense of added responsibility with which this honour fills (I had almost said burdens) me as I think of the great issues of national life and policy involved in the present and immediate future conduct of our Government. I shall seek, as I have always sought, to justify the extraordinary confidence thus reposed in me by striving to purge my heart and purpose of every personal and of every misleading party motive and devoting every energy I have to the service of the nation as a whole, praying that I may continue to have the counsel and support of all forward-looking men at every turn of the difficult business.

For I do not doubt that the people of the United States will wish the Democratic Party to continue in control of the Government. They are not in the habit of rejecting those who have actually served them for those who are making doubtful and conjectural promises of service. Least of all are they likely to substitute those who promised to render them particular services and

SOURCE: R. S. Baker and W. E. Dodd (eds.), *The Public Papers of Woodrow Wilson: The New Democracy* (New York: Harper and Bros., 1926), II, 275–281. Reprinted by permission of Harper and Row, Publishers.

proved false to that promise for those who have actually rendered those very services.

Boasting is always an empty business, which pleases nobody but the boaster, and I have no disposition to boast of what the Democratic Party has accomplished. It has merely done its duty. It has merely fulfilled its explicit promises. But there can be no violation of good taste in calling attention to the manner in which those promises have been carried out or in adverting to the interesting fact that many of the things accomplished were what the opposition party had again and again promised to do but had left undone. Indeed that is manifestly part of the business of this year of reckoning and assessment. There is no means of judging the future except by assessing the past. Constructive action must be weighed against destructive comment and reaction. The Democrats either have or have not understood the varied interests of the country. The test is contained in the record.

What is that record? What were the Democrats called into power to do? What things had long waited to be done, and how did the Democrats do them? It is a record of extraordinary length and variety, rich in elements of many kinds, but consistent in principle throughout and susceptible of brief recital.

The Republican Party was put out of power because of failure, practical failure and moral failure; because it had served special interests and not the country at large; because, under the leadership of its preferred and established guides, of those who still make its choices, it had lost touch with the thoughts and the needs of the Nation and was living in a past age and under a fixed illusion, the illusion of greatness. It had framed tariff laws based upon a fear of foreign trade, a fundamental doubt as to American skill, enterprise, and capacity, and a very tender regard for the profitable privileges of those who had gained control of domestic markets and domestic credits; and yet had enacted antitrust laws which hampered the very things they meant to foster, which were stiff and inelastic, and in part unintelligible. It had permitted the country throughout the long period of its control to stagger from one financial crisis to another under the operation of a national banking law of its own framing

which made stringency and panic certain and the control of the
larger business operations of the country by the bankers of a few
reserve centers inevitable; had made as if it meant to reform the
law but had faint-heartedly failed in the attempt, because it could
not bring itself to do the one thing necessary to make the reform
genuine and effectual, namely, break up the control of small
groups of bankers. It had been oblivious, or indifferent, to the
fact that the farmers, upon whom the country depends for its
food and in the last analysis for its prosperity, were without
standing in the matter of commercial credit, without the protection of standards in their market transactions, and without systematic knowledge of the markets themselves; that the labourers
of the country, the great army of men who man the industries
it was professing to father and promote, carried their labour
as a mere commodity to market, were subject to restraint by
novel and drastic process in the courts, were without assurance
of compensation for industrial accidents, without federal assistance in accommodating labour disputes, and without national
aid or advice in finding the places and the industries in which
their labour was most needed. The country had no national
system of road construction and development. Little intelligent
attention was paid to the army, and not enough to the navy. The
other republics of America distrusted us, because they found
that we thought first of the profits of American investors and only
as an afterthought of impartial justice and helpful friendship.
Its policy was provincial in all things; its purposes were out of
harmony with the temper and purpose of the people and the
timely development of the nation's interests.

So things stood when the Democratic Party came into power.
How do they stand now? Alike in the domestic field and in the
wide field of the commerce of the world, American business and
life and industry have been set free to move as they never
moved before.

The tariff has been revised, not on the principle of repelling
foreign trade, but upon the principle of encouraging it, upon
something like a footing of equality with our own in respect of
the terms of competition, and a Tariff Board has been created
whose function it will be to keep the relations of American with

foreign business and industry under constant observation, for the guidance alike of our business men and of our Congress. American energies are now directed towards the markets of the world.

The laws against trusts have been clarified by definition, with a view to making it plain that they were not directed against big business but only against unfair business and the pretense of competition where there was none; and a Trade Commission has been created with powers of guidance and accommodation which have relieved business men of unfounded fears and set them upon the road of hopeful and confident enterprise.

By the Federal Reserve Act the supply of currency at the disposal of active business has been rendered elastic, taking its volume, not from a fixed body of investment securities, but from the liquid assets of daily trade; and these assets are assessed and accepted, not by distant groups of bankers in control of unavailable reserves, but by bankers at the many centers of local exchange who are in touch with local conditions everywhere.

Effective measures have been taken for the re-creation of an American merchant marine and the revival of the American carrying trade indispensable to our emancipation from the control which foreigners have so long exercised over the opportunities, the routes, and the methods of our commerce with other countries.

The Interstate Commerce Commission has been reorganized to enable it to perform its great and important functions more promptly and more efficiently. We have created, extended and improved the service of the parcels post.

So much we have done for business. What other party has understood the task so well or executed it so intelligently and energetically? What other party has attempted it at all? The Republican leaders, apparently, know of no means of assisting business but "protection." How to stimulate it and put it upon a new footing of energy and enterprise they have not suggested.

For the farmers of the country we have virtually created commercial credit, by means of the Federal Reserve Act and the Rural Credits Act. They now have the standing of other business men in the money market. We have successfully regulated speculation in "futures" and established standards in the marketing of grains. By an intelligent Warehouse Act we have assisted to make the standard crops available as never before both for systematic marketing and as a security for loans from the banks. We have greatly added to the work of neighborhood demonstration on the farm itself of improved methods of cultivation, and, through the intelligent extension of the functions of the Department of Agriculture, have made it possible for the farmer to learn systematically where his best markets are and how to get at them.

The workingmen of America have been given a veritable emancipation, by the legal recognition of a man's labour as part of his life, and not a mere marketable commodity; by exempting labour organizations from processes of the courts which treated their members like fractional parts of mobs and not like accessible and responsible individuals; by releasing our seamen from involuntary servitude; by making adequate provision for compensation for industrial accidents; by providing suitable machinery for mediation and conciliation in industrial disputes; and by putting the Federal Department of Labor at the disposal of the workingman when in search of work.

We have effected the emancipation of the children of the country by releasing them from hurtful labour. We have instituted a system of national aid in the building of highroads such as the country has been feeling after for a century. We have sought to equalize taxation by means of an equitable income tax. We have taken the steps that ought to have been taken at the outset to open up the resources of Alaska. We have provided for national defense upon a scale never before seriously proposed upon the responsibility of an entire political party. We have driven the tariff lobby from cover and obliged it to substitute solid argument for private influence.

This extraordinary recital must sound like a platform, a list of sanguine promises; but it is not. It is a record of promises made four years ago and now actually redeemed in constructive legislation.

These things must profoundly disturb the thoughts and confound the plans of those who have made themselves believe that the Democratic Party neither understood nor was ready to assist the business of the country in the great enterprises which it is its evident and inevitable destiny to undertake and carry

through. The breaking up of the lobby must especially discon-
cert them; for it was through the lobby that they sought and
were sure they had found the heart of things. The game of
privilege can be played successfully by no other means.

This record must equally astonish those who feared that the
Democratic Party had not opened its heart to comprehend the
demands of social justice. We have in four years come very near
to carrying out the platform of the Progressive Party as well as
our own; for we also are progressives.

There is one circumstance connected with this program which
ought to be very plainly stated. It was resisted at every step by
the interests which the Republican Party had catered to and
fostered at the expense of the country, and these same interests
are now earnestly praying for a reaction which will save their
privileges,—for the restoration of their sworn friends to power
before it is too late to recover what they have lost. They fought
with particular desperation and infinite resourcefulness the reform of the banking and currency system, knowing that to be the
citadel of their control; and most anxiously are they hoping and
planning for the amendment of the Federal Reserve Act by the
concentration of control in a single bank which the old familiar
group of bankers can keep under their eye and direction. But
while the "big men" who used to write the tariffs and command
the assistance of the Treasury have been hostile—all but a few
with vision—the average business man knows that he has been
delivered, and that the fear that was once every day in his
heart that the men who controlled credit and directed enterprise
from the committee rooms of Congress would crush him, is there
no more, and will not return—unless the party that consulted
only the "big men" should return to power—the party of masterly
inactivity and cunning resourcefulness in standing pat to resist
change.

The Republican Party is just the party that *cannot* meet the
new conditions of a new age. It does not know the way and
it does not wish new conditions. It tried to break away from the
old leaders and could not. They still select its candidates and
dictate its policy, still resist change, still hanker after the old conditions, still know no methods of encouraging business but the

old methods. When it changes its leaders and its purposes and brings its ideas up to date it will have the right to ask the American people to give it power again; but not until then. A new age, in an age of revolutionary change, needs new purposes and new ideas.

PART III

The 1920's

H ARDING saw his election as a popular mandate for a return to normalcy (Selection 9), but the 1920's were not simply a return to the "good old days" of laissez-faire government. Secretary of Commerce Herbert Hoover, the chief prophet of the "new era," stood for positive government action to promote business efficiency and co-operation and thus foster prosperity (Selection 10).

With progressivism in eclipse, pre-war reformers had to re-examine their premises and policies (Selection 11). At the same time, the decade of the 1920's was a period of far-reaching social changes. The anxieties and hostilities aroused among many old-stock Americans were reflected in the rapid growth of the Ku Klux Klan. In the 1928 presidential election, Al Smith's Roman Catholicism was the leading issue. But the election symbolized in microcosm the larger cultural conflict taking place between the older rural and small-town America and the new urban America (Selection 12).

The Depression following the 1929 stock market crash ended Republican political hegemony. Hoover, more than any of his predecessors, sought to have the government cushion the impact of the Depression. At first, he hoped to solve the crisis by limited government action encouraging voluntary business co-operation. But the steadily worsening situation forced him to support a larger measure of direct government intervention. His suspicions of big government and his commitment to balancing the budget,

however, led him to resist the growing demand for massive
government spending to lift the country out of the Depression
(Selection 13).

9 / WARREN G. HARDING AND THE
RETURN TO NORMALCY

*Harding set the tone for his administration
in his inaugural address, March 4, 1921.*

Our supreme task is the resumption of our onward, normal
way. . . .

We can reduce the abnormal expenditures, and we will. We
can strike at war taxation, and we must. We must face the grim
necessity, with full knowledge that the task is to be solved, and
we must proceed with a full realization that no statute enacted
by man can repeal the inexorable laws of nature. Our most
dangerous tendency is to expect too much of government, and
at the same time do for it too little.

We contemplate the immediate task of putting our public
household in order. We need a rigid and yet sane economy,
combined with fiscal justice, and it must be attended by individual
prudence and thrift, which are so essential to this trying hour
and reassuring for the future.

The business world reflects the disturbance of war's reaction.
Herein flows the lifeblood of material existence. The economic
mechanism is intricate and its parts interdependent, and has
suffered the shocks and jars incident to abnormal demands,
credit inflations, and price upheavals. The normal balances have

SOURCE: *Supplement to the Messages and Papers of the Presidents Covering the Term of Warren G. Harding . . . and the First Term of Calvin
Coolidge . . .* (Washington: Bureau of National Literature, 1925), 8925-
8929.

been impaired, the channels of distribution have been clogged, the relations of labor and management have been strained. We must seek the readjustment with care and courage. Our people must give and take. Prices must reflect the receding fever of war activities. Perhaps we never shall know the old levels of wages again, because war invariably readjusts compensations, and the necessaries of life will show their inseparable relationship, but we must strive for normalcy to reach stability. All the penalties will not be light, nor evenly distributed. There is no way of making them so. There is no instant step from disorder to order. We must face a condition of grim reality, charge off our losses and start afresh. It is the oldest lesson of civilization. I would like government to do all it can to mitigate; then, in understanding, in mutuality of interest, in concern for the common good, our tasks will be solved. No altered system will work a miracle. Any wild experiment will only add to the confusion. Our best assurance lies in efficient administration of our proven system.

The forward course of the business cycle is unmistakable. Peoples are turning from destruction to production. Industry has sensed the changed order and our own people are turning to resume their normal, onward way. The call is for productive America to go on. I know that Congress and the Administration will favor every wise Government policy to aid the resumption and encourage continued progress.

I speak for administrative efficiency, for lightened tax burdens, for sound commercial practices, for adequate credit facilities, for sympathetic concern for all agricultural problems, for the omission of unnecessary interference of Government with business, for an end to Government's experiment in business, and for more efficient business in Government administration. With all of this must attend a mindfulness of the human side of all activities, so that social, industrial, and economic justice will be squared with the purposes of a righteous people.

. . . Common welfare is the goal of our national endeavor. Wealth is not inimical to welfare; it ought to be its friendliest agency. There never can be equality of rewards or possessions so long as the human plan contains varied talents and differing degrees of industry and thrift, but ours ought to be a country free from great blotches of distressed poverty. We ought to find a way to guard against the perils and penalties of unemployment. We want an America of homes, illumined with hope and happiness, where mothers, freed from the necessity for long hours of toil beyond their own doors, may preside as befits the hearthstone of American citizenship. We want the cradle of American childhood rocked under conditions so wholesome and so hopeful that no blight may touch it in its development, and we want to provide that no selfish interest, no material necessity, no lack of opportunity shall prevent the gaining of that education so essential to best citizenship.

There is no short cut to the making of these ideals into glad realities. The world has witnessed again and again the futility and the mischief of ill-considered remedies for social and economic disorders. But we are mindful today as never before of the friction of modern industrialism, and we must learn its causes and reduce its evil consequences by sober and tested methods. Where genius has made for great possibilities, justice and happiness must be reflected in a greater common welfare.

Service is the supreme commitment of life. I would rejoice to acclaim the era of the Golden Rule and crown it with the autocracy of service. I pledge an administration wherein all the agencies of Government are called to serve, and ever promote an understanding of Government purely as an expression of the popular will.

10 / HERBERT HOOVER:

PROPHET OF THE "NEW ERA"

*In his speech accepting the 1928 Republican
presidential nomination, Hoover expounds his philosophy
and prophesies the end of poverty in the United States.*

Our problems of the past seven years have been problems of
reconstruction; our problems of the future are problems of construction. They are problems of progress. New and gigantic forces
have come into our national life. The Great War released ideas
of government in conflict with our principles. We have grown to
financial and physical power which compels us into a new
setting among nations. Science has given us new tools and a
thousand inventions. Through them have come to each of us
wider relationships, more neighbors, more leisure, broader vision,
higher ambitions, greater problems. To insure that these tools
shall not be used to limit liberty has brought a vast array of
questions in government.

The points of contact between the government and the people
are constantly multiplying. Every year wise governmental policies
become more vital in ordinary life. As our problems grow so do
our temptations grow to venture away from those principles
upon which our republic was founded and upon which it has
grown to greatness. Moreover we must direct economic progress
in support of moral and spiritual progress. . . .

The Republican Party came into authority nearly eight years
ago. It is necessary to remind ourselves of the critical conditions
of that time. We were confronted with an incompleted peace

SOURCE: Herbert Hoover, *The New Day: Campaign Speeches of Herbert
Hoover, 1928* (Stanford, California: Stanford University Press, 1928), pp.
10–17, 30–35, 40–42. Reprinted by permission of the Hoover Foundation.

and involved in violent and dangerous disputes both at home and abroad. The Federal Government was spending at the rate of five and one-half billions per year; our national debt stood at the staggering total of twenty-four billions. The foreign debts were unsettled. The country was in a panic from overexpansion due to the war and the continued inflation of credit and currency after the Armistice, followed by a precipitant nation-wide deflation which in half a year crashed the prices of commodities by nearly one-half. Agriculture was prostrated; land was unsalable; commerce and industry were stagnated; our foreign trade ebbed away; five millions of unemployed walked the streets. Discontent and agitation against our democracy were rampant. Fear for the future haunted every heart.

No party ever accepted a more difficult task of reconstruction than did the Republican Party in 1921. The record of these seven and one-half years constitutes a period of rare courage in leadership and constructive action. Never has a political party been able to look back upon a similar period with more satisfaction. Never could it look forward with more confidence that its record would be approved by the electorate.

Peace has been made. The healing processes of good will have extinguished the fires of hate. Year by year in our relations with other nations we have advanced the ideals of law and of peace, in substitution for force. By rigorous economy federal expenses have been reduced by two billions per annum. The national debt has been reduced by six and a half billions. The foreign debts have been settled in large part and on terms which have regard for our debtors and for our taxpayers. Taxes have been reduced four successive times. These reductions have been made in the particular interest of the small taxpayers. For this purpose taxes upon articles of consumption and popular service have been removed. The income tax rolls today show a reduction of eighty per cent in the total revenue collected on incomes under $10,000 per year, while they show a reduction of only twenty-five per cent in revenues from incomes above that amount. Each successive reduction in taxes has brought a reduction in the cost of living to all our people.

Commerce and industry have revived. Although the agricultural, coal, and textile industries still lag in their recovery and still require our solicitude and assistance, yet they have made substantial progress. While other countries engaged in the war are only now regaining their pre-war level in foreign trade, our exports, even if we allow for the depreciated dollar, are fifty-eight per cent greater than before the war. Constructive leadership and co-operation by the government have released and stimulated the energies of our people. Faith in the future has been restored. Confidence in our form of government has never been greater.

PEOPLE'S WIDENING OPPORTUNITY

But it is not through the recitation of wise policies in government alone that we demonstrate our progress under Republican guidance. To me the test is the security, comfort, and opportunity that have been brought to the average American family. During this less than eight years our population has increased by eight per cent. Yet our national income has increased by over thirty billions of dollars per year or more than forty-five per cent. Our production—and therefore our consumption—of goods has increased by over twenty-five per cent. It is easily demonstrated that these increases have been widely spread among our whole people. Home ownership has grown. While during this period the number of families has increased by about 2,300,000, we have built more than 3,500,000 new and better homes. In this short time we have equipped nearly nine million more homes with electricity, and through it drudgery has been lifted from the lives of women. The barriers of time and distance have been swept away and life made freer and larger by the installation of six million more telephones, seven million radio sets, and the service of an additional fourteen million automobiles. Our cities are growing magnificent with beautiful buildings, parks, and playgrounds. Our countryside has been knit together with splendid roads.

We have doubled the use of electrical power and with it we have taken sweat from the backs of men. The purchasing power of wages has steadily increased. The hours of labor have de-

creased. The twelve-hour day has been abolished. Great progress
has been made in stabilization of commerce and industry. The
job of every man has thus been made more secure. Unemployment in the sense of distress is widely disappearing.

Our Prosperity Wisely Enjoyed

Most of all, I like to remember what this progress has meant
to America's children. The portal of their opportunity has been
ever widening. While our population has grown but eight per
cent, we have increased by eleven per cent the number of
children in our grade schools, by sixty-six per cent the number in
our high schools, and by seventy-five per cent the number in our
institutions of higher learning.

With all our spending we have doubled savings deposits in
our banks and building and loan associations. We have nearly
doubled our life insurance. Nor have our people been selfish.
They have met with a full hand the most sacred obligation of
man—charity. The gifts of America to churches, to hospitals, and
institutions for the care of the afflicted, and to relief from great
disasters have surpassed by hundreds of millions any totals for
any similar period in all human record.

One of the oldest and perhaps the noblest of human aspirations
has been the abolition of poverty. By poverty I mean the grinding
by undernourishment, cold, and ignorance, and fear of old age
of those who have the will to work. We in America today are
nearer to the final triumph over poverty than ever before in the
history of any land. The poorhouse is vanishing from among us.
We have not yet reached the goal, but, given a chance to go
forward with the policies of the last eight years, we shall soon
with the help of God be in sight of the day when poverty will
be banished from this nation. There is no guarantee against
poverty equal to a job for every man. That is the primary
purpose of the economic policies we advocate.

I especially rejoice in the effect of our increased national
efficiency upon the improvement of the American home. That
is the sanctuary of our loftiest ideals, the source of the spiritual
energy of our people. The bettered home surroundings, the

expanded schools and playgrounds, and the enlarged leisure which have come with our economic progress have brought to the average family a fuller life, a wider outlook, a stirred imagination, and a lift in aspirations. . . .

THE GOVERNMENT AND BUSINESS

With impressive proof on all sides of magnificent progress, no one can rightly deny the fundamental correctness of our economic system. Our pre-eminent advance over nations in the last eight years has been due to distinctively American accomplishments. We do not owe these accomplishments to our vast natural resources. These we have always had. They have not increased. What has changed is our ability to utilize these resources more effectively. It is our human resources that have changed. Man for man and woman for woman, we are today more capable, whether in the work of farm, factory, or business, than ever before. It lies in our magnificent educational system, in the hardworking character of our people, in the capacity of far-sighted leadership in industry, the ingenuity, the daring of the pioneers of new inventions, in the abolition of the saloon, and the wisdom of our national policies.

With the growth and increasing complexity of our economic life the relations of government and business are multiplying daily. They are yearly more dependent upon each other. Where it is helpful and necessary, this relation should be encouraged. Beyond this it should not go. It is the duty of government to avoid regulation as long as equal opportunity to all citizens is not invaded and public rights violated. Government should not engage in business in competition with its citizens. Such actions extinguish the enterprise and initiative which has been the glory of America and which has been the root of its pre-eminence among the nations of the earth. On the other hand, it is the duty of business to conduct itself so that government regulation or government competition is unnecessary.

Business is practical, but it is founded upon faith—faith among our people in the integrity of business men, and faith that it will receive fair play from the government. It is the duty of government to maintain that faith. Our whole business system would break down in a day if there was not a high sense of moral responsibility in our business world. The whole practice and ethics of business has made great strides of improvement in the last quarter of a century, largely due to the effort of business and the professions themselves. One of the most helpful signs of recent years is the stronger growth of associations of workers, farmers, business men, and professional men with a desire to cure their own abuses and a purpose to serve public interest. Many problems can be solved through co-operation between government and these self-governing associations to improve methods and practices. When business cures its own abuses it is true self-government, which comprises more than political institutions. . . .

PROPER PROMOTION OF BUSINESS A GOVERNMENT FUNCTION

The government can be of invaluable aid in the promotion of business. The ideal state of business is freedom from those fluctuations from boom to slump which bring on one hand the periods of unemployment and bankruptcy and, on the other, speculation and waste. Both are destructive to progress and fraught with great hardship to every home. By economy in expenditures, wise taxation, and sound fiscal finance it can relieve the burdens upon sound business and promote financial stability. By sound tariff policies it can protect our workmen, our farmers, and our manufacturers from lower standards of living abroad. By scientific research it can promote invention and improvement in methods. By economic research and statistical service it can promote the elimination of waste and contribute to stability in production and distribution. By promotion of foreign trade it can expand the markets for our manufacturers and farmers and thereby contribute greatly to stability and employment.

Our people know that the production and distribution of goods on a large scale is not wrong. Many of the most important comforts of our people are only possible by mass production and distribution. Both small and big business have their full place.

The test of business is not its size—the test is whether there is honest competition, whether there is freedom from domination, whether there is integrity and usefulness of purpose. As Secretary of Commerce I have been greatly impressed by the fact that the foundation of American business is the independent business man. The Department by encouragement of his associations and by provision of special services has endeavored to place him in a position of equality in information and skill with larger operations. Alike with our farmers his is the stronghold of American individuality. It is here that our local communities receive their leadership. It is here that we refresh our leadership for larger enterprise. We must maintain his opportunity and his individual service. He and the public must be protected from any domination or from predatory business.

. . . . .

There is one of the ideals of America upon which I wish at this time to lay especial emphasis. For we should constantly test our economic, social, and governmental system by certain ideals which must control them. The founders of our republic propounded the revolutionary doctrine that all men are created equal and all should have equality before the law. This was the emancipation of the individual. And since these beginnings, slowly, surely, and almost imperceptibly, this nation has added a third ideal almost unique to America—the ideal of equal opportunity. This is the safeguard of the individual. The simple life of early days in our republic found but few limitations upon equal opportunity. By the crowding of our people and the intensity and complexity of their activities it takes today a new importance.

Equality of opportunity is the right of every American—rich or poor, foreign or native-born, irrespective of faith or color. It is the right of every individual to attain that position in life to which his ability and character entitle him. By its maintenance we will alone hold open the door of opportunity to every new generation, to every boy and girl. It tolerates no privileged classes or castes or groups who would hold opportunity as their prerogative. Only from confidence that this right will be upheld

can flow that unbounded courage and hope which stimulate each
individual man and woman to endeavor and to achievement.
The sum of their achievement is the gigantic harvest of national
progress.

NOT SOCIALISM

This ideal of individualism based upon equal opportunity to
every citizen is the negation of socialism. It is the negation of
anarchy. It is the negation of despotism. It is as if we set a race.
We, through free and universal education, provide the training
of the runners; we give to them an equal start; we provide in
the government the umpire of fairness in the race. The winner is
he who shows the most conscientious training, the greatest
ability, and the greatest character. Socialism bids all to end the
race equally. It holds back the speedy to the pace of the slowest.
Anarchy would provide neither training nor umpire. Despotism
picks those who should run and those who should win.

Conservative, progressive, and liberal thought and action have
their only real test in whether they contribute to equal opportunity, whether they hold open the door of opportunity. If they
do not they are false in their premise no matter what their name
may be.

It was Abraham Lincoln who firmly enunciated this ideal as
the equal chance. The Sherman Law was enacted in endeavor to
hold open the door of equal opportunity in business. The commissions for regulation of public utilities were created to prevent
discrimination in service and prevent extortion in rates—and
thereby the destruction of equal opportunity.

Equality of opportunity is a fundamental principle of our
nation. With it we must test all our policies. The success or
failure of this principle is the test of our government.

11 / WHAT HAPPENED TO PROGRESSIVISM IN THE TWENTIES?

When long-time reformer Frederic C. Howe asked in his autobiography, The Confessions of a Reformer *(1925), where the pre-war radicals were,* The Survey, *in its February 1, 1926 issue, published the answers from a number of well-known reformers of the pre-war era. The following were among the replies.*

WILLIAM ALLEN WHITE, KANSAS EDITOR

The old reformer in the new order faces a new situation. He cannot bring to bear upon the new situation the old psychology. It won't work. The dissidence of discontent will not bite into this situation. Twenty, thirty, even forty years ago economic and social injustices were much more obvious and seemed more cruel than they are today. Since 1917, in America at least, great improvement seems to have come in the distribution of wealth. Perhaps the rich are vastly richer, but certainly the poor are getting more necessities, comforts, and even luxuries out of life than they got before. They are not getting enough, but they are getting too many of the needs and comforts of life to make a very serious cause at the present time. I should like to see them get more. But when I talk to the average man who looks at life in the average way, at the average condition of the average industrial worker, the average man puts his hand to his mouth and swallows his yawn and walks off. You cannot dramatize the injustices of the present situation. Hence the reformer's occupation is gone. The radical is unable to appeal to the emotions of

SOURCE: "Where Are the Pre-War Radicals?", *The Survey*, LV, 9 (February 1, 1926), 556–562, 564–566.

the people. New times will produce new causes, and sooner or later new issues will call out those qualities in heart and mind which made the old idealists popular and forceful in the land. But their time is not now.

NEWTON W. BAKER, FORMER REFORM MAYOR OF CLEVELAND AND SECRETARY OF WAR UNDER WILSON

An intelligent answer requires us to recall at the outset that many of the things about which Mr. Howe was radical have been accomplished. American municipal government, which was a disgrace twenty-five years ago, is now both more honest and more efficient. The principle of municipal home rule has been adopted into state constitutions. Many cities have made and re-made their own charters and a series of informing experiments has been made in municipal institutions, so that city government is freer from bossism, more responsive to popular control and more efficient than it used to be. With these changes has come the full acceptance of the program of municipal activity for which radicals used to contend—better public schools, parks, bath houses and public control of public utility monopolies.

In the second place, we must admit that some of the things radicals contended for have been tried and found of less value in practice than they promised in theory. Among these are the initiative and referendum, the recall, the non-partisan primary, the commission form of government and proportional representation. That some of these have proved useful is clear, but their absolute importance is plainly less than was once supposed.

In the third place, when the great national test came after the World War, the radicals developed a wholly unsuspected lack of capacity to cooperate. When the war was over, real liberal cooperation would have captured the future for the world, but every radical and every liberal, apparently, had his own theory or his own grievance, and the conservative reaction marched through the liberal ranks, which were broken into fragments by their own dissensions.

In the fourth place, after the immeasurable destruction of the World War, a destruction alike of physical property and faith in human institutions, the stricken and terrified world demanded a respite. Instead of more destruction of things and faith, it wanted a chance to build again on its shattered foundation. Most of the radicals of the older day have responded to the call for constructive effort.

Lastly the experience of the Russian people under a degrading despotism, with radicals in the saddle, has tempered the welcome of radical ideas in other parts of the world.

None of the foregoing means that there is less room in the world or less need in the world for liberalism. Liberalism is a state of mind and not a creed. A liberal uses his fellow men for their benefit and not for his own. He judges political purposes by their effect on the common good and he has in his mind's eye, as the ultimate object of his concern, "the forgotten man," remote, obscure and inaudible in high places. Liberalism of this quality is imperishable and it has many brave services yet to perform for the American people.

RAY STANNARD BAKER, FORMER MUCKRAKER AND WILSON ADMIRER

I can answer "Here" to your roll-call of the "pre-war radicals." If I was indeed a radical then, I am still a radical, and no hopeless radical either, for my belief in certain great fundamentals of human relationship has not changed. I believed then that the basis of all advance in civilization was human understanding and human sympathy. I believe it still more vitally now. I am therefore more radical, not less.

Where I was mistaken as a "pre-war radical" was in thinking that what I wanted could be had by adopting certain easy devices of social inventions—otherwise, by short-cuts. What I have gained since is the knowledge that though the thing is true the time appointed is long. There are no miracles in progress; there is only the plodding but beautiful adventure of inquiry and education. Civilization does not come by control but by self-control. We cannot make the hurrah of elections and the enactment of laws take the place of personal conviction.

I deny being a "disillusioned radical"; but rather a deeper

radical in the very sense of the word "root." We must go down deep where men live and try first of all to understand them. We "pre-war radicals" were just like all the other politicians; we were more interested in bossing people than in knowing them; we wanted to boss our neighbors into our own little plans for goodness, or efficiency, or justice. We did not understand that growth does not come from without or above, but from within and deep down.

Don't blame us then because we are no longer so sure as we were, or so noisy; think of us as having gone back to get acquainted with life, of liking better for a while to ask questions than to answer them; of *trying to understand*. And don't worry; you will hear of us again later (not us in any personal or ego-tistical sense, but of us who believe that understanding is the key-note of civilization); we shall be coming up from the soil all muscular with new power. For this is the truth of the matter: people are infinitely worth knowing, worth living among, worth working with; they are the only material we have out of which to build a New Earth. This is the greatest of all creative ad-ventures; and better worth while than ever it was before in history; for the material is more alive, more malleable, more interesting. That it cannot at once, overnight, be shaped to our ideas of perfection, is no cause for sickly disillusionment, but for new enthusiasm and new effort. The true creator sees that while the stone is harder than he thought, the image within it is vastly greater, and nobler.

NORMAN HOPGOOD, FORMER EDITOR OF "COLLIER'S"

Granted that a certain group of liberals have more or less dis-integrated I do not find it possible to become hectic over their lessened prominence. Things happen in history. Wilson executed most of his own program and that of the Bull Moose, which gave us a chance to see how much our cures were worth. The war came along and handed us new problems of considerable magnitude.

The greatest world-problem now is peace. Labor elements and liberal elements in England, France, and Germany are attending to that. The greatest American problem I cannot pick out, because there does not seem to be any. For my part, free speech and free thought interest me more than any other issue and I find an active group of people to work with along those lines, most of these people being pre-war.

The hard difficulty we encountered in the La Follette campaign was lack of an issue. A definite cure was offered for the too much readiness of the Supreme Court to upset certain kinds of legislation, and the cure was probably wrong. At least it is likely that the soundest cure is time and circumstance. An old-fashioned cure for the problem of monopoly was pressed, and convinced almost nobody. The government ownership of railroads was trotted out of the stable but failed to cause excitement.

I went on the stump for La Follette and would do it tomorrow for his son. But it is the spirit I should be supporting, the honesty, the indifference to wealth. With most of the definite conceptions, such as the form of farm relief, the method of curbing trusts, isolationism, I should disagree.

Many of those of whom you are asking the question have found matters about which to remain busy. Eugene Debs has done a noble job, in jail and out. Roger Baldwin never sleeps in his work for old-fashioned Jeffersonian freedom. Victor Berger is in Congress and is trying to have Russia recognized. I do not know that Ray Stannard Baker was ever any better employed than now that he is in large part studying other sources of progress than political ones. Will Irwin gives his life to peace. Lincoln Steffens sticks to some views that the world cares little for, but I am perfectly satisfied to leave some of his years to his baby. The baby is worth it, and so is the wife.

It is true that the United States is happy making money. Labor has higher real wages than ever before. Figures are easy to fight with but I believe at least skilled labor gets 20 or 25 per cent more than it did in 1913 for the same effort. It is a mechanical age. The muck-raking in which I took part in the years before 1912 was an asset in its place and time, but there is no use crying because our particular medicine is not needed forever. Other jobs approach and they will be seen through by other men.

ROGER N. BALDWIN, FOUNDER OF THE AMERICAN CIVIL LIBERTIES UNION

The political radicals Fred Howe talks about were gripped by the romantic notion that "the People could rule." They voiced the old American faith that privileged classes could be controlled by the "Public." As a humble member of the reformers' crew of those hopeful days, I believed it too. Most of us have since been as disillusioned as Howe.

There is no "Public"; the "People" as a political party are unorganizable. Only economic classes can be organized. The only power that works is class power. The "combined manufacturers and bankers of the United States," as Woodrow Wilson put it, is the class that politically controls us. The world has lost faith in parliaments; political democracy is recognized only as a form under which capitalism controls society, just as feudalism controlled it through kings. Political liberalism is dead.

There can be no more reformers of the Tom Johnson, Sam Jones school; no more crusades for the initiative, referendum and other devices for popular control; no more political muck-raking. The pre-war radicals have been put out of business by the industrial autocrats. Political democracy and industrial autocracy can't exist together.

But a new radicalism has taken the place of the old. It is the radicalism of a new class rising to power on the failures of capitalism and on the democratic urge. That class is the organized producers—labor and the farmers. Fred Howe finally identified himself with them. He saw that radicals of today must put their roots into that class, not into a phantom public. Hundreds of others who want to serve their generation, and who ten or twenty years ago would have gone into political reform or social work, now tie up with labor and its allied interests. The pre-war radicals in the working-class still carry on. Recruits from youth constantly add to their number, despite the discouragement of these days of reaction.

The same fine faith and love of their fellow men which marked Fred Howe's friends in the days of political reform find expression in these new working-class movements. Radicalism does not die; its forms change.

FREMONT OLDER, CRUSADING EDITOR OF THE SAN FRANCISCO "CALL"

Some of them are in jail, some of them with little hope left are still on the job, but more of them have been inoculated by the money madness that has seized America.

In the old pre-war days, say about 1910, I was in the midst of the big job of "saving the world," and had not the slightest doubt it could be done quickly. That was the year Hiram Johnson made his famous campaign for Governor of California, fighting all the entrenched political machines and corporation power that had been established for forty years. He swept the state, and the enthusiasm that followed his election further stimulated me in my belief that the millennium was not far off. But a few years later the war came and ended it all.

In those days a large part of my activities were devoted to the labor movement in California. I recall that I then had a feeling that there was a biological difference between the poor man and the rich man, and that somehow the poor were more altruistic, had more compassion and pity for their fellow men than the wealthy. I am not clear, now, where I got that idea, possibly from reading one of Jane Addams' books describing the poor that she came in contact with around Hull House in Chicago. Wherever I got it, it was deep-seated, and I had a profound faith in labor. I thought all that was necessary to bring about a mild millennium was to raise wages. Improved living conditions would give the poor a chance to express these fine qualities that I felt they possessed, and there would be no further difficulty in quickly making the world a finer place to live in.

The high wages came during the war, and what happened? The workers became more conservative. They bought automobiles, lived in better houses, dressed better, and acquired the habits of the well-to-do.

This fact was brought home to me very forcibly when I was making a big effort to establish the innocence of Mooney and

Billings in California. Ten out of the twelve most prominent labor leaders in San Francisco were either inactive, uninterested in the Mooney case, or actively opposing the movement to free them.

When the revolution came in Russia everyone knows what happened to labor. Led by Gompers, the American Federation of Labor became more violently hostile to the movement for freedom in Russia than the most reactionary groups among the wealthy.

This condition has persisted ever since. Every election has shown labor voting almost solidly with capital.

It was during those grilling years that I put in trying to establish the innocence of Mooney and Billings that I learned my lesson about human nature and discovered that practically the only difference between the poor classes and the rich classes was that one had money and the other had not.

I have only lost my faith in man, not my pity for him. That is stronger than ever. If there is to be any improvement, it will not be accomplished by labor, as Fred Howe thinks, but by a very slow process of education through the coming centuries. The money standard will outlast any one living today.

GEORGE W. ALGER, LONGTIME HEAD OF THE REFORM CLUB OF NEW YORK AND A PIONEER CHAMPION OF LABOR LEGISLATION

1—Radicalism tends to flourish more in periods of depression and discontent and a radical leader gets his message as well as his following from such an atmosphere. We are now in a period of wide-spread general prosperity and there is less interest in purely political questions than at any time during the past twenty years. This is evidenced by the failure of an increasingly large part of our population to even vote.

2—The old programs of pre-war radicalism have either resulted in the accomplishment of their purposes, for example, the social justice programs which included workmen's compensation laws and the like, or the public has become more or less convinced that certain purposes on these old programs were either not important or not desirable. A large part of pre-war radicalism dealt with political machinery intended to make the mass power of the uninformed common man apply to problems which he was incompetent to decide. This program is no longer appealing. There is less interest in these so-called democratic methods of deciding public matters than ever before. The old program, for example, for the initiative, referendum and recall has lost practically all the enthusiasm which it originally had back of it. The results, where this program has been tried, have not been sufficiently alluring to keep the continued interest of the people in it.

3—The war has made a complete change in politics and in economics. New political issues have not yet crystalized but old political issues are very much in the discard. So far as pre-war radicals are concerned, many of them have, under the test of the war, lost both public confidence and their political following. Those who were bad Americans during the war, who, even after our entrance upon the war, continued to act rather as representatives of German groups in their own constituencies and who embarrassed the public authorities of the country to the best of their abilities during the war have largely lost their standing except among a very negligible group. Post-war tests applied to some of the pre-war radicals have still further discredited them. We are faced with great international problems and many of the pre-war radicals are showing today a provincialism and parochialism which brings into question their judgment on other matters as well. Witness, for example, the greatest of our provincials Borah, and Hiram Johnson whose public bad manners are only equal to his parochialism.

4—You cannot have a general lack of interest in politics and public questions and have a particularly vital radicalism. Moreover, the terms "radical" and "progressive" have been applied by the press to cover people who are in no sense radicals or progressive and who are simply demagogues, who contribute nothing but wild proposals which receive newspaper consideration only because they are extreme and whose main function is to keep alive a bone-headed conservatism, the so-called 100 per cent American proposition whose early demise will be exceedingly helpful.

JOHN HAYNES HOLMES, MINISTER OF THE COMMUNITY CHURCH IN NEW YORK

"This movement that promised so much twenty years ago" has collapsed and its leaders are gone for two reasons:

1—We have discovered that America is no longer, probably never was, the country that we loved. The liberals of the last generation believed passionately in America as a country unique among the nations of the earth. It was a democracy—its government belonged to the people—its shores were a refuge for the oppressed—its destiny was to be fulfillment of the social visions of the ages. Here humanity was at last to find itself! If the liberals hated and fought the municipal corruptionists, the monopolists, the bankers, it was because these were despoilers of the dream. Then came the War—and America was seen to be just like every other country! The America we loved was gone, and in its place was just one more cruel imperialism. This discovery ended a movement which had for its purpose the protection and vindication of an ideal America.

2—Closely related to the above is the present dispersion of interest over the wider area of the world. Idealism is not dead. It is still with us, only it fixes its attention now upon the British Labour Party, upon the League of Nations, upon Soviet Russia, upon Gandhi and India. America is temporarily abandoned as the last triumphant stronghold of capitalistic imperialism, while we feed our hopes and advance our cause in these far-flung fields across the seas. And this is well—for the hope of the world today is not to be found in any one nation and people anywhere but in all nations and people everywhere. America is in for a long period of reaction; victories for the future must now be won elsewhere. But America will follow where we once hoped that she would lead, and thus find her place at last in the commonwealth of man.

CLARENCE DARROW, FAMED LAWYER

I have no doubt but what the world war is largely responsible for the reactionary tendency of the day. This is a condition that has followed all great wars. To engage in such a contest requires a cultivation of intense patriotism. When nations begin mobilizing, they start with the liars. They write about their enemies and they write about themselves. Everything is good at home and bad with their enemies. Some fairly intelligent people do not know any better than to believe it. I believed part of it myself, but am gradually getting over it. After the war, the spirit of super-patriotism remains. This is easily used to the advantage of the strong. Religious superstitions likewise grow; the leaders have a positive doctrine which involves unlimited promises. Then too, people are generally prosperous, or seem to be, during a great war. All the slack is taken up. Every man is busy. Production is great. Wages and commodities are high. Every one likes it until they wake up, which is several years after.

Following the War of the Rebellion, it was eight years before the people began to realize that somebody had to pay.

One must always remember that human beings do not reason—enough to hurt. They live from their emotions and so far as they do reason, this is controlled by their emotions. They are patriotic when they are getting plenty to eat and begin to grumble when times are hard. The grumbling will come later—not very much later; and after that, again will come bragging, blustering and one hundred per cent patriotism, and so on—world without end.

12 / AL SMITH AND THE CLASH

OF CULTURES

> *The Ku Klux Klan took a leading part in the campaign*
> *against Al Smith in presidential election of 1928. But*
> *even many old-stock Americans hostile to the Klan*
> *—such as famed editor William Allen White—*
> *were repelled by the New Yorker. In this excerpt from*
> *a letter of January 12, 1929, to Justice Louis D. Brandeis,*
> *White explains that more than simply Smith's religion*
> *was responsible for his defeat.*

I think thousands of western progressives balked at Smith, first because he was going too fast; second because he zigzagged on the wrong side of traffic on prohibition; and third because he represented a strange, unfamiliar, and to many narrow minds, an abhorrent tendency in our national life. Partly it was religion that symbolized the distrust. But I think it was chiefly an instinctive feeling for the old rural order and old rural ways, the tremendous impact of a desire for the good opinion of the old lady next door. I think inevitably in this century we shall see another moral censor than she, new moral standards. But still the old order holds fast in spite of our urban and industrial development.

SOURCE: Walter Johnson (ed.), *Selected Letters of William Allen White, 1899–1943* (New York: Henry Holt and Company, 1947), p. 290. Reprinted by permission of the Estate of William Allen White.

13 / HERBERT HOOVER
AND THE GREAT DEPRESSION

*In his speech of December 5, 1929, before a conference of
business leaders at the Chamber of Commerce of the
United States, Hoover appealed for business
co-operation to overcome the crisis.*

This body represents the industries of the United States. You
have been invited to create a temporary organization for the purpose of systematically spreading into industry as a whole the
measures which have been taken by some of our leading industries to counteract the effect of the recent panic in the stock
market. There has necessarily been some unemployment, starting
with diversion of capital from the channels of business into the
speculation, and after the break by some reduction in the demand
for luxuries and semi-necessities from those who met with losses.
But the large effect was to create undue pessimism, fear, uncer-
tainty and hesitation in business. These emotions, being emotions,
if they had been allowed to run their course would, by feeding on
themselves, create difficulties. The American mind is prone to re-
vert to previous occasions when we were much less able to organize to meet such situtations.

These are potential difficulties which cannot be cured with
words. If we could do so, the merest description of the fundamental stability of our vast organism of production and distribution, touched with the light of the future of the United States,
would cure it instantly. The cure for such storms is action; the
cure for unemployment is to find jobs.

SOURCE: William S. Meyers, *The State Papers and Other Public Writings
of Herbert Hoover* (Garden City, N.Y.: Doubleday, Doran, and Company
1934), I, 181–184. Reprinted by permission of the Hoover Foundation.

We have, fortunately, since our previous crashes established the Federal Reserve System. The first step in recovering confidence was made by the powerful effectiveness of that system, and the strong position of the banks, the result of which has been steadily diminishing interest rates, with a smooth and rapid return into the channels of business of the money previously absorbed in the speculative market. This is reversal of our historic experience and is a magnificent tribute to the System. Capital is becoming more abundant in all parts of the country, the bond market is growing stronger each day and already public issues held back for months have begun to appear.

The second action necessary to maintain progress was the standard set by leading employers that so far as they were concerned there would be no movement to reduce wages, and a corresponding assurance from the leaders of labor that not only would they use their utmost influence to allay labor conflict, but would also coöperate with the employers in the present situation. These assurances have been given and thereby we not only assure the consuming power of the country but we remove fear from millions of homes.

The third line of action has been to undertake through voluntary organization of industry the continuity and expansion of the construction and maintenance work of the country, so as to take up any slack in employment which arises in other directions. The extension and organization of this work are the purpose of this meeting. The greatest tool which our economic system affords for the establishment of stability is the construction and maintenance work, the improvements and betterments, and general clean-up of plants in preparation for cheaper production and the increased demand of the future. It has long been agreed by both business men and economists that this great field of expenditure could, by its acceleration in time of need, be made into a great balance wheel of stability. It is agreed that its temporary speeding up to absorb otherwise idle labor brings great subsequent benefits and no liabilities. A very considerable part of our wage earners are employed directly and indirectly in construction and the preparation and transportation of its materials. In the inevitable periods when the demand for consumable goods increases and labor is fully employed, construction and maintenance can slacken and we actually again gain in stability. No one would advocate the production of consumable goods beyond the daily demand; that in itself only stirs up future difficulty.

I am glad to report that such a program has met with universal approval of all those in responsible positions. Our railways and utilities and many of our larger manufacturers have shown a most distinguished spirit in undertaking to maintain and even to expand their construction and betterment programs. The state, county, and municipal governments are responding in the most gratifying way to the requests to coöperate with the Federal Government in every prudent expansion of public works. Much construction work had been postponed during the past few months by reason of the shortage of mortgage money due to the diversion of capital to speculative purposes, which should soon be released.

It is to make this movement systematic in all branches of the industrial world that we are here—that is the task. I believe that with the great back logs which are already assured by the public service institutions and the governmental works you will be able to build up the construction and maintenance activities for 1930 to a higher level than that of 1929, and that is what we require.

Another of the great balance wheels of stability is our foreign trade. But in stimulating our exports we should be mainly interested in development work abroad such as roads and utilities, which increase the standards of living of peoples and thus the increased demand for goods from every nation, for we gain in prosperity by a prosperous world, not by displacing others.

All of these efforts have one end—to assure employment and to remove the fear of unemployment.

The very fact that you gentlemen come together for these broad purposes represents an advance in the whole conception of the relationship of business to public welfare. You represent the business of the United States, undertaking through your own voluntary action to contribute something very definite to the advancement of stability and progress in our economic life. This is a far cry from the arbitrary and dog-eat-dog attitude of the business world of some thirty or forty years ago. And this is not dictation or interference by the Government with business. It is a request from the Government that you coöperate in prudent measures to solve a national problem. A great responsibility and a great opportunity rest upon the business and economic organization of the country. The task is one fitted to its fine initiative and courage.

Beyond this, a great responsibility for stability and prosperity rests with the whole people. I have no desire to preach. I may, however, mention one good old word—work.

The pressure of events forced Hoover to accept a larger measure of federal intervention. In his press statement of May 12, 1932, he explained his proposal for expanding the powers of the Reconstruction Finance Corporation.

The policy steadfastly adhered to up to the present time has been that responsibility for relief to distress belongs to private organizations, local communities, and the states. That fundamental policy is not to be changed. But since the fear has arisen that existing relief measures and resources may prove inadequate in certain localities and to insure against any possible breakdown in those localities it is proposed that authority be granted to the Reconstruction Finance Corporation to assist such states as may need it by underwriting only state bonds or by loaning directly to such states as may not be in position temporarily to sell securities in the market. The funds so obtained to be used for relief purposes and the total limited to $250,000,000 or $300,000,000.

The second part of the program contemplates providing the machinery whereby employment may be increased through restoring normal occupations rather than works of artificial character. Without entering the field of industry or public expansion, there are a large number of economically sound and self-supporting projects of a constructive replacement character that would

SOURCE: Meyers, *The State Papers . . . of Herbert Hoover,* II, 187–188. Reprinted by permission of the Hoover Foundation.

unquestionably be carried forward were it not for the present situation existing in the capital markets and the inadequate functioning of the credit machinery of the country. They exist both in the field of public bodies and of industry. There is no dearth of capital, and on the other hand there is a real demand for capital for productive purposes that have been held in abeyance. The problem is to make the existing capital available and to stimulate its use in constructive capital activities. This involves under existing conditions resort to special machinery which is adapted to furnish the necessary element of confidence.

It is proposed to use the instrumentality of the Reconstruction Finance Corporation which has a nation-wide organization by authorizing the Corporation either to underwrite or make loans for income producing and self-sustaining enterprises which will increase employment whether undertaken by public bodies or by private enterprises.

In order to safeguard the program beyond all question, it is proposed that there must be proper security for the loans, that as said projects must be income-producing, that borrowers must have sufficient confidence to furnish part of the capital, and that the project must contribute to early and substantial employment.

It is proposed to provide the necessary funds as they are required by the sale of securities of the Reconstruction Corporation and its total borrowing powers to be increased up to $3,000,000,-000. It is not proposed to issue Government bonds. It is hoped that this further process of speeding up the economic machine will not involve any such sum. But in view of the early adjournment of Congress it is desirable to provide an ample margin.

It is necessary to sharply distinguish between the use of capital for the above purposes and its use for unproductive public works. This proposal represents a flow of funds into productive enterprises, which is not taking place today because of abnormal conditions. These being loans on security and being self-liquidating in character, do not constitute a charge against the tax-payer or the public credit. The issue of bonds for public works, non-productive of revenue, is a direct charge either upon the tax-payer or upon the public credit, the interest on which and the ultimate redemption of which must be met from taxation.

An examination shows that to increase Federal Government construction work during the next year beyond the amounts already provided for would be to undertake works of largely artificial character far in advance of public return and would represent a wasteful use of capital and public credit.

Hoover remained adamantly against demands for a massive federal public works program. In his letter to Herbert S. Crocker, president of the American Society of Civil Engineers, May 21, 1932, he explained why.

I am in receipt of your kind letter of May 19th, and I have also the presentation of the sub-committee of the Society suggesting that the depression can be broken by a large issue of Federal Government bonds to finance a new program of huge expansion of "public works" construction, in addition to the already large programs now provided for in the current budgets. The same proposals have been made from other quarters and have been given serious consideration during the past few days.

The back of the depression cannot be broken by any single Government undertaking. That can only be done with the coöperation of business, banking, industry, and agriculture in conjunction with the Government. The aid the Government may give includes: (a) The quick, honest balancing of the Federal Budget through drastic reduction of less necessary expenses and the minimum increase in taxes; (b) The avoidance of issue of further Treasury securities as the very keystone of national and international confidence upon which all employment rests; (c) The continuation of the work of the Reconstruction Corporation which has overcome the financial strain on thousands of small banks, releasing credit to their communities, the strengthening of building and loan associations, the furnishing of credit to agriculture, the protection of trustee institutions and the support of financial

SOURCE: Meyers, *The State Papers . . . of Herbert Hoover,* II, 189–195. Reprinted by permission of the Hoover Foundation.

stability of the railways; (d) The expansion of credit by the
Federal Reserve Banks; (e) The organized translation of these
credits into actualities for business and public bodies; (f) Un-
ceasing effort at sound strengthening of the foundations of agriculture; (g) The continuation of such public works in aid to unemployment as do not place a strain on the taxpayer and do not
necessitate Government borrowing; (h) Continuation of national,
community and individual efforts in relief of distress; (i) The
introduction of the five day week in government which would
save the discharge of 100,000 employees and would add 30,000
to the present list; (j) The passage of the Home Loan discount
bank legislation which would protect home owners from foreclosure and would furnish millions of dollars of employment in
home improvement without cost to the Treasury; (k) Financial
aid by means of loans from the Reconstruction Corporation to
such states as, due to the long strain, are unable to continue to
finance distress relief; (l) The extension of the authority of the
Reconstruction Corporation not only in a particular to which I
called attention last December—that is, loans on sound security
to industry where they would sustain and expand employment—
but also in view of the further contraction of credit to increase its
authority to expand the issue of its own securities up to $3,000,-
000,000 for the purpose of organized aid to "income-producing
works" throughout the Nation, both of public and private character.

1—The vice in that segment of the proposals made by your
society and others for further expansion of "public works" is that
they include public works of remote usefulness; they impose un-
bearable burdens upon the taxpayer; they unbalance the Budget
and demoralize Government credit. A larger and far more effective relief to unemployment at this stage can be secured by increased aid to "income-producing works." I wish to emphasize
this distinction between what for purposes of this discussion we
may term "income-producing works" (also referred to as "self-
liquidating works") on the one hand and non-productive "public
works" on the other. By "income-producing works" I mean such
projects of states, counties and other sub-divisions as water-works,
toll-bridges, toll-tunnels, docks and any other such activities

which charge for their service and whose earning capacity provides a return upon the investment. With the return of normal times, the bonds of such official bodies based upon such projects can be disposed of to the investing public and thus make the intervention of the Reconstruction Corporation purely an emergency activity. I include in this class aid to established industry where it would sustain and increase employment with the safeguard that loans for these purposes should be made on sound security and the proprietors of such industries should provide a portion of the capital. Non-productive "public works" in the sense of the term here used include: public buildings, highways, streets, river and harbor improvement, military and naval construction, etc., which bring no direct income and comparatively little relief to unemployment.

. . . . . .

2—These proposals of huge expansion of "public works" have a vital relation to balancing the Federal Budget and to the stabilizing of national credit. The financing of "income-producing works" by the Reconstruction Corporation is an investment operation, requires no congressional appropriation, does not unbalance the Budget, is not a drain upon the Treasury, does not involve the direct issue of Government bonds, does not involve added burdens upon the taxpayer either now or in the future. It is an emergency operation which will liquidate itself with the return of the investor to the money markets.

The proposal to build non-productive "public works" of the category I have described necessitates making increased appropriations by the Congress. These appropriations must be financed by immediate increased taxation or by the issuance of Government bonds. Whatever the method employed, they are inescapably a burden upon the taxpayer. If such a course is adopted beyond the amounts already provided in the Budget now before Congress for the next fiscal year, it will upset all possibility of balancing the Budget; it will destroy confidence in Government securities and make for the instability of the Government which in result will deprive more people of employment than will be gained.

3—I have for many years advocated the speeding up of public works in times of depression as an aid to business and unemployment. That has been done upon a huge scale and is proceeding at as great a pace as fiscal stability will warrant. All branches of Government—Federal, state and municipal—have greatly expanded their "public works" and have now reached a stage where they have anticipated the need for many such works for a long time to come. Therefore, the new projects which might be undertaken are of even more remote usefulness. . . . We cannot thus squander ourselves into prosperity.

. . . . .

4—To sum up. It is generally agreed that the balancing of the Federal Budget and unimpaired national credit is indispensable to the restoration of confidence and to the very start of economic recovery. The Administration and Congress have pledged themselves to this end. A "public works" program such as is suggested by your committee and by others, through the issuance of Federal bonds creates at once an enormous further deficit.

What is needed is the return of confidence and a capital market through which credit will flow in the thousand rills with its result of employment and increased prices. That confidence will be only destroyed by action in these directions. These channels will continue clogged by fears if we continue attempts to issue large amounts of Government bonds for purposes of nonproductive works.

Such a program as these huge Federal loans for "public works" is a fearful price to pay in putting a few thousand men temporarily at work and dismissing many more thousands of others from their present employment. There is vivid proof of this since these proposals of public works financed by Government bonds were seriously advanced a few days ago. Since then United States Government bonds have shown marked weakness on the mere threat. And it is followed at once by a curtailment of the ability of states, municipalities and industry to issue bonds and thus a curtailment of activities which translate themselves into decreased employment.

It will serve no good purpose and will fool no one to try to cover appearances by resorting to a so-called "extraordinary budget." That device is well known. It brought the governments of certain foreign countries to the brink of financial disaster. It means a breach of faith to holders of all Government securities, an unsound financial program and a severe blow to returning confidence and further contraction of economic activities in the country.

What you want and what I want is to restore normal employment. I am confident that if the program I have proposed to the Congress is expeditiously completed and we have the coöperation of the whole community, we will attain the objective for which we have been searching so long.

PART IV

The New Deal

In his inaugural address, F.D.R. sought to reassure the panic-stricken nation about the future (Selection 14). In the "Hundred Days" that followed, the administration and Congress moved swiftly to provide relief for the distressed and to stimulate the recovery of the economy.

During the "Hundred Days," Roosevelt faced almost no opposition. By 1934, however, the administration was under attack from the right and the left. On the right, disgruntled conservatives organized in the American Liberty League assailed the New Deal as dangerously radical (Selection 15). The most formidable threat from the left was probably Huey Long's "Share Our Wealth" movement (Selection 16). The administration's response was a move to the left in 1935–1936 in what historians have called the Second New Deal (Selection 17). After his landslide victory in the 1936 elections, F.D.R. pledged in his second inaugural to continue the fight to uplift the one-third of the nation that was ill-fed, ill-clothed, and ill-housed (Selection 18).

But the 1936 elections marked the high tide of the New Deal. Roosevelt's defeat in the "court packing" fight seriously damaged his prestige and his increasing preoccupation with the Axis threat led him to softpedal his domestic reform program in order to win support for his foreign policy (Selection 19).

14 / F.D.R. REASSURES THE COUNTRY

In his inaugural address, March 4, 1933,
Roosevelt sought to revive public confidence.

I am certain that my fellow Americans expect that on my in-
duction into the Presidency I will address them with a candor
and a decision which the present situation of our Nation impels.
This is preeminently the time to speak the truth, the whole truth,
frankly and boldly. Nor need we shrink from honestly facing
conditions in our country today. This great Nation will endure as
it has endured, will revive and will prosper. So, first of all, let me
assert my firm belief that the only thing we have to fear is fear
itself—nameless, unreasoning, unjustified terror which paralyzes
needed efforts to convert retreat into advance. In every dark hour
of our national life a leadership of frankness and vigor has met
with that understanding and support of the people themselves
which is essential to victory. I am convinced that you will again
give that support to leadership in these critical days.

In such a spirit on my part and on yours we face our common difficulties. They concern, thank God, only material things.
Values have shrunken to fantastic levels; taxes have risen; our
ability to pay has fallen; government of all kinds is faced by
serious curtailment of income; the means of exchange are frozen
in the currents of trade; the withered leaves of industrial enterprise lie on every side; farmers find no markets for their produce;
the savings of many years in thousands of families are gone.

SOURCE: Samuel I. Rosenman (ed.), *The Public Papers and Addresses of
Franklin D. Roosevelt: Volume Two, The Year of Crisis, 1933* (New York:
Random House, 1938), pp. 11–16. Copyright 1938 by Franklin D. Roose-
velt, and renewed 1965 by Elliott Roosevelt, the Honorable James Roosevelt,
and Franklin Delano Roosevelt, Jr. Reprinted by permission of the Hon.
Samuel I. Rosenman and Random House Inc.

More important, a host of unemployed citizens face the grim problem of existence, and an equally great number toil with little return. Only a foolish optimist can deny the dark realities of the moment.

Yet our distress comes from no failure of substance. We are stricken by no plague of locusts. Compared with the perils which our forefathers conquered because they believed and were not afraid, we have still much to be thankful for. Nature still offers her bounty and human efforts have multiplied it. Plenty is at our doorstep, but a generous use of it languishes in the very sight of the supply. Primarily this is because rulers of the exchange of mankind's goods have failed through their own stubbornness and their own incompetence, have admitted their failure, and have abdicated. Practices of the unscrupulous money changers stand indicted in the court of public opinion, rejected by the hearts and minds of men.

True they have tried, but their efforts have been cast in the pattern of an outworn tradition. Faced by failure of credit they have proposed only the lending of more money. Stripped of the lure of profit by which to induce our people to follow their false leadership, they have resorted to exhortations, pleading tearfully for restored confidence. They know only the rules of a generation of self-seekers. They have no vision, and when there is no vision the people perish.

The money changers have fled from their high seats in the temple of our civilization. We may now restore that temple to the ancient truths. The measure of the restoration lies in the extent to which we apply social values more noble than mere monetary profit.

Happiness lies not in the mere possession of money; it lies in the joy of achievement, in the thrill of creative effort. The joy and moral stimulation of work no longer must be forgotten in the mad chase of evanescent profits. These dark days will be worth all they cost us if they teach us that our true destiny is not to be ministered unto but to minister to ourselves and to our fellow men.

Recognition of the falsity of material wealth as the standard of success goes hand in hand with the abandonment of the false belief that public office and high political position are to be valued only by the standards of pride of place and personal profit; and there must be an end to a conduct in banking and in business which too often has given to a sacred trust the likeness of callous and selfish wrongdoing. Small wonder that confidence languishes, for it thrives only on honesty, on honor, on the sacredness of obligations, on faithful protection, on unselfish performance; without them it cannot live.

Restoration calls, however, not for changes in ethics alone. This Nation asks for action, and action now.

Our greatest primary task is to put people to work. This is no unsolvable problem if we face it wisely and courageously. It can be accomplished in part by direct recruiting by the Government itself, treating the task as we would treat the emergency of a war, but at the same time, through this employment, accomplishing greatly needed projects to stimulate and reorganize the use of our natural resources.

Hand in hand with this we must frankly recognize the overbalance of population in our industrial centers and, by engaging on a national scale in a redistribution, endeavor to provide a better use of the land for those best fitted for the land. The task can be helped by definite efforts to raise the values of agricultural products and with this the power to purchase the output of our cities. It can be helped by preventing realistically the tragedy of the growing loss through foreclosure of our small homes and our farms. It can be helped by insistence that the Federal, State, and local governments act forthwith on the demand that their cost be drastically reduced. It can be helped by the unifying of relief activities which today are often scattered, uneconomical, and unequal. It can be helped by national planning for and supervision of all forms of transportation and of communications and other utilities which have a definitely public character. There are many ways in which it can be helped, but it can never be helped merely by talking about it. We must act and act quickly.

Finally, in our progress toward a resumption of work we require two safeguards against a return of the evils of the old order: there must be a strict supervision of all banking and credits and investments, so that there will be an end to speculation with other people's money; and there must be provision for an adequate but sound currency.

These are the lines of attack. I shall presently urge upon a new Congress, in special session, detailed measures for their fulfillment, and I shall seek the immediate assistance of the several States.

Through this program of action we address ourselves to putting our own national house in order and making income balance outgo. Our international trade relations, through vastly important, are in point of time and necessity secondary to the establishment of a sound national economy. I favor as a practical policy the putting of first things first. I shall spare no effort to restore world trade by international economic readjustment, but the emergency at home cannot wait on that accomplishment.

The basic thought that guides these specific means of national recovery is not narrowly nationalistic. It is the insistence, as a first consideration, upon the interdependence of the various elements in and parts of the United States—a recognition of the old and permanently important manifestation of the American spirit of the pioneer. It is the way to recovery. It is the immediate way. It is the strongest assurance that the recovery will endure.

In the field of world policy I would dedicate this Nation to the policy of the good neighbor—the neighbor who resolutely respects himself and, because he does so, respects the rights of others—the neighbor who respects his obligations and respects the sanctity of his agreements in and with a world of neighbors.

If I read the temper of our people correctly, we now realize as we have never realized before our interdependence on each other; that we cannot merely take but we must give as well; that if we are to go forward, we must move as a trained and loyal army willing to sacrifice for the good of a common discipline, because without such discipline no progress is made, no leadership becomes effective. We are, I know, ready and willing to submit our lives and property to such discipline, because it makes possible a leadership which aims at a larger good. This I propose to offer, pledging that the larger purposes will bind upon us all as a sacred obligation with a unity of duty hitherto evoked only in time of armed strife.

With this pledge taken, I assume unhesitatingly the leadership of this great army of our people dedicated to a disciplined attack upon our common problems.

Action in this image and to this end is feasible under the form of government which we have inherited from our ancestors. Our Constitution is so simple and practical that it is possible always to meet extraordinary needs by changes in emphasis and arrangement without loss of essential form. That is why our constitutional system has proved itself the most superbly enduring political mechanism the modern world has produced. It has met every stress of vast expansion of territory, of foreign wars, of bitter internal strife, of world relations.

It is to be hoped that the normal balance of Executive and legislative authority may be wholly adequate to meet the unprecedented task before us. But it may be that an unprecedented demand and need for undelayed action may call for temporary departure from that normal balance of public procedure.

I am prepared under my constitutional duty to recommend the measures that a stricken Nation in the midst of a stricken world may require. These measures, or such other measures as the Congress may build out of its experience and wisdom, I shall seek, within my constitutional authority, to bring to speedy adoption.

But in the event that the Congress shall fail to take one of these two courses, and in the event that the national emergency is still critical, I shall not evade the clear course of duty that will then confront me. I shall ask the Congress for the one remaining instrument to meet the crisis—broad Executive power to wage a war against the emergency, as great as the power that would be given to me if we were in fact invaded by a foreign foe.

For the trust reposed in me I will return the courage and the devotion that befit the time. I can do no less.

We face the arduous days that lie before us in the warm courage of national unity; with the clear consciousness of seeking old and precious moral values; with the clean satisfaction that comes from the stern performance of duty by old and young alike. We aim at the assurance of a rounded and permanent national life.

We do not distrust the future of essential democracy. The

people of the United States have not failed. In their need they have registered a mandate that they want direct, vigorous action. They have asked for discipline and direction under leadership. They have made me the present instrument of their wishes. In the spirit of the gift I take it.

15 / THUNDER ON THE RIGHT

The organization of the American Liberty League on August 15, 1934, reflected the growing conservative disenchantment with the New Deal. Its platform follows.

1.

To preserve American institutions which safeguard, to citizens in all walks of life, the right to liberty and the pursuit of happiness. Therefore to uphold American principles which oppose the tendency shown in many countries to restrict freedom of speech, freedom of the press, religious liberty, the right to peaceable assembly and the right to petition the government; and to combat the growth of bureaucracy, the spread of monopoly, the socialization of industry and the regimentation of American life.

2.

To maintain the right of an equal opportunity for all to work, earn, save and acquire property in order that every man may enjoy the fruit of his own ability and labor, and thus have, in his declining years, the peace of mind that comes from a sense of security for himself and for his wife and children who may survive him.

3.

To uphold the principle that the levying of taxes, the appropriation of public funds and the designation of the purposes for

SOURCE: *American Liberty League: Its Platform* (Washington: American Liberty League Pamphlet No. 9, 1935), pp. 1–2.

which they are to be expended are exclusively the functions of
the Congress and should not be exercised by administrative officials.

4.

To advocate economy in government by abolishing useless commissions and offices, consolidating departments and bureaus and
eliminating extravagance; to advocate a sound fiscal policy and
the maintenance of a sound and stable currency to be preserved
at all hazards.

5.

To further the restoration of employment and the rehabilitation of agriculture, business and industry, and to oppose all unnecessary interference and competition by government with legitimate industry.

6.

To oppose all measures that may threaten the security of the
invested savings of the millions of savings bank depositors, holders of insurance policies and other investors. Also to support governmental policies that will protect invested funds that go to the
maintenance of churches, colleges, hospitals and all institutions
that care for the aged, the poor, the orphans and the afflicted.

7.

To support government in the obligation to provide for those
who, because of involuntary unemployment or disability, cannot
provide for themselves.

8.

To uphold the American principle that laws be made only by
the direct representatives of the people in the Congress, and that
the laws be interpreted only by the Courts, and to oppose the
delegation of either of these functions to executive departments,
commissions or bureau heads.

9.

To provide for the rank and file of the American people, who
are unorganized and too often have no voice in legislation that

affects their welfare, an opportunity, through united effort and a service of public information, to offset the influence of any and all groups working for selfish purposes.

10.

Finally, to preserve for succeeding generations the principles of the Declaration of Independence, the safeguards of personal liberty and the opportunity for initiative and enterprise provided under the Constitution. These are the foundation stones upon which America has built the most successful governmental structure thus far devised.

16 / THUNDER ON THE LEFT

One of the most colorful and effective of the so-called Southern demagogues, Huey Long first made Louisiana his personal fiefdom and then reached for national power with his "Share Our Wealth" movement.

To members and well-wishers of the Share Our Wealth Society:

For twenty years I have been in the battle to provide that, so long as America has, or can produce, an abundance of the things which make life comfortable and happy, that none should own so much of the things which he does not need and cannot use as to deprive the balance of the people of a reasonable proportion of the necessities and conveniences of life. The whole line of my political thought has always been that America must face the time when the whole country would shoulder the obligation which it owes to every child born on earth—that is, a fair chance to life, liberty, and happiness.

I had been in the United States Senate only a few days when I began my effort to make the battle for a distribution of wealth

SOURCE: *Congressional Record,* 74th Cong., 1st sess. (1935), pp. 8040–8043.

among all the people a national issue for the coming elections. On July 2, 1932, pursuant to a promise made, I heard Franklin Delano Roosevelt, accepting the nomination of the Democratic Party at the Chicago convention for President of the United States, use the following words:

"Throughout the Nation, men and women, forgotten in the political philosophy of the Government for the last years, look to us here for guidance and for a more equitable opportunity to share in the distribution of the national wealth."

It therefore seemed that all we had to do was to elect our candidate and that then my object in public life would be accomplished. . . .

It is not out of place for me to say that the support which I brought to Mr. Roosevelt to secure his nomination and election . as President—and without which it was hardly probable he would ever have been nominated—was on the assurances which I had that he would take the proper stand for the redistribution of wealth in the campaign. He did that much in the campaign; but after his election, what then? I need not tell you the story. We have not time to cry over our disappointments, over promises which others did not keep, and over pledges which were broken.

We have not a moment to lose.

It was after my disappointment over the Roosevelt policy, after he became President, that I saw the light. I soon began to understand that, regardless of what we had been promised, our only chance of securing the fulfillment of such pledges was to organize the men and the women of the United States so that they were a force capable of action, and capable of requiring such a policy from the lawmakers and from the President after they took office. That was the beginning of the Share Our Wealth Society movement. . . .

Even after the present President of the United States had thrown down the pledge which he had made time after time, and rather indicated the desire, instead, to have all the common people of America fed from a half-starvation dole, while the plutocrats of the United States were allowed to wax richer and richer, even after that, I made the public proposition that if he would return to his promise and carry out the pledge given to the people and to me that, regardless of all that had passed, I would again support his administration to the limit of my ability.

Of course, however, I was not blind; I had long since come to the understanding that he was chained to other purposes and to other interests which made impossible his keeping the words which he uttered to the people.

I delayed using this form of call to the members and well-wishers of the Share Our Wealth Society until we had progressed so far as to convince me that we could succeed either before or in the next national election of November 1936. Until I became certain that the spirit of the people could be aroused throughout the United States, and that, without any money—because I have none, except such little as I am given—the people could be persuaded to perfect organizations throughout the counties and communities of the country, I did not want to give false hopes to any of those engaged with me in this noble work. But I have seen and checked back enough, based upon the experiences which I have had in my public career, to know that we can, with much more ease, win the present fight, either between now and the next national campaign, or else in the next national campaign—I say with much more ease than many other battles which I have won in the past but which did not mean near so much.

We now have enough societies and enough members, to say nothing of the well-wishers, who—if they will put their shoulders to the wheel and give us one-half of the time which they do not need for anything else—can force the principles of the Share Our Wealth Society to the forefront, to where no person participating in national affairs can ignore them further.

Now, here is what I ask the officers and members and well-wishers of all the Share Our Wealth Societies to do—two things, to wit:

First. If you have a Share Our Wealth Society in your neighborhood—or, if you have not one, organize one—meet regularly, and let all members, men and women, go to work as quickly and as hard as they can to get every person in the neighborhood to become a member and to go out with them to get more members for the society. If members do not want to go into the society already organized in their community, let them organize another society.

We must have them as members in the movement, so that, by having their cooperation, on short notice we can all act as one person for the one object and purpose of providing that in the land of plenty there shall be comfort for all. The organized 600 families who control the wealth of America have been able to keep the 125,000,000 people in bondage because they have never once known how to effectually strike for their fair demands.

Second. Get a number of members of the Share Our Wealth Society to immediately go into all other neighborhoods of your county and into the neighborhoods of the adjoining counties, so as to get the people in the other communities and in the other counties to organize more Share Our Wealth Societies there; that will mean we can soon get about the work of perfecting a complete, unified organization that will not only hear promises but will compel the fulfillment of pledges made to the people.

It is impossible for the United States to preserve itself as a republic or as a democracy when 600 families own more of this Nation's wealth—in fact, twice as much—as all the balance of the people put together. Ninety-six percent of our people live below the poverty line, while 4 percent own 87 percent of the wealth. America can have enough for all to live in comfort and still permit millionaires to own more than they can ever spend and to have more than they can ever use; but America cannot allow the multimillionaires and the billionaires, a mere handful of them, to own everything unless we are willing to inflict starvation upon 125,000,000 people.

We looked upon the year 1929 as the year when too much was produced for the people to consume. We were told, and we believed, that the farmers raised too much cotton and wool for the people to wear and too much food for the people to eat. Therefore, much of it went to waste, some rotted, and much of it was burned or thrown into the river or into the ocean. But, when we picked up the bulletin of the Department of Agriculture for that year 1929, we found that, according to the diet which they said everyone should eat in order to be healthy, multiplying it by 120,000,000, the number of people we had in 1929, had all of our people had the things which the Government said they should eat in order to live well, we did not have enough even in 1929 to

feed the people. In fact, these statistics show that in some instances we had from one-third to one-half less than the people
needed, particularly of milk, eggs, butter, and dried fruits.

But why in the year 1929 did it appear we had too much? Because the people could not buy the things they wanted to eat,
and needed to eat. That showed the need for and duty of the
Government then and there, to have forced a sharing of our
wealth, and a redistribution, and Roosevelt was elected on the
pledge to do that very thing.

But what was done? Cotton was plowed under the ground.
Hogs and cattle were burned by the millions. The same was done
to wheat and corn, and farmers were paid starvation money not
to raise and not to plant because of the fact that we did not want
so much because of people having no money with which to buy.
Less and less was produced, when already there was less produced than the people needed if they ate what the Government
said they needed to sustain life. God forgive those rulers who
burned hogs, threw milk in the river, and plowed under cotton
while little children cried for meat and milk and something to put
on their naked backs! . . .

Will we allow the political sports, the high heelers, the wise-
acres, and those who ridicule us in our misery and poverty to
keep us from organizing these societies in every hamlet so that
they may bring back to life this law and custom of God and of
this country? Is there a man or woman with a child born on the
earth, or who expects ever to have a child born on earth, who is
willing to have it raised under the present-day practices of piracy,
where it comes into life burdened with debt, condemned to a system of slavery by which the sweat of its brow throughout its existence must go to satisfy the vanity and the luxury of a leisurely
few, who can never be made to see that they are destroying the
root and branch of the greatest country ever to have risen? Our
country is calling; the laws of the Lord are calling; the graves of
our forefathers would open today if their occupants could see the
bloom and flower of their creation withering and dying because
the greed of the financial masters of this country has starved and
withheld from mankind those things produced by his own labor.
To hell with the ridicule of the wise street-corner politician. Pay

no attention to any newspaper or magazine that has sold its columns to perpetuate this crime against the people of America. Save this country. Save mankind. Who can be wrong in such a work, and who cares what consequences may come following the mandates of the Lord, of the Pilgrims, of Jefferson, Webster, and Lincoln? He who falls in this fight falls in the radiance of the future. Better to make this fight and lose than to be a party to a system that strangles humanity.

It took the genius of labor and the lives of all Americans to produce the wealth of this land. If any man, or 100 men, wind up with all that has been produced by 120,000,000 people, that does not mean that those 100 men produced the wealth of the country; it means that those 100 men stole, directly or indirectly, what 125,-000,000 people produced. Let no one tell you that the money masters made this country. They did no such thing. Very few of them ever hewed the forest; very few ever hacked a crosstie; very few ever nailed a board; fewer of them ever laid a brick. Their fortunes came from manipulated finance, control of government, rigging of markets, the spider webs that have grabbed all businesses; they grab the fruits of the land, the conveniences and the luxuries that are intended for 125,000,000 people, and run their heelers to our meetings to set up the cry, "We earned it honestly." The Lord says they did no such thing. The voices of our forefathers say they did no such thing. In this land of abundance, they have no right to impose starvation, misery, and pestilence for the purpose of vaunting their own pride and greed. . . .

We are calling upon people whose souls cannot be cankered by the lure of wealth and corruption. We are calling upon people who have at heart, above their own nefarious possessions, the welfare of this country and of its humanity. We are calling upon them, we are calling upon you, we are calling upon the people of America, upon the men and women who love this country, and who would save their children and their neighbors from calamity and distress, to call in the people whom they know, to acquaint them with the purposes of this society and secure organization and cooperation among everyone willing to lend his hand to this worthy work. Fear of ridicule? Fear of reprisal? Fear of being taken off of the starvation dole? It is too late for our people to have such fears. I have undergone them all. There is nothing under the canopy of heaven which has not been sent to ridicule and embarrass my efforts in this work. And yet, despite such ridicule, face to face in any argument I have yet to see the one of them who dares to gainsay the principle to share our wealth. On the contrary, when their feet are put to the fire, each and every one of them declare that they are in favor of sharing the wealth, and the redistribution of wealth. But then some get suddenly ignorant and say they do not know how to do it. Oh, ye of little faith! God told them how. Apparently they are too lazy in mind or body to want to learn, so long as their ignorance is for the benefit of the 600 ruling families of America who have forged chains of slavery around the wrists and ankles of 125,000,000 freeborn citizens. Lincoln freed the black man, but today the white and the black are shackled far worse than any colored person in 1860. . . .

Here is the whole sum and substance of the share-our-wealth movement:

1. Every family to be furnished by the Government a homestead allowance, free of debt, of not less than one-third the average family wealth of the country, which means, at the lowest, that every family shall have the reasonable comforts of life up to a value of from $5,000 to $6,000. No person to have a fortune of more than 100 to 300 times the average family fortune, which means that the limit to fortunes is between $1,500,000 and $5,000,000, with annual capital levy taxes imposed on all above $1,000,000.

2. The yearly income of every family shall be not less than one-third of the average family income, which means that, according to the estimates of the statisticians of the United States Government and Wall Street, no family's annual income would be less than from $2,000 to $2,500. No yearly income shall be allowed to any person larger than from 100 to 300 times the size of the average family income, which means that no person would be allowed to earn in any year more than from $600,000 to $1,800,000, all to be subject to present income-tax laws.

3. To limit or regulate the hours of work to such an extent as to prevent overproduction; the most modern and efficient ma-

chinery would be encouraged, so that as much would be produced as possible so as to satisfy all demands of the people, but to also allow the maximum time to the workers for recreation, convennience, education, and luxuries of life.

4. An old-age pension to the persons over 60.

5. To balance agricultural production with what can be consumed according to the laws of God, which includes the preserving and storage of surplus commodities to be paid for and held by the Government for the emergencies when such are needed. Please bear in mind, however, that when the people of America have had money to buy things they needed, we have never had a surplus of any commodity. This plan of God does not call for destroying any of the things raised to eat or wear, nor does it countenance wholesale destruction of hogs, cattle, or milk.

6. To pay the veterans of our wars what we owe them and to care for their disabled.

7. Education and training for all children to be equal in opportunity in all schools, colleges, universities, and other institutions for training in the professions and vocations of life; to be regulated on the capacity of children to learn, and not on the ability of parents to pay the costs. Training for life's work to be as much universal and thorough for all walks in life as has been the training in the arts of killing.

8. The raising of revenue and taxes for the support of this program to come from the reduction of swollen fortunes from the top, as well as for the support of public works to give employment whenever there may be any slackening necessary in private enterprise.

I now ask those who read this circular to help us at once in this work of giving life and happiness to our people—not a starvation dole upon which someone may live in misery from week to week. Before this miserable system of wreckage has destroyed the life germ of respect and culture in our American people let us save what was here, merely by having none too poor and none too rich. The theory of the Share Our Wealth Society is to have enough for all, but not to have one with so much that less than enough remains for the balance of the people.

Please, therefore, let me ask you who read this document—

please help this work before it is too late for us to be of help to our people. We ask you now, (1) help to get your neighbor into the work of this society and (2) help get other Share Our Wealth societies started in your county and in adjoining counties and get them to go out to organize other societies.

To print and mail out this circular costs about 60 cents per hundred, or $6 per thousand. Anyone who reads this who wants more circulars of this kind to use in the work, can get them for that price by sending the money to me, and I will pay the printer for him. Better still, if you can have this circular reprinted in your own town or city.

Let everyone who feels he wishes to help in our work start right out and go ahead. One man or woman is as important as any other. Take up the fight! Do not wait for someone else to tell you what to do. There are no high lights in this effort. We have no State managers and no city managers. Everyone can take up the work, and as many societies can be organized as there are people to organize them. One is the same as another. The reward and compensation is the salvation of humanity. Fear no opposition. "He who falls in this fight falls in the radiance of the future!"

Yours sincerely,

HUEY P. LONG,
United States Senator, Washington, D. C.

17 / THE SECOND NEW DEAL

F.D.R.'s State of the Union message to Congress, January 4, 1935, inaugurated the administration's swing to the left in 1935 and 1936.

[T]he Constitution wisely provides that the Chief Executive shall report to Congress on the state of the Union, for through you, the chosen legislative representatives, our citizens every-

SOURCE: *Congressional Record*, 74th Cong., 1st sess. (1935), pp. 116–118.

where may fairly judge the progress of our governing. I am confident that today, in the light of the events of the past two years, you do not consider it merely a trite phrase when I tell you that I am truly glad to greet you and that I look forward to common counsel, to useful cooperation, and to genuine friendships between us.

We have undertaken a new order of things, yet we progress to it under the framework and in the spirit and intent of the American Constitution. We have proceeded throughout the Nation a measurable distance on the road toward this new order. Materially, I can report to you substantial benefits to our agricultural population, increased industrial activity, and profits to our merchants. Of equal moment, there is evident a restoration of that spirit of confidence and faith which marks the American character. Let him who, for speculative profit or partisan purpose, without just warrant would seek to disturb or dispel this assurance, take heed before he assumes responsibility for any act which slows our onward steps.

Throughout the world change is the order of the day. In every Nation economic problems, long in the making, have brought crises of many kinds for which the masters of old practice and theory were unprepared. In most Nations social justice, no longer a distant ideal, has become a definite goal, and ancient Governments are beginning to heed the call.

Thus, the American people do not stand alone in the world in their desire for change. We seek it through tested liberal traditions, through processes which retain all of the deep essentials of that republican form of representative government first given to a troubled world by the United States.

As the various parts in the program begun in the Extraordinary Session of the Seventy-third Congress shape themselves in practical administration, the unity of our program reveals itself to the Nation. The outlines of the new economic order, rising from the disintegration of the old, are apparent. We test what we have done as our measures take root in the living texture of life. We see where we have built wisely and where we can do still better.

The attempt to make a distinction between recovery and reform is a narrowly conceived effort to substitute the appearance of reality for reality itself. When a man is convalescing from illness, wisdom dictates not only cure of the symptoms but also removal of their cause.

It is important to recognize that while we seek to outlaw specific abuses, the American objective of today has an infinitely deeper, finer, and more lasting purpose than mere repression. Thinking people in almost every country of the world have come to realize certain fundamental difficulties with which civilization must reckon. Rapid changes—the machine age, the advent of universal and rapid communication, and many other new factors —have brought new problems. Succeeding generations have attempted to keep pace by reforming in piecemeal fashion this or that attendant abuse. As a result, evils overlap and reform becomes confused and frustrated. We lose sight, from time to time, of our ultimate human objectives.

Let us for a moment strip from our simple purpose the confusion that results from a multiplicity of detail and from millions of written and spoken words.

We find our population suffering from old inequalities, little changed by past sporadic remedies. In spite of our efforts and in spite of our talk we have not weeded out the overprivileged and we have not effectively lifted up the underprivileged. Both of these manifestations of injustice have retarded happiness. No wise man has any intention of destroying what is known as the "profit motive," because by the profit motive we mean the right by work to earn a decent livelihood for ourselves and for our families.

We have, however, a clear mandate from the people, that Americans must forswear that conception of the acquisition of wealth which, through excessive profits, creates undue private power over private affairs and, to our misfortune, over public affairs as well. In building toward this end we do not destroy ambition, nor do we seek to divide our wealth into equal shares on stated occasions. We continue to recognize the greater ability of some to earn more than others. But we do assert that the ambition of the individual to obtain for him and his a proper security, a reasonable leisure, and a decent living throughout life is an ambition to be preferred to the appetite for great wealth and great power.

I recall to your attention my message to the Congress last June in which I said, "Among our objectives I place the security of the men, women, and children of the Nation first." That remains our first and continuing task; and in a very real sense every major legislative enactment of this Congress should be a component part of it.

In defining immediate factors which enter into our quest, I have spoken to the Congress and the people of three great divisions:

First. The security of a livelihood through the better use of the national resources of the land in which we live.

Second. The security against the major hazards and vicissitudes of life.

Third. The security of decent homes.

I am now ready to submit to the Congress a broad program designed ultimately to establish all three of these factors of security —a program which because of many lost years will take many future years to fulfill.

A study of our national resources, more comprehensive than any previously made, shows the vast amount of necessary and practicable work which needs to be done for the development and preservation of our natural wealth for the enjoyment and advantage of our people in generations to come. The sound use of land and water is far more comprehensive than the mere planting of trees, building of dams, distributing of electricity, or retirement of submarginal land. It recognizes that stranded populations, either in the country or the city, cannot have security under the conditions that now surround them.

To this end we are ready to begin to meet this problem—the intelligent care of population throughout our Nation, in accordance with an intelligent distribution of the means of livelihood for that population. A definite program for putting people to work, of which I shall speak in a moment, is a component part of this greater program of security of livelihood through the better use of our national resources.

Closely related to the broad problem of livelihood is that of security against the major hazards of life. Here also a comprehensive survey of what has been attempted or accomplished in many Nations and in many States proves to me that the time has come for action by the National Government. I shall send to you, in a few days, definite recommendations based on these studies. These recommendations will cover the broad subjects of unemployment insurance and old-age insurance, of benefits for children, for mothers, for the handicapped, for maternity care, and for other aspects of dependency and illness where a beginning can now be made.

The third factor—better homes for our people—has also been the subject of experimentation and study. Here, too, the first practical steps can be made through the proposals which I shall suggest in relation to giving work to the unemployed.

Whatever we plan and whatever we do should be in the light of these three clear objectives of security. We cannot afford to lose valuable time in haphazard public policies which cannot find a place in the broad outlines of these major purposes. In that spirit I come to an immediate issue made for us by hard and inescapable circumstance—the task of putting people to work. In the spring of 1933 the issue of destitution seemed to stand apart; today, in the light of our experience and our new national policy, we find we can put people to work in ways which conform to, initiate, and carry forward the broad principles of that policy.

The first objectives of emergency legislation of 1933 were to relieve destitution, to make it possible for industry to operate in a more rational and orderly fashion, and to put behind industrial recovery the impulse of large expenditures in government undertakings. The purpose of the National Industrial Recovery Act to provide work for more people succeeded in a substantial manner within the first few months of its life, and the Act has continued to maintain employment gains and greatly improved working conditions in industry.

The program of public works provided for in the Recovery Act launched the Federal Government into a task for which there was little time to make preparation and little American experience to follow. Great employment has been given and is being given by these works.

More than two billions of dollars have also been expended in direct relief to the destitute. Local agencies, of necessity, determined the recipients of this form of relief. With inevitable exceptions, the funds were spent by them with reasonable efficiency, and as a result actual want of food and clothing in the great majority of cases has been overcome.

But the stark fact before us is that great numbers still remain unemployed.

A large proportion of these unemployed and their dependents have been forced on the relief rolls. The burden on the Federal Government has grown with great rapidity. We have here a human as well as an economic problem. When humane considerations are concerned, Americans give them precedence. The lessons of history, confirmed by the evidence immediately before me, show conclusively that continued dependence upon relief induces a spiritual and moral disintegration fundamentally destructive to the national fibre. To dole out relief in this way is to administer a narcotic, a subtle destroyer of the human spirit. It is inimical to the dictates of sound policy. It is in violation of the traditions of America. Work must be found for able-bodied but destitute workers.

The Federal Government must and shall quit this business of relief.

I am not willing that the vitality of our people be further sapped by the giving of cash, of market baskets, of a few hours of weekly work cutting grass, raking leaves, or picking up papers in the public parks. We must preserve not only the bodies of the unemployed from destitution but also their self-respect, their self-reliance, and courage and determination. This decision brings me to the problem of what the Government should do with approximately five million unemployed now on the relief rolls.

About one million and a half of these belong to the group which in the past was dependent upon local welfare efforts. Most of them are unable for one reason or another to maintain themselves independently—for the most part, through no fault of their own. Such people, in the days before the great depression, were cared for by local efforts—by States, by counties, by towns, by cities, by churches, and by private welfare agencies. It is my thought that in the future they must be cared for as they were before. I stand ready, through my own personal efforts and through the public influence of the office that I hold, to help these local agencies to get the means necessary to assume this burden.

The security legislation which I shall propose to the Congress will, I am confident, be of assistance to local effort in the care of this type of cases. Local responsibility can and will be resumed, for, after all, common sense tells us that the wealth necessary for this task existed and still exists in the local community, and the dictates of sound administration require that this responsibility be in the first instance a local one.

There are, however, an additional three and one half million employable people who are on relief. With them the problem is different and the responsibility is different. This group was the victim of a Nation-wide depression caused by conditions which were not local but national. The Federal Government is the only governmental agency with sufficient power and credit to meet this situation. We have assumed this task, and we shall not shrink from it in the future. It is a duty dictated by every intelligent consideration of national policy to ask you to make it possible for the United States to give employment to all of these three and one-half million employable people now on relief, pending their absorption in a rising tide of private employment.

It is my thought that, with the exception of certain of the normal public building operations of the Government, all emergency public works shall be united in a single new and greatly enlarged plan.

With the establishment of this new system we can supersede the Federal Emergency Relief Administration with a coordinated authority which will be charged with the orderly liquidation of our present relief activities and the substitution of a national chart for the giving of work.

This new program of emergency public employment should be governed by a number of practical principles.

1—All work undertaken should be useful—not just for a day or a year, but useful in the sense that it affords permanent improvement in living conditions or that it creates future new wealth for the Nation.

2—Compensation on emergency public projects should be in the form of security payments which should be larger than the amount now received as a relief dole, but, at the same time, not so large as to encourage the rejection of opportunities for private employment or the leaving of private employment to engage in Government work.

3—Projects should be undertaken on which a large percentage of direct labor can be used.

4—Preference should be given to those projects which will be self-liquidating in the sense that there is a reasonable expectation that the Government will get its money back at some future time.

5—The projects undertaken should be selected and planned so as to compete as little as possible with private enterprises. This suggests that if it were not for the necessity of giving useful work to the unemployed now on relief these projects in most instances would not now be undertaken.

6—The planning of projects would seek to assure work during the coming fiscal year to the individuals now on relief, or until such time as private employment is available. In order to make adjustment to increasing private employment, work should be planned with a view to tapering it off in proportion to the speed with which the emergency workers are offered positions with private employers.

7—Effort should be made to locate projects where they will serve the greatest unemployment needs as shown by present relief rolls, and the broad program of the National Resources Board should be freely used for guidance in selection. Our ultimate objective being the enrichment of human lives, the Government has the primary duty to use its emergency expenditures as much as possible to serve those who cannot secure the advantages of private capital.

Ever since the adjournment of the Seventy-third Congress the Administration has been studying from every angle the possibility and the practicability of new forms of employment. As a result of these studies I have arrived at certain very definite convictions as to the amount of money that will be necessary for the sort of public projects that I have described. I shall submit these figures in my budget message. I assure you now they will be within the sound credit of the Government.

The work itself will cover a wide field, including clearance of slums, which for adequate reasons cannot be undertaken by private capital; in rural housing of several kinds, where, again, private capital is unable to function; in rural electrification; in the reforestation of the great watersheds of the nation; in an intensified program to prevent soil erosion and to reclaim blighted areas; in improving existing road systems and in constructing national highways designed to handle modern traffic; in the elimination of grade crossings; in the extension and enlargement of the successful work of the Civilian Conservation Corps; in non-Federal works, mostly self-liquidating and highly useful to local divisions of Government; and on many other projects which the nation needs and cannot afford to neglect.

This is the method which I propose to you in order that we may better meet this present-day problem of unemployment. Its greatest advantage is that it fits logically and usefully into the long-range permanent policy of providing the three types of security which constitute as a whole an American plan for the betterment of the future of the American people.

I shall consult with you from time to time concerning other measures of national importance. Among the subjects that lie immediately before us are the consolidation of Federal regulatory administration over all forms of transportation, the renewal and clarification of the general purposes of the National Industrial Recovery Act, the strengthening of our facilities for the prevention, detection, and treatment of crime and criminals, the restoration of sound conditions in the public utilities field through abolition of the evil features of holding companies, the gradual tapering off of the emergency credit activities of Government, and improvement in our taxation forms and methods.

We have already begun to feel the bracing effect upon our economic system of a restored agriculture. The hundreds of millions of additional income that farmers are receiving are finding their way into the channels of trade. The farmers' share of the national income is slowly rising. The economic facts justify the widespread opinion of those engaged in agriculture that our provisions for maintaining a balanced production give at this time the most adequate remedy for an old and vexing problem. For the present, and especially in view of abnormal world conditions, agricultural adjustment with certain necessary improvements in methods should continue.

18 / THE NEW DEAL AT HIGH TIDE

In the wake of his overwhelming victory in the 1936
elections, Roosevelt outlined in his second
inaugural address, January 20, 1937,
a bold program to uplift the one-third of the
nation living in poverty.

When four years ago we met to inaugurate a President, the republic, single-minded in anxiety, stood in spirit here. We dedicated ourselves to the fulfillment of a vision—to speed the time when there would be for all the people that security and peace essential to the pursuit of happiness. We of the Republic pledged ourselves to drive from the temple of our ancient faith those who had profaned it; to end by action, tireless and unafraid, the stagnation and despair of that day. We did those first things first.

Our covenant with ourselves did not stop there. Instinctively we recognized a deeper need—the need to find through government the instrument of our united purpose to solve for the individual the ever-rising problems of a complex civilization. Re-

SOURCE: Samuel I. Rosenman (ed.), *The Public Papers and Addresses of Franklin D. Roosevelt: 1937 Volume, The Constitution Prevails* (New York: Macmillan, 1941), pp. 1–6. Reprinted by permission of the Honorable Samuel I. Rosenman.

peated attempts at their solution without the aid of government had left us baffled and bewildered. For, without that aid, we had been unable to create those moral controls over the services of science which are necessary to make science a useful servant instead of a ruthless master of mankind. To do this we knew that we must find practical controls over blind economic forces and blindly selfish men.

We of the Republic sensed the truth that democratic government has innate capacity to protect its people against disasters once considered inevitable, to solve problems once considered unsolvable. We would not admit that we could not find a way to master economic epidemics just as, after centuries of fatalistic suffering, we had found a way to master epidemics of disease. We refused to leave the problems of our common welfare to be solved by the winds of chance and the hurricanes of disaster.

In this we Americans were discovering no wholly new truth; we were writing a new chapter in our book of self-government.

This year marks the one hundred and fiftieth anniversary of the Constitutional Convention which made us a nation. At that Convention our forefathers found the way out of the chaos which followed the Revolutionary War; they created a strong government with powers of united action sufficient then and now to solve problems utterly beyond individual or local solution. A century and a half ago they established the Federal Government in order to promote the general welfare and secure the blessings of liberty to the American people.

Today we invoke those same powers of government to achieve the same objectives.

Four years of new experience have not belied our historic instinct. They hold out the clear hope that government within communities, government within the separate States, and government of the United States can do the things the times require, without yielding its democracy. Our tasks in the last four years did not force democracy to take a holiday.

Nearly all of us recognize that as intricacies of human relationships increase, so power to govern them also must increase—power to stop evil; power to do good. The essential democracy of our Nation and the safety of our people depend not upon the absence of power, but upon lodging it with those whom the people can change or continue at stated intervals through an honest and free system of elections. The Constitution of 1787 did not make our democracy impotent.

In fact, in these last four years, we have made the exercise of all power more democratic; for we have begun to bring private autocratic powers into their proper subordination to the public's government. The legend that they were invincible—above and beyond the processes of a democracy—has been shattered. They have been challenged and beaten.

Our progress out of the depression is obvious. But that is not all that you and I mean by the new order of things. Our pledge was not merely to do a patchwork job with second-hand materials. By using the new materials of social justice we have undertaken to erect on the old foundations a more enduring structure for the better use of future generations.

In that purpose we have been helped by achievements of mind and spirit. Old truths have been relearned; untruths have been unlearned. We have always known that heedless self-interest was bad morals; we know now that it is bad economics. Out of the collapse of a prosperity whose builders boasted their practicality has come the conviction that in the long run economic morality pays. We are beginning to wipe out the line that divides the practical from the ideal; and in so doing we are fashioning an instrument of unimagined power for the establishment of a morally better world.

This new understanding undermines the old admiration of worldly success as such. We are beginning to abandon our tolerance of the abuse of power by those who betray for profit the elementary decencies of life.

In this process evil things formerly accepted will not be so easily condoned. Hard-headedness will not so easily excuse hard-heartedness. We are moving toward an era of good feeling. But we realize that there can be no era of good feeling save among men of good will.

For these reasons I am justified in believing that the greatest change we have witnessed has been the change in the moral climate of America.

Among men of good will, science and democracy together offer an ever-richer life and ever-larger satisfaction to the individual. With this change in our moral climate and our rediscovered ability to improve our economic order, we have set our feet upon the road of enduring progress.

Shall we pause now and turn our back upon the road that lies ahead? Shall we call this the promised land? Or, shall we continue on our way? For "each age is a dream that is dying, or one that is coming to birth."

Many voices are heard as we face a great decision. Comfort says, "Tarry a while." Opportunism says, "This is a good spot." Timidity asks, "How difficult is the road ahead?"

True, we have come far from the days of stagnation and despair. Vitality has been preserved. Courage and confidence have been restored. Mental and moral horizons have been extended.

But our present gains were won under the pressure of more than ordinary circumstance. Advance became imperative under the goad of fear and suffering. The times were on the side of progress.

To hold to progress today, however, is more difficult. Dulled conscience, irresponsibility, and ruthless self-interest already reappear. Such symptoms of prosperity may become portents of disaster! Prosperity already tests the persistence of our progressive purpose.

Let us ask again: Have we reached the goal of our vision of that fourth day of March, 1933? Have we found our happy valley?

I see a great nation, upon a great continent, blessed with a great wealth of natural resources. Its hundred and thirty million people are at peace among themselves; they are making their country a good neighbor among the nations. I see a United States which can demonstrate that, under democratic methods of government, national wealth can be translated into a spreading volume of human comforts hitherto unknown, and the lowest standard of living can be raised far above the level of mere subsistence.

But here is the challenge to our democracy: In this nation I see tens of millions of its citizens—a substantial part of its whole population—who at this very moment are denied the greater part of what the very lowest standards of today call the necessities of life.

I see millions of families trying to live on incomes so meager that the pall of family disaster hangs over them day by day.

I see millions whose daily lives in city and on farm continue under conditions labeled indecent by a so-called polite society half a century ago.

I see millions denied education, recreation, and the opportunity to better their lot and the lot of their children.

I see millions lacking the means to buy the products of farm and factory and by their poverty denying work and productiveness to many other millions.

I see one-third of a nation ill-housed, ill-clad, ill-nourished.

It is not in despair that I paint you that picture. I paint it for you in hope—because the nation, seeing and understanding the injustice in it, proposes to paint it out. We are determined to make every American citizen the subject of his country's interest and concern; and we will never regard any faithful, law-abiding group within our borders as superfluous. The test of our progress is not whether we add more to the abundance of those who have much; it is whether we provide enough for those who have too little.

If I know aught of the spirit and purpose of our nation, we will not listen to Comfort, Opportunism, and Timidity. We will carry on.

Overwhelmingly, we of the Republic are men and women of good will; men and women who have more than warm hearts of dedication; men and women who have cool heads and willing hands of practical purpose as well. They will insist that every agency of popular government use effective instruments to carry out their will.

Government is competent when all who compose it work as trustees for the whole people. It can make constant progress when it keeps abreast of all the facts. It can obtain justified support and legitimate criticism when the people receive true information of all that government does.

If I know aught of the will of our people, they will demand

that these conditions of effective government shall be created and maintained. They will demand a nation uncorrupted by cancers of injustice and, therefore, strong among the nations in its example of the will to peace.

Today we reconsecrate our country to long-cherished ideals in a suddenly changed civilization. In every land there are always at work forces that drive men apart and forces that draw men together. In our personal ambitions we are individualists. But in our seeking for economic and political progress as a nation, we all go up, or else we all go down, as one people.

To maintain a democracy of effort requires a vast amount of patience in dealing with differing methods, a vast amount of humility. But out of the confusion of many voices rises an understanding of dominant public need. Then political leadership can voice common ideals, and aid in their realization.

In taking again the oath of office as President of the United States, I assume the solemn obligation of leading the American people forward along the road over which they have chosen to advance.

While this duty rests upon me I shall do my utmost to speak their purpose and to do their will, seeking Divine guidance to help us each and every one to give light to them that sit in darkness and to guide our feet into the way of peace.

19 / THE END OF THE NEW DEAL

In his State of the Union message to Congress of January 4, 1939, F.D.R. called a halt to the New Deal reform program to concentrate the nation's full energies upon meeting the threat from without.

[I]n reporting on the state of the Nation, I have felt it necessary on previous occasions to advise the Congress of disturbance abroad and of the need of putting our own house in order in the

SOURCE: *Congressional Record,* 76th Cong., 1st sess. (1939), pp. 74–76.

face of storm signals from across the seas. As this Seventy-sixth Congress opens there is need for further warning.

A war which threatened to envelop the world in flames has been averted; but it has become increasingly clear that world peace is not assured.

All about us rage undeclared wars—military and economic. All about us grow more deadly armaments—military and economic. All about us are threats of new aggression—military and economic.

Storms from abroad directly challenge three institutions indispensable to Americans, now as always. The first is religion. It is the source of the other two—democracy and international good faith.

Religion, by teaching man his relationship to God, gives the individual a sense of his own dignity and teaches him to respect himself by respecting his neighbors.

Democracy, the practice of self-government, is a covenant among free men to respect the rights and liberties of their fellows.

International good faith, a sister of democracy, springs from the will of civilized nations of men to respect the rights and liberties of other nations of men.

In a modern civilization, all three—religion, democracy, and international good faith—complement and support each other.

Where freedom of religion has been attacked, the attack has come from sources opposed to democracy. Where democracy has been overthrown, the spirit of free worship has disappeared. And where religion and democracy have vanished, good faith and reason in international affairs have given way to strident ambition and brute force.

An ordering of society which relegates religion, democracy and good faith among nations to the background can find no place within it for the ideals of the Prince of Peace. The United States rejects such an ordering, and retains its ancient faith.

There comes a time in the affairs of men when they must prepare to defend, not their homes alone, but the tenets of faith and humanity on which their churches, their governments and their very civilization are founded. The defense of religion, of democracy and of good faith among nations is all the same fight. To save one we must now make up our minds to save all.

We know what might happen to us of the United States if the new philosophies of force were to encompass the other continents and invade our own. We, no more than other nations, can afford to be surrounded by the enemies of our faith and our humanity. Fortunate it is, therefore, that in this Western Hemisphere we have, under a common ideal of democratic government, a rich diversity of resources and of peoples functioning together in mutual respect and peace.

That hemisphere, that peace, and that ideal we propose to do our share in protecting against storms from any quarter. Our people and our resources are pledged to secure that protection. From that determination no American flinches.

This by no means implies that the American republics disassociate themselves from the nations of other continents—it does not mean the Americas against the rest of the world. We as one of the republics reiterate our willingness to help the cause of world peace. We stand on our historic offer to take counsel with all other nations of the world to the end that aggression among them be terminated, that the race of armaments cease and that commerce be renewed.

But the world has grown so small and weapons of attack so swift that no nation can be safe in its will to peace so long as any other powerful nation refuses to settle its grievances at the council table.

For if any government bristling with implements of war insists on policies of force, weapons of defense give the only safety.

In our foreign relations we have learned from the past what not to do. From new wars we have learned what we must do.

We have learned that effective timing of defense, and the distant points from which attacks may be launched are completely different from what they were twenty years ago.

We have learned that survival cannot be guaranteed by arming after the attack begins—for there is new range and speed to offense.

We have learned that long before any overt military act, aggression begins with preliminaries of propaganda, subsidized penetration, the loosening of ties of good will, the stirring of prejudice, and the incitement to disunion.

We have learned that God-fearing democracies of the world which observe the sanctity of treaties and good faith in their dealings with other nations cannot safely be indifferent to international lawlessness anywhere. They cannot forever let pass, without effective protest, acts of aggression against sister nations —acts which automatically undermine all of us.

Obviously they must proceed along practical, peaceful lines. But the mere fact that we rightly decline to intervene with arms to prevent acts of aggression does not mean that we must act as if there were no aggression at all. Words may be futile, but war is not the only means of commanding a decent respect for the opinions of mankind. There are many methods short of war, but stronger and more effective than mere words, of bringing home to aggressor governments the aggregate sentiments of our own people.

At the very least, we can and should avoid any action, or any lack of action, which will encourage, assist, or build up an aggressor. We have learned that when we deliberately try to legislate neutrality, our neutrality laws may operate unevenly and unfairly—may actually give aid to an aggressor and deny it to the victim. The instinct of self-preservation should warn us that we ought not to let that happen any more.

And we have learned something else—the old, old lesson that probability of attack is mightily decreased by the assurance of an ever-ready defense. Since 1931 world events of thunderous import have moved with lightning speed. During these eight years many of our people clung to the hope that the innate decency of mankind would protect the unprepared who showed their innate trust in mankind. Today we are all wiser—and sadder.

Under modern conditions what we mean by "adequate defense"—a policy subscribed to by all of us—must be divided into three elements. First, we must have armed forces and defenses strong enough to ward off sudden attack against strategic positions and key facilities essential to ensure sustained resistance and ultimate victory. Secondly, we must have the organization and location of those key facilities so that they may be immediately utilized and rapidly expanded to meet all needs without danger of serious interruption by enemy attack.

In the course of a few days I shall send you a special message making recommendations for those two essentials of defense against danger which we cannot safely assume will not come.

If these first two essentials are reasonably provided for, we must be able confidently to invoke the third element, the underlying strength of citizenship—the self-confidence, the ability, the imagination, and the devotion that give the staying power to see things through.

A strong and united nation may be destroyed if it is unprepared against sudden attack. But even a nation well armed and well organized from a strictly military standpoint may, after a period of time, meet defeat if it is unnerved by self-distrust, endangered by class prejudice, by dissension between capital and labor, by false economy, and by other unsolved social problems at home.

In meeting the troubles of the world we must meet them as one people—with a unity born of the fact that for generations those who have come to our shores, representing many kindreds and tongues, have been welded by common opportunity into a united patriotism. If another form of government can present a united front in its attack on a democracy, the attack must and will be met by a united democracy. Such a democracy can and must exist in the United States.

A dictatorship may command the full strength of a regimented nation. But the united strength of a democratic nation can be mustered only when its people, educated by modern standards to know what is going on and where they are going, have conviction that they are receiving as large a share of opportunity for development, as large a share of material success and of human dignity as they have a right to receive.

Our Nation's program of social and economic reform is therefore a part of defense as basic as armaments themselves.

Against the background of events in Europe, in Africa, and in

Asia during these recent years, the pattern of what we have accomplished since 1933 appears in even clearer focus.

For the first time we have moved upon deep-seated problems affecting our national strength and have forged national instruments adequate to meet them.

Consider what the seemingly piecemeal struggles of these six years add up to in terms of realistic national preparedness.

We are conserving and developing natural resources—land, water, power, forests.

We are trying to provide necessary food, shelter, and medical care for the health of our population.

We are putting agriculture—our system of food and fibre supply—on a sounder basis.

We are strengthening the weakest spot in our system of industrial supply—its long-smouldering labor difficulties.

We have cleaned up our credit system so that depositor and investor alike may more readily and willingly make their capital available for peace or war.

We are giving to our youth new opportunities for work and education.

We have sustained the morale of all the population by the dignified recognition of our obligations to the aged, the helpless, and the needy.

Above all, we have made the American people conscious of their interrelationship and their interdependence. They sense a common destiny and a common need of each other. Differences of occupation, geography, race, and religion no longer obscure the nation's fundamental unity in thought and in action.

We have our difficulties, true; but we are a wiser and a tougher Nation than we were in 1929 or 1932.

Never have there been six years of such far-flung internal preparedness in our history. And this has been done without any dictator's power to command, without conscription of labor or confiscation of capital, without concentration camps, and without a scratch on freedom of speech, freedom of the press, or the rest of the Bill of Rights.

We see things now that we could not see along the way. The

tools of government which we had in 1933 are outmoded. We have had to forge new tools for a new role of government operating in a democracy—a role of new responsibility for new needs and increased responsibility for old needs, long neglected.

Some of these tools had to be roughly shaped and still need some machining down. Many of those who fought bitterly against the forging of these new tools welcome their use today. The American people, as a whole, have accepted them. The Nation looks to the Congress to improve the new machinery which we have permanently installed, provided that in the process the social usefulness of the machinery is not destroyed or impaired.

All of us agree that we should simplify and improve laws if experience and operation clearly demonstrate the need. For instance, all of us want better provision for our older people under our social security legislation. For the medically needy we must provide better care.

Most of us agree that for the sake of employer and employee alike we must find ways to end factional labor strife and employer-employee disputes.

Most of us recognize that none of these tools can be put to maximum effectiveness unless the executive processes of government are revamped—reorganized, if you will—into more effective combination. And even after such reorganization it will take time to develop administrative personnel and experience in order to use our new tools with a minimum of mistakes. The Congress, of course, needs no further information on this.

With this exception of legislation to provide greater Government efficiency, and with the exception of legislation to ameliorate our railroad and other transportation problems, the past three Congresses have met in part or in whole the pressing needs of the new order of things.

We have now passed the period of internal conflict in the launching of our program of social reform. Our full energies may now be released to invigorate the processes of recovery in order to preserve our reforms, and to give every man and woman who wants to work a real job at a living wage.

But time is of paramount importance. The deadline of danger

from within and from without is not within our control. The
hourglass may be in the hands of other nations. Our own hourglass tells us that we are off on a race to make democracy work,
so that we may be efficient in peace and therefore secure in
self-defense. . . .

PART V

Post-World War II America

After the war, President Harry S Truman sought to reinvigorate domestic reform as the champion of the "Fair Deal" (Selection 20). Although he won an upset victory in the 1948 presidential race, his program was repeatedly frustrated by a bipartisan conservative majority in Congress. In addition, he found himself increasingly on the defensive in the face of attacks by Republican Senator Joseph R. McCarthy of Wisconsin, who exploited popular anxieties growing out of the Cold War and the Korean conflict (Selection 21).

Truman's successor, Dwight D. Eisenhower, stood for what he called "modern Republicanism." In practice, that meant no turning-back of the clock on the major New Deal reforms, but proceeding slowly with any new programs (Selection 22). Disappointed liberals condemned his presidency as eight largely wasted years (Selection 23).

In 1960, John F. Kennedy narrowly defeated Vice President Richard Nixon for the presidency and pledged his administration to the conquest of the "New Frontier" (Selection 24). But he was unable to make much headway with Congress before his death. In 1964, the Republican right wing captured the G.O.P. and nominated Barry Goldwater for the presidency. The Goldwater rhetoric—most notably his acceptance speech (Selection 25)—so frightened millions of moderates that Lyndon Johnson won a landslide victory. In his State of the Union message of January 4, 1965, Johnson outlined his far-reaching program to build "the Great Society" (Selection 26).

Probably the most striking feature of the postwar era has been the so-called civil rights revolution, for which the most important breakthrough came with the Supreme Court's decision in *Brown* v. *Board of Education of Topeka* (1954) outlawing public school segregation. Although the years after 1954 saw the passage of new and stronger legislation to assure the Negro legal equality, time increasingly showed that legal equality was of marginal benefit to the millions of poverty-stricken Negroes throughout the South and in the Northern urban ghettos. In his Howard University speech on June 4, 1965, President Johnson called for a program of massive governmental assistance to help the Negro overcome the legacy of slavery and discrimination (Selection 27).

But the cost of the Vietnam war and a growing white backlash have prevented the implementation of the chief executive's more ambitious recommendations, and the problem of what Daniel P. Moynihan has called the Negro "underclass" remains our foremost domestic problem for the years ahead (Selection 28).

20 / HARRY S TRUMAN AND THE

FAIR DEAL

> *In his State of the Union message to Congress, January 5, 1949, President Harry S Truman outlined his Fair Deal program.*

I am happy to report to this Eighty-first Congress that the state of the Union is good. Our Nation is better able than ever before to meet the needs of the American people, and to give them their fair chance in the pursuit of happiness. This great Republic is foremost among the nations of the world in the search for peace.

SOURCE: *Public Papers of the Presidents of the United States: Harry S Truman, 1949* (Washington: Government Printing Office, 1964), pp. 1–7.

During the last sixteen years, our people have been creating a society which offers new opportunities for every man to enjoy his share of the good things of life.

In this society, we are conservative about the values and principles which we cherish; but we are forward-looking in protecting those values and principles and in extending their benefits. We have rejected the discredited theory that the fortunes of the Nation should be in the hands of a privileged few. We have abandoned the "trickle-down" concept of national prosperity. Instead, we believe that our economic system should rest on a democratic foundation and that wealth should be created for the benefit of all.

The recent election shows that the people of the United States are in favor of this kind of society and want to go on improving it.

The American people have decided that poverty is just as wasteful and just as unnecessary as preventable disease. We have pledged our common resources to help one another in the hazards and struggles of individual life. We believe that no unfair prejudice or artificial distinction should bar any citizen of the United States of America from an education, or from good health, or from a job that he is capable of performing.

The attainment of this kind of society demands the best efforts of every citizen in every walk of life, and it imposes increasing responsibilities on the Government.

The Government must work with industry, labor, and the farmers in keeping our economy running at full speed. The Government must see that every American has a chance to obtain his fair share of our increasing abundance. These responsibilities go hand in hand.

We cannot maintain prosperity unless we have a fair distribution of opportunity and a widespread consumption of the products of our factories and farms.

Our Government has undertaken to meet these responsibilities.

We have made tremendous public investments in highways, hydroelectric power projects, soil conservation, and reclamation. We have established a system of social security. We have enacted laws protecting the rights and the welfare of our working people and the income of our farmers. These Federal policies have paid for themselves many times over. They have strengthened the material foundations of our democratic ideals. Without them, our present prosperity would be impossible.

Reinforced by these policies, our private enterprise system has reached new heights of production. Since the boom year of 1929, while our population has increased by only 20 percent, our agricultural production has increased by 45 percent, and our industrial production has increased by 75 percent. We are turning out far more goods and more wealth per worker than we have ever done before.

This progress has confounded the gloomy prophets—at home and abroad—who predicted the downfall of American capitalism. The people of the United States, going their own way, confident in their own powers, have achieved the greatest prosperity the world has ever seen.

But, great as our progress has been, we still have a long way to go.

As we look around the country, many of our shortcomings stand out in bold relief.

We are suffering from excessively high prices.

Our production is still not large enough to satisfy our demands.

Our minimum wages are far too low.

Small business is losing ground to growing monopoly.

Our farmers still face an uncertain future. And too many of them lack the benefits of our modern civilization.

Some of our natural resources are still being wasted.

We are acutely short of electric power, although the means for developing such power are abundant.

Five million families are still living in slums and firetraps. Three million families share their homes with others.

Our health is far behind the progress of medical science. Proper medical care is so expensive that it is out of the reach of the great majority of our citizens.

Our schools, in many localities, are utterly inadequate.

Our democratic ideals are often thwarted by prejudice and intolerance.

Each of these shortcomings is also an opportunity—an opportunity for the Congress and the President to work for the good of the people.

Our first great opportunity is to protect our economy against the evils of "boom and bust."

This objective cannot be attained by government alone. Indeed, the greater part of the task must be performed by individual efforts under our system of free enterprise. We can keep our present prosperity, and increase it, only if free enterprise and free government work together to that end.

We cannot afford to float along ceaselessly on a postwar boom until it collapses. It is not enough merely to prepare to weather a recession if it comes. Instead, government and business must work together constantly to achieve more and more jobs and more and more production—which mean more and more prosperity for all the people.

The business cycle is man-made; and men of good will, working together, can smooth it out.

So far as business is concerned, it should plan for steady, vigorous expansion—seeking always to increase its output, lower its prices, and avoid the vices of monopoly and restriction. So long as business does this, it will be contributing to continued prosperity, and it will have the help and encouragement of the Government.

The Employment Act of 1946 pledges the Government to use all its resources to promote maximum employment, production, and purchasing power. This means that the Government is firmly committed to protect business and the people against the dangers of recession and against the evils of inflation. This means that the Government must adapt its plans and policies to meet changing circumstances.

At the present time, our prosperity is threatened by inflationary pressures at a number of critical points in our economy. And the Government must be in a position to take effective action at these danger spots. To that end, I recommend that the Congress enact legislation for the following purposes:

First, to continue the power to control consumer credit and enlarge the power to control bank credit.

Second, to grant authority to regulate speculation on the commodity exchanges.

Third, to continue export control authority and to provide adequate machinery for its enforcement.

Fourth, to continue the priorities and allocation authority in the field of transportation.

Fifth, to authorize priorities and allocations for key materials in short supply.

Sixth, to extend and strengthen rent control.

Seventh, to provide standby authority to impose price ceilings for scarce commodities which basically affect essential industrial production or the cost of living, and to limit unjustified wage adjustments which would force a break in an established price ceiling.

Eighth, to authorize an immediate study of the adequacy of production facilities for materials in critically short supply, such as steel; and, if found necessary, to authorize Government loans for the expansion of production facilities to relieve such shortages, and to authorize the construction of such facilities directly, if action by private industry fails to meet our needs.

The Economic Report, which I shall submit to the Congress shortly, will discuss in detail the economic background for these recommendations.

One of the most important factors in maintaining prosperity is the Government's fiscal policy. At this time, it is essential not only that the Federal budget be balanced, but also that there be a substantial surplus to reduce inflationary pressures, and to permit a sizable reduction in the national debt, which now stands at $252 billion. I recommend, therefore, that the Congress enact new tax legislation to bring in an additional $4 billion of Government revenue. This should come principally from additional corporate taxes. A portion should come from revised estate and gift taxes. Consideration should be given to raising personal income rates in the middle and upper brackets.

If we want to keep our economy running in high gear, we must be sure that every group has the incentive to make its full contribution to the national welfare. At present, the working men and women of the Nation are unfairly discriminated against by a statute that abridges their rights, curtails their constructive efforts, and hampers our system of free collective bargaining. That statute is the Labor-Management Relations Act of 1947, sometimes called the Taft-Hartley Act.

That act should be repealed!

The Wagner Act should be reenacted. However, certain improvements, which I recommended to the Congress two years ago, are needed. Jurisdictional strikes and unjustified secondary boycotts should be prohibited. The use of economic force to decide issues arising out of the interpretation of existing contracts should be prevented. Without endangering our democratic freedoms, means should be provided for setting up machinery for preventing strikes in vital industries which affect the public interest.

The Department of Labor should be rebuilt and strengthened and those units properly belonging within that department should be placed in it.

The health of our economy and its maintenance at high levels further require that the minimum wage fixed by law should be raised to at least 75 cents an hour.

If our free enterprise economy is to be strong and healthy, we must reinvigorate the forces of competition. We must assure small business the freedom and opportunity to grow and prosper. To this purpose, we should strengthen our antitrust laws by closing those loopholes that permit monopolistic mergers and consolidations.

Our national farm program should be improved—not only in the interest of the farmers, but for the lasting prosperity of the whole Nation. Our goals should be abundant farm production and parity income for agriculture. Standards of living on the farm should be just as good as anywhere else in the country.

Farm price supports are an essential part of our program to achieve these ends. Price supports should be used to prevent farm price declines which are out of line with general price levels, to facilitate adjustments in production to consumer demands, and to promote good land use. Our price support legislation must be adapted to these objectives. The authority of the Commodity Credit Corporation to provide adequate storage space for crops should be restored. Our program for farm prosperity should also seek to expand the domestic market for agricultural products, particularly among low-income groups, and to increase and stabilize foreign markets.

We should give special attention to extending modern conveniences and services to our farms. Rural electrification should be pushed forward. And in considering legislation relating to housing, education, health, and social security, special attention should be given to rural problems.

Our growing population and the expansion of our economy depend upon the wise management of our land, water, forest, and mineral wealth. In our present dynamic economy, the task of conservation is not to lockup our resources but to develop and improve them. Failure, today, to make the investments which are necessary to support our progress in the future would be false economy.

We must push forward the development of our rivers for power, irrigation, navigation, and flood control. We should apply the lessons of our Tennessee Valley experience to our other great river basins.

I again recommend action be taken by the Congress to approve the St. Lawrence Seaway and Power project. This is about the fifth time I have recommended it.

We must adopt a program for the planned use of the petroleum reserves under the sea, which are—and must remain—vested in the Federal Government. We must extend our programs of soil conservation. We must place our forests on a sustained yield basis, and encourage the development of new sources of vital minerals.

In all this we must make sure that the benefits of these public undertakings are directly available to the people. Public power should be carried to consuming areas by public transmission lines where necessary to provide electricity at the lowest possible rates. Irrigation waters should serve family farms and not land speculators.

The Government has still other opportunities—to help raise the standard of living of our citizens. These opportunities lie in the fields of social security, health, education, housing, and civil rights.

The present coverage of the social security laws is altogether inadequate; the benefit payments are too low. One-third of our workers are not covered. Those who receive old-age and survivors insurance benefits receive an average payment of only $25 a month. Many others who cannot work because they are physically disabled are left to the mercy of charity. We should expand our social security program, both as to the size of the benefits and the extent of coverage, against the economic hazards due to unemployment, old age, sickness, and disability.

We must spare no effort to raise the general level of health in this country. In a nation as rich as ours, it is a shocking fact that tens of millions lack adequate medical care. We are short of doctors, hospitals, nurses. We must remedy these shortages. Moreover, we need—and we must have without further delay— a system of prepaid medical insurance which will enable every American to afford good medical care.

It is equally shocking that millions of our children are not receiving a good education. Millions of them are in overcrowded, obsolete buildings. We are short of teachers, because teachers' salaries are too low to attract new teachers, or to hold the ones we have. All these school problems will become much more acute as a result of the tremendous increase in the enrollment in our elementary schools in the next few years. I cannot repeat too strongly my desire for prompt Federal financial aid to the States to help them operate and maintain their school systems.

The governmental agency which now administers the programs of health, education, and social security should be given full departmental status.

The housing shortage continues to be acute. As an immediate step, the Congress should enact the provisions for low-rent public housing, slum clearance, farm housing, and housing research which I have repeatedly recommended. The number of low-rent public housing units provided for in the legislation should be increased to 1 million units in the next seven years. Even this number of units will not begin to meet our need for new housing.

Most of the houses we need will have to be built by private enterprise, without public subsidy. By producing too few rental units and too large a proportion of high-priced houses, the building industry is rapidly pricing itself out of the market. Building costs must be lowered.

The Government is now engaged in a campaign to induce all segments of the building industry to concentrate on the production of lower priced housing. Additional legislation to encourage such housing will be submitted.

The authority which I have requested, to allocate materials in short supply and to impose price ceilings on such materials, could be used, if found necessary, to channel more materials into homes large enough for family life at prices which wage earners can afford.

The driving force behind our progress is our faith in our democratic institutions. That faith is embodied in the promise of equal rights and equal opportunities which the founders of our Republic proclaimed to their countrymen and to the whole world.

The fulfillment of this promise is among the highest purposes of government. The civil rights proposals I made to the Eightieth Congress, I now repeat to the Eighty-first Congress. They should be enacted in order that the Federal Government may assume the leadership and discharge the obligations clearly placed upon it by the Constitution.

I stand squarely behind those proposals.

Our domestic programs are the foundation of our foreign policy. The world today looks to us for leadership because we have so largely realized, within our borders, those benefits of democratic government for which most of the people of the world are yearning.

We are following a foreign policy which is the outward expression of the democratic faith we profess. We are doing what we can to encourage free states and free peoples throughout the world, to aid the suffering and afflicted in foreign lands, and to strengthen democratic nations against aggression.

The heart of our foreign policy is peace. We are supporting a world organization to keep peace and a world economic policy to create prosperity for mankind. Our guiding star is the principle of international cooperation. To this concept we have made a national commitment as profound as anything in history.

To it we have pledged our resources and our honor.

Until a system of world security is established upon which we can safely rely, we cannot escape the burden of creating and maintaining armed forces sufficient to deter aggression. We have made great progress in the last year in the effective organization of our Armed Forces, but further improvements in our national security legislation are necessary. Universal training is essential to the security of the United States.

During the course of this session I shall have occasion to ask the Congress to consider several measures in the field of foreign policy. At this time, I recommend that we restore the Reciprocal Trade Agreements Act to full effectiveness, and extend it for three years. We should also open our doors to displaced persons without unfair discrimination.

It should be clear by now to all citizens that we are not seeking to freeze the status quo. We have no intention of preserving the injustices of the past. We welcome the constructive efforts being made by many nations to achieve a better life for their citizens. In the European recovery program, in our good-neighbor policy and in the United Nations, we have begun to batter down those national walls which block the economic growth and the social advancement of the peoples of the world.

We believe that if we hold resolutely to this course, the principle of international cooperation will eventually command the approval even of those nations which are now seeking to weaken or subvert it.

We stand at the opening of an era which can mean either great achievement or terrible catastrophe for ourselves and for all mankind.

The strength of our Nation must continue to be used in the interest of all our people rather than a privileged few. It must continue to be used unselfishly in the struggle for world peace and the betterment of mankind the world over.

This is the task before us.

It is not an easy one. It has many complications, and there will be strong opposition from selfish interests.

I hope for cooperation from farmers, from labor, and from business. Every segment of our population and every individual has a right to expect from our Government a fair deal.

In 1945, when I came down before the Congress for the first time on April 16, I quoted to you King Solomon's prayer that he wanted wisdom and the ability to govern his people as they should be governed. I explained to you at that time that the task before me was one of the greatest in the history of the world, and that it was necessary to have the complete cooperation of the Congress and the people of the United States.

Well now, we are taking a new start with the same situation. It is absolutely essential that your President have the complete co-operation of the Congress to carry out the great work that must be done to keep the peace in this world, and to keep this country prosperous.

The people of this great country have a right to expect that the Congress and the President will work in closest cooperation with one objective—the welfare of the people of this Nation as a whole.

In the months ahead I know that I shall be able to cooperate with this Congress.

Now, I am confident that the Divine Power which has guided us to this time of fateful responsibility and glorious opportunity will not desert us now.

With that help from Almighty God which we have humbly acknowledged at every turning point in our national life, we shall be able to perform the great tasks which He now sets before us.

21 / MC CARTHYISM

*Liberal Catholic journalist John Cogley
assesses the man and the phenemenon.*

Senator McCarthy seems to have been retired to the back pages
since the historic censure action, despite several drastic, and
somewhat pitiable, attempts on his part to make new headlines.
Again it can be said that the nation has survived a hurricane.
Quite a number of personal reputations and not a few American
traditions lie among the wreckage, of course. But basic American
institutions are still safe.

In the heat of such national controversy as McCarthy stirred
up, it is almost impossible to make a reasoned judgment; intro-
spection and soul-searching, under such circumstances, seem to
be out of the question. Now, though, in the lull following the
storm, our recent experiences with the man who has been called
the most successful demagogue in American history should provide some understanding of ourselves. . . .

First of all, there is the fairly obvious fact that McCarthyism
was not truly an ism in the meaningful sense of the word. The
Senator had no program. McCarthyism represented a dangerous
mood rather than an ideological assault. It was not opposed, as a
matter of principle, to American institutions. It was, rather, recklessly disinterested in them. Indeed, it interpreted a steady concern with the fate of certain democratic rights and procedures as
at best a weakness and perhaps even witless subversion. The
coupling of "Fifth Amendment" with "Communist" was more than
a semantic device. It was an impiety which betrayed the basically radical nature of the movement.

The McCarthy movement demonstrated a deep-rooted distrust

SOURCE: John Cogley, "McCarthyism Revisited," *The Commonweal,* LXII,
6 (May 13, 1955), 151. Reprinted by permission of *The Commonweal.*

of American institutions, even while it lavished verbal praise upon them. It was the McCarthyist position, for instance, that freedom of the press as it was practiced in this country led to innumerable local editions of the *Daily Worker*. It was the McCarthyist position that academic freedom had in fact led to treasonable doctrines' being taught at America's greatest universities. It was the McCarthyist position that political freedom had resulted in "twenty years of treason."

But for all this discontent with the actual workings of democracy, there was no forthright attack on democratic methods or democratic institutions. Clearly the U.S. was going to hell in a basket. But the next logical step was never taken. No one suggested that we should change our democratic framework. The McCarthy assault was not abstract but focused on the concrete results of democracy.

Such attacks can always be made and will probably have a certain validity. For it is of the nature of democracy that the wrongheaded will get a hearing with the wise; that the guilty will have the refuge of civil liberties along with the innocent; that the liar will share the platform with the truth-teller. Democracy is a dangerous business, and we should have known this before Senator McCarthy dramatized it. We should have known that we cannot have democracy without constant hazard.

Once McCarthy—with some truth and a great deal of distortion—pointed out that democracy was perilous, a large group of Americans seemed to verge on losing their faith in democracy, or at least in democratic procedures. For instance, take the question of the Fifth Amendment. It was, early in the game, clear to most of us that Communists were relying heavily on the protection it afforded. As case after case piled up, there was a strong tendency among the McCarthy followers to belittle and even to abandon the Fifth Amendment, because it was being abused and misused. Of course it was being abused and misused. So have free speech, academic freedom, religious freedom, political freedom, free enterprise. They always will be. This is the price we pay for liberty, as on a deeper level human freedom means the possibility of sin.

The abuse of democratic institutions should have been taken for granted. The price should have been paid willingly. But as long as people think that democracy is "safe" and fool-proof, ripe pickings for the next Senator McCarthy who comes along will remain.

This, it seems to me, is an essential lesson to be learned from the McCarthy experience. The nation at one time was divided right down the middle on the question. One group, cherishing the illusion that political folly and subversion (the distinction was never very clearly etched) must be attributable to extra-democratic processes, were outraged to learn the "revelations" which other people unearthed and McCarthy exploited. When they came upon the fact that the use of democratic methods does not always assure democratic triumphs, they grew suspicious of democratic methods and sullenly demanded changes which would have seriously affected our traditions of civil liberty. They demanded blacklists, university screening boards, absurd security checks, etc.

The other group, cherishing civil liberties, also seemed unable to face up to the fact that democracy means hazard. They reacted at first by denying or belittling subversion. Later, in desperation, they took to burdening Senator McCarthy with sins he was not guilty of and came too readily to the defense of his targets, with little or no discrimination. It would seem that this group, too, could not find it in themselves to face up to the perils of democracy.

Unfortunately, Senator McCarthy was not defeated on principle. The basic issues the controversy raised still remain to be settled. Until they are, either Senator McCarthy or a reasonable facsimile may reappear at any time—and who knows with what success?

22 / DWIGHT D. EISENHOWER AND

MODERN REPUBLICANISM

President Eisenhower expounds his philosophy
in an address to the Republican National
Conference, June 7, 1957.

. . . Representative government can succeed only where there are healthy, responsible political parties. These parties must have at the center and core of their being the same dedication to the service of our nation as inspires the men of our armed services.

This sense of patriotism is felt by both of America's great parties—in this matter let no one anywhere in the world think Americans are divided.

But one thing more is necessary: A political party must stand for something—policies that it believes will advance the best interests of the entire nation. It must stand for principles and programs that the sovereign voters of the country can clearly see, identify and judge.

So what do we as Republicans stand for?

Why have we joined together in a national organization? And why do hundreds and thousands of Republicans work side by side—often without recognition or distinction or reward—in tasks assigned by this organization to which we all belong?

We do this because we have been drawn together by a set of common beliefs and principles respecting government and its relationship to other governments, to our own economy and to each individual citizen.

These beliefs are plainly stated in our Declarations of Faith and

SOURCE: *Public Papers of the Presidents of the United States: Dwight D. Eisenhower, 1957* (Washington: Government Printing Office, 1958), pp. 448–451.

our Declarations of Determination which are the Republican National Platform of 1956. As we read and re-read that platform—a practice which I commend to all of you—it becomes very clear that the modern Republican Party stands one hundred percent for the basic principles of Republicanism that have been its guide since the days of its founding.

Some of the features of those beliefs:

We believe in integrity in government—not government by crony.

We believe that whatever can be done by private effort should be done by private effort rather than by the government—and not the other way round.

We believe that, if a job must be done by government, it should whenever possible be done by State and local government rather than by the Federal government—and not the other way round. We oppose unnecessary centralization of power.

We believe in a sound dollar—not a rubber dollar.

And therefore, we believe that a government should operate on a balanced budget and not go into debt except in emergencies—we reject deficit spending as a fiscal policy for America.

We believe that we should work to reduce taxes—not raise them; as we also seek to reduce our huge national debt.

And as we think, ladies and gentlemen, over the record of the past four years, let us not forget that the greatest tax cut in history was granted by the Republicans in power in Congress and the Administration. And we have paid something on our national debt.

We believe in vigorous and impartial enforcement of the laws.

We believe that private business is a healthy force which is the foundation of our prosperity, and should be respected and encouraged—not bullied and abused. And the fact that the four-year period since the re-introduction of this attitude into government has also been the period of the greatest sustained growth in jobs, production and incomes of all modern peace times is not, may I say, a mere congenial coincidence.

We believe that government can and should discharge its constitutional duty to promote the general well-being of its citizens—and can do so without excessive centralization.

We believe that to preserve our own freedom we must concern ourselves with the security of other free nations constantly exposed to the threat of domination by international communism. Nothing today can present more danger to us than a retreat to the folly of isolationism.

We believe in the pre-eminence of the individual citizen and his rights—with the government his servant, not his master or his keeper.

It is principles like these, then, that not only draw us together, but also set us apart from the easy-spending, paternalistic, business-baiting inflationists who were so influential for years before 1953.

23 / THE EISENHOWER YEARS—

A CRITICAL APPRAISAL

Noted student of the presidency Sidney Hyman assesses the Eisenhower administration.

[The Eisenhower administration's] . . . dominating tendencies have been to act as if domestic and foreign affairs were separate matters; as if religion was a substitute for politics in a condition of no war and no peace; as if a balanced budget was the paramount means of meeting the Soviet economic offensive; as if we could win the newly emergent nations to the practices of democracy by ringing democratic manifestoes—while withholding from them a full measure of the material assistance they need as a flooring for democratic growth. The Eisenhower Administration has acted as if decisions of our choosing correspond to the best interest of our allies; as if the sensibilities of our non-voting con-

SOURCE: Sidney Hyman, "The Failure of the Eisenhower Presidency," *The Progressive*, XXIV, 5 (May, 1960), 12–13. Reprinted by permission of *The Progressive*.

stituents could be ignored whenever their wishes collided with the voting constituency of America; as if information which belonged in the public domain as an indispensable prerequisite for democratic debate, should be withheld from the nation on the theory that President "knows best."

Yet the heart of the trouble with the Eisenhower Presidency is something else again. It has been its failure to accept the reality of the shift in executive-legislative relations that has occurred within the Constitution. It has not firmly grasped the responsibility of Presidential leadership from above, yet it has refused to allow Congress to improvise a substitute leadership from below to fill the vacuum. It has not marched at the head of affairs to force events into being of a kind favorable to America and the Grand Alliance. It has bent the weight of its energies to the end of stopping things which have been put into motion elsewhere. What it has done throughcut is to seek the best of both worlds: to claim all the credit for the sunshine and to blame everyone else for the rain; to allow no voice but its own to be heard, yet to make Congress assume a large measure of the responsibility for all miscarriages of Administration policy.

The full proof of these charges would require a day-to-day listing of the actions of the Eisenhower Administration since it came to power in 1953. But a few representative instances, chosen without reference to any time sequence, will make an adequate case.

Item. In the last session of the Congress, the President exercised his veto power 150 times, yet lent his approval to the Republican policy of calling the Democratic-controlled 86th Congress a "do-nothing Congress." How could it do anything when the veto power is equal to two-thirds the combined strength of the entire Congress, and a majority of that size is rarely on the same side of legislation? How could Congress attend, for example, to the needs of education, housing, and urban re-development when measures of this kind were beaten down by Executive veto—all in the name of a balanced budget?

Item. The Senate Preparedness Subcommittee on Armed Services sat day after day, week after week, heard hundreds of witnesses, took testimony from dozens of men, and unanimously

made seventeen recommendations urging this nation to accelerate its defense program. Few of the recommendations have been
carried out by the President. Moreover, at least one billion dollars
of defense money the Congress has appropriated has been im-
pounded, sunk, or hidden by the President while Congress is
virtually powerless to make him do what it wants done.

Item. The President repeatedly talked of how important it was
to provide long term economic assistance to the underdeveloped
countries. In the last session, the Foreign Relations Committee,
which was of the same mind, labored long and hard and issued a
nearly unanimous report which would have enabled the Development Loan Fund to plan its operations on a long-term basis. Yet,
when there was a crucial vote on the floor of the Senate, the White
House, swayed by the Treasury Department and the Bureau of the
Budget (over the opposition of the State Department), sent word
to party lieutenants to cut down the Development Loan proposal.
And it was cut down.

Item. When Charles E. Wilson was Secretary of Defense, Congress appropriated about $175 million for basic research. When
asked why he had not spent the money, Wilson was quoted as
saying that in his mind basic research was what you were doing
when you did not know what to do. There was no word of correction from the White House. When asked about the lagging
space program, Wilson said he had enough troubles on earth.
There was no word of correction from the White House.

Item. After the Suez war, to whose onset the Administration
contributed through its own blunders, the Eisenhower Doctrine
was proclaimed as the nostrum which would set everything right
in the Middle East. Congress was not consulted in the period
while that Doctrine was being formulated within the Executive.
The terms were first leaked to the press, and once they were in
public print, the Administration invoked the holy name of bi-
partisanship to insure its adoption by Congress, just as it had
previously done in the case of the Formosa Resolution.

In both cases, Congress was informed that it had to support
the position of the Administration because otherwise the Russians
and the rest of the world would think we were sorely divided.
That support was forthcoming not because the leaders of Con-

gress were convinced of the wisdom of the Administration's course. They were not at all convinced of the wisdom of the Administration's policy. They were convinced that the course was either dangerous or meaningless. Yet in Lebanon, just as in Quemoy and Matsu, Congress suddenly discovered that the Eisenhower Doctrine was *its* doctrine, and, the Formosa Resolution was *its* resolution.

Item. The Administration repeatedly emphasized the imperative necessity of maintaining "fiscal solvency." To be sure, at one point, it developed a deficit of $12.5 billion. At that same point, the Democratic members of Congress observed that something like $4 billion in dividend income in this country goes unreported; if there was a dividend withholding tax, as in the case of many other sources of income, the government would collect at least a billion dollars of the dividend-based revenues that were due it. This Democratic proposal was killed by the Administration, as was the case with another proposal that there be a tightening up of the tax-free expense allowances. Yet, for all its own negligence in enforcing existing tax laws, the Administration at every turn blasted the Democrats for being "reckless spenders."

Item. The President has spoken eloquently about the virtues of democracy. He would most certainly agree that free and open discussion is a leading factor in the actual workings of democracy. Yet his general tendency has been to shut off all debate by asserting that he knows more than "almost anyone" about military matters. Those who disagree with his judgments are, to him, "noisy extremists." They are, he says, unpatriotic because they have "the tendency to disparage our country" with their "spurious" assertions. The earnest men who are worried about our country's security are told by him that they are "political morticians exhibiting a breast-beating pessimism."

There is a case to be made for Mr. Eisenhower, albeit a small one. After twenty years of innovation under the Presidencies of Franklin D. Roosevelt and Harry S. Truman in meeting the social, political, and military revolutions of the day, perhaps the time was ripe for a Presidency that would devote itself to consolidating the gains made. Perhaps we all needed a breather in which to look around and to reappraise where we stood as individuals in relationship to our own government, and where our government stood in relation to other nations. In such an interval of pause, existing programs could have been refined, the fast setting mold of habit could have been breached to allow for an entry of fresh air, the whole administrative machinery of government could have been renovated. Moreover, at any time, there is a place for a veto, for a disengagement from dangerous points of exposure, and for a political dialectic in which the negative arm is stronger than the affirmative arm.

If President Eisenhower had in fact been a consolidator in some such manner; if he had in fact used his negative arm to stop dangerous tendencies or to withdraw from them, his Presidency would have had a material relevance to the hour at which we stand in our history. Yet his has been the period of a falling apart, of a loss of élan and dash, of a veto for the sake of saying no, of a widening breach between power and responsibility. The legacy he leaves to his successor in the White House, whoever he may be, is unenviable. Demands long postponed or ignored will burst upon the President in the 1960's. If President Eisenhower's successor rises to meet them, as he must if we are to continue to be a major power, it seems fairly certain that he will be damned for somehow violating the Constitution because he might insist on acting not like Mr. Eisenhower but like a President. It seems fairly certain that he will be damned for being a divisive influence, a source of acrimonious dispute, and worse. Yet one must hope that the next President will have the courage and the magnanimity to make his office respond to the needs of the time; to reunite power and responsibility in it; and to revive our sagging constitutional morality by restoring discussion itself to the governmental process.

24 / JOHN F. KENNEDY AND THE NEW FRONTIER

In his State of the Union message to Congress, January 11, 1962, President Kennedy outlined his New Frontier program.

In the past year, I have travelled not only across our own land but to other lands—to the North and the South, and across the seas. And I have found—as I am sure you have, in your travels —that people everywhere, in spite of occasional disappointments, look to us—not to our wealth or power, but to the splendor of our ideals. For our Nation is commissioned by history to be either an observer of freedom's failure or the cause of its success. Our overriding obligation in the months ahead is to fulfill the world's hopes by fulfilling our own faith.

I. STRENGTHENING THE ECONOMY

That task must begin at home. For if we cannot fulfill our own ideals here, we cannot expect others to accept them. And when the youngest child alive today has grown to the cares of manhood, our position in the world will be determined first of all by what provisions we make today—for his education, his health, and his opportunities for a good home and a good job and a good life.

At home, we began the year in the valley of recession—we completed it on the high road of recovery and growth. With the help of new congressionally approved or administratively increased stimulants to our economy, the number of major surplus

SOURCE: *Public Papers of the Presidents of the United States: John F. Kennedy, 1962* (Washington: Government Printing Office, 1963), pp. 5–9.

labor areas has declined from 101 to 60; nonagricultural employment has increased by more than a million jobs; and the average factory work-week has risen to well over 40 hours. At year's end the economy which Mr. Khrushchev once called a "stumbling horse" was racing to new records in consumer spending, labor income, and industrial production.

We are gratified—but we are not satisfied. Too many unemployed are still looking for the blessings of prosperity. As those who leave our schools and farms demand new jobs, automation takes old jobs away. To expand our growth and job opportunities, I urge on the Congress three measures:

1—First, the Manpower Training and Development Act, to stop the waste of able-bodied men and women who want to work, but whose only skill has been replaced by a machine, or moved with a mill, or shut down with a mine;

2—Second, the Youth Employment Opportunities Act, to help train and place not only the one million young Americans who are both out of school and out of work, but the twenty-six million young Americans entering the labor market in this decade; and

3—Third, the 8 percent tax credit for investment in machinery and equipment, which, combined with planned revisions of depreciation allowances, will spur our modernization, our growth, and our ability to compete abroad.

Moreover—pleasant as it may be to bask in the warmth of recovery—let us not forget that we have suffered three recessions in the last seven years. The time to repair the roof is when the sun is shining—by filling three basic gaps in our anti-recession protection. We need:

1—First, Presidential standby authority, subject to congressional veto, to adjust personal income tax rates downward within a specified range and time, to slow down an economic decline before it has dragged us all down;

2—Second, Presidential standby authority, upon a given rise in the rate of unemployment, to accelerate Federal and federally-aided capital improvement programs; and

3—Third, a permanent strengthening of our unemployment compensation system—to maintain for our fellow citizens searching for a job who cannot find it, their purchasing power and their living standards without constant resort—as we have seen in recent years by the Congress and the administrations—to temporary supplements.

If we enact this six-part program, we can show the whole world that a free economy need not be an unstable economy—that a free system need not leave men unemployed—and that a free society is not only the most productive but the most stable form of organization yet fashioned by man.

II. Fighting Inflation

But recession is only one enemy of a free economy—inflation is another. Last year, 1961, despite rising production and demand, consumer prices held almost steady—and wholesale prices declined. This is the best record of overall price stability of any comparable period of recovery since the end of World War II.

Inflation too often follows in the shadow of growth—while price stability is made easy by stagnation or controls. But we mean to maintain both stability and growth in a climate of freedom.

Our first line of defense against inflation is the good sense and public spirit of business and labor—keeping their total increases in wages and profits in step with productivity. There is no single statistical test to guide each company and each union. But I strongly urge them—for their country's interest, and for their own—to apply the test of the public interest to these transactions.

Within this same framework of growth and wage-price stability:

—This administration has helped keep our economy competitive by widening the access of small business to credit and Government contracts, and by stepping up the drive against monopoly, price-fixing, and racketeering;

—We will submit a Federal Pay Reform bill aimed at giving our classified, postal, and other employees new pay scales more comparable to those of private industry;

—We are holding the fiscal 1962 budget deficit far below the level incurred after the last recession in 1958; and, finally,

—I am submitting for fiscal 1963 a balanced Federal Budget.

This is a joint responsibility, requiring Congressional cooperation on appropriations, and on three sources of income in particular:

1—First, an increase in postal rates, to end the postal deficit;

2—Secondly, passage of the tax reforms previously urged, to
remove unwarranted tax preferences, and to apply to dividends
and to interest the same withholding requirements we have long
applied to wages; and

3—Third, extension of the present excise and corporation tax
rates, except for those changes—which will be recommended in
a message—affecting transportation.

III. Getting America Moving

But a stronger nation and economy require more than a balanced Budget. They require progress in those programs that spur
our growth and fortify our strength.

Cities

A strong America depends on its cities—America's glory, and
sometimes America's shame. To substitute sunlight for conges-
tion and progress for decay, we have stepped up existing urban
renewal and housing programs, and launched new ones—re-
doubled the attack on water pollution—speeded aid to airports,
hospitals, highways, and our declining mass transit systems—and
secured new weapons to combat organized crime, racketeering,
and youth delinquency, assisted by the coordinated and hard-
hitting efforts of our investigative services: the FBI, the Internal
Revenue, the Bureau of Narcotics, and many others. We shall
need further anti-crime, mass transit, and transportation legislation—and new tools to fight air pollution. And with all this effort
under way, both equity and commonsense require that our nation's urban areas—containing three-fourths of our population—
sit as equals at the Cabinet table. I urge a new Department of
Urban Affairs and Housing.

Agriculture and Resources

A strong America also depends on its farms and natural resources. American farmers took heart in 1961—from a billion

dollar rise in farm income—and from a hopeful start on reducing the farm surpluses. But we are still operating under a patchwork accumulation of old laws, which cost us $1 billion a year in CCC carrying charges alone, yet fail to halt rural poverty or boost farm earnings.

Our task is to master and turn to fully fruitful ends the magnificent productivity of our farms and farmers. The revolution on our own countryside stands in the sharpest contrast to the repeated farm failures of the Communist nations and is a source of pride to us all. Since 1950 our agricultural output per man-hour has actually doubled! Without new, realistic measures, it will someday swamp our farmers and our taxpayers in a national scandal or a farm depression.

I will, therefore, submit to the Congress a new comprehensive farm program—tailored to fit the use of our land and the supplies of each crop to the long-range needs of the sixties—and designed to prevent chaos in the sixties with a program of commonsense.

We also need for the sixties—if we are to bequeath our full national estate to our heirs—a new long-range conservation and recreation program—expansion of our superb national parks and forests—preservation of our authentic wilderness areas—new starts on water and power projects as our population steadily increases—and expanded REA generation and transmission loans.

Civil Rights

But America stands for progress in human rights as well as economic affairs, and a strong America requires the assurance of full and equal rights to all its citizens, of any race or of any color. This administration has shown as never before how much could be done through the full use of Executive powers—through the enforcement of laws already passed by the Congress—through persuasion, negotiation, and litigation, to secure the constitutional rights of all: the right to vote, the right to travel without hindrance across State lines, and the right to free public education.

I issued last March a comprehensive order to guarantee the right to equal employment opportunity in all Federal agencies and contractors. The Vice President's Committee thus created has done much, including the voluntary "Plans for Progress" which, in all sections of the country, are achieving a quiet but striking success in opening up to all races new professional, supervisory, and other job opportunities.

But there is much more to be done—by the Executive, by the courts, and by the Congress. Among the bills now pending before you, on which the executive departments will comment in detail, are appropriate methods of strengthening these basic rights which have our full support. The right to vote, for example, should no longer be denied through such arbitrary devices on a local level, sometimes abused, such as literacy tests and poll taxes. As we approach the 100th anniversary, next January, of the Emancipation Proclamation, let the acts of every branch of the Government —and every citizen—portray that "righteousness does exalt a nation."

Health and Welfare

Finally, a strong America cannot neglect the aspirations of its citizens—the welfare of the needy, the health care of the elderly, the education of the young. For we are not developing the Nation's wealth for its own sake. Wealth is the means—and people are the ends. All our material riches will avail us little if we do not use them to expand the opportunities of our people.

Last year, we improved the diet of needy people—provided more hot lunches and fresh milk to school children—built more college dormitories—and, for the elderly, expanded private housing, nursing homes, health services, and social security. But we have just begun.

To help those least fortunate of all, I am recommending a new public welfare program, stressing services instead of support, rehabilitation instead of relief, and training for useful work instead of prolonged dependency.

To relieve the critical shortage of doctors and dentists—and this is a matter which should concern us all—and expand research, I urge action to aid medical and dental colleges and scholarships and to establish new National Institutes of Health.

To take advantage of modern vaccination achievements, I am proposing a mass immunization program, aimed at the virtual elimination of such ancient enemies of our children as polio, diphtheria, whooping cough, and tetanus.

To protect our consumers from the careless and the unscrupulous, I shall recommend improvements in the Food and Drug laws —strengthening inspection and standards, halting unsafe and worthless products, preventing misleading labels, and cracking down on the illicit sale of habit-forming drugs.

But in matters of health, no piece of unfinished business is more important or more urgent than the enactment under the social security system of health insurance for the aged.

For our older citizens have longer and more frequent illnesses, higher hospital and medical bills and too little income to pay them. Private health insurance helps very few—for its cost is high and its coverage limited. Public welfare cannot help those too proud to seek relief but hard-pressed to pay their own bills. Nor can their children or grandchildren always sacrifice their own health budgets to meet this constant drain.

Social security has long helped to meet the hardships of retirement, death, and disability. I now urge that its coverage be extended without further delay to provide health insurance for the elderly.

Education

Equally important to our strength is the quality of our education. Eight million adult Americans are classified as functionally illiterate. This is a disturbing figure—reflected in Selective Service rejection rates—reflected in welfare rolls and crime rates. And I shall recommend plans for a massive attack to end this adult illiteracy.

I shall also recommend bills to improve educational quality, to stimulate the arts, and, at the college level, to provide Federal loans for the construction of academic facilities and federally financed scholarships.

If this Nation is to grow in wisdom and strength, then every able high school graduate should have the opportunity to develop his talents. Yet nearly half lack either the funds or the facilities to attend college. Enrollments are going to double in our colleges in the short space of ten years. The annual cost per student is skyrocketing to astronomical levels—now averaging $1,650 a year, although almost half of our families earn less than $5,000. They cannot afford such costs—but this Nation cannot afford to maintain its military power and neglect its brainpower.

But excellence in education must begin at the elementary level. I sent to the Congress last year a proposal for Federal aid to public school construction and teachers' salaries. I believe that bill, which passed the Senate and received House Committee approval, offered the minimum amount required by our needs and —in terms of across-the-board aid—the maximum scope permitted by our Constitution. I therefore see no reason to weaken or withdraw that bill: and I urge its passage at this session.

"Civilization," said H. G. Wells, "is a race between education and catastrophe." It is up to you in this Congress to determine the winner of that race.

These are not unrelated measures addressed to specific gaps or grievances in our national life. They are the pattern of our intentions and the foundation of our hopes. "I believe in democracy," said Woodrow Wilson, "because it releases the energy of every human being." The dynamic of democracy is the power and the purpose of the individual, and the policy of this administration is to give to the individual the opportunity to realize his own highest possibilities.

Our program is to open to all the opportunity for steady and productive employment, to remove from all the handicap of arbitrary or irrational exclusion, to offer to all the facilities for education and health and welfare, to make society the servant of the individual and the individual the source of progress, and thus to realize for all the full promise of American life.

25 / BARRY GOLDWATER AND THE
NEW CONSERVATISM

*Goldwater's speech accepting the 1964 Republican
presidential nomination, July 16, 1964, frightened
moderates throughout the country into supporting
Democratic nominee Lyndon B. Johnson.*

My good friend and great Republican, Dick Nixon and your
charming wife, Pat; my running mate—that wonderful Republican who has served us so well for so long—Bill Miller and his
wife, Stephanie; to Thruston Morton, who's done such a com-
mendable job in chairmaning this convention; to Mr. Herbert
Hoover who I hope is watching, and to the great American and
his wife, General and Mrs. Eisenhower. To my own wife, my
family, and to all of my fellow Republicans here assembled, and
Americans across this great nation:

From this moment, united and determined, we will go forward
together dedicated to the ultimate and undeniable greatness of
the whole man.

Together we will win.

I accept your nomination with a deep sense of humility. I
accept, too, the responsibility that goes with it, and I seek your
continued help and your continued guidance. My fellow Republicans, our cause is too great for any man to feel worthy of it.
Our task would be too great for any man did he not have with
him the heart and the hands of this great Republican party.

And I promise you tonight that every fibre of my being is
consecrated to our cause, that nothing shall be lacking from the

SOURCE: *Vital Speeches of the Day*, XXX, 21 (August 15, 1964), 642–
644. Reprinted by permission of *Vital Speeches of the Day*.

struggle that can be brought to it by enthusiasm, by devotion and plain hard work.

In this world no person, no party can guarantee anything, but what we can do and what we shall do is to deserve victory and victory will be ours. The Good Lord raised this mighty Republican Republic to be a home for the brave and to flourish as the land of the free—not to stagnate in the swampland of collectivism, not to cringe before the bully of Communism.

Now my fellow Americans, the tide has been running against freedom. Our people have followed false prophets. We must, and we shall, return to proven ways—not because they are old, but because they are true.

We must, and we shall, set the tide running again in the cause of freedom. And this party, with its every action, every word, every breath and every heart beat, has but a single resolve, and that is freedom.

Freedom made orderly for this nation by our constitutional government. Freedom under a government limited by laws of nature and of nature's God. Freedom balanced so that order lacking liberty will not become the slavery of the prison cell; balanced so that liberty lacking order will not become the license of the mob and of the jungle.

Now, we Americans understand freedom, we have earned it; we have lived for it, and we have died for it. This nation and its people are freedom's models in a searching world. We can be freedom's missionaries in a doubting world.

But, ladies and gentlemen, first we must renew freedom's mission in our own hearts and in our own homes.

During four futile years the Administration which we shall replace has distorted and lost that faith. It has talked and talked and talked and talked the words of freedom but it has failed and failed and failed in the works of freedom.

Now failure cements the wall of shame in Berlin; failures blot the sands of shame at the Bay of Pigs; failures marked the slow death of freedom in Laos; failures infest the jungles of Vietnam, and failures haunt the houses of our once great alliances and undermine the greatest bulwark ever erected by free nations, the NATO community.

Failures proclaim lost leadership, obscure purpose, weakening wills and the risk of inciting our sworn enemies to new aggressions and to new excesses.

And because of this Administration we are tonight a world divided. We are a nation becalmed. We have lost the brisk pace of diversity and the genius of individual creativity. We are plodding along at a pace set by centralized planning, red tape, rules without responsibility and regimentation without recourse.

Rather than useful jobs in our country, people have been offered bureaucratic make-work; rather than moral leadership, they have been given bread and circuses; they have been given spectacles, and yes, they've even been given scandals.

Tonight there is violence in our streets, corruption in our highest offices, aimlessness among our youth, anxiety among our elderly, and there's a virtual despair among the many who look beyond material success toward the inner meaning of their lives. And where examples of morality should be set, the opposite is seen. Small men seeking great wealth or power have too often and too long turned even the highest levels of public service into mere personal opportunity.

Now, certainly simple honesty is not too much to demand of men in government. We find it in most. Republicans demand it from everyone.

They demand it from everyone no matter how exalted or protected his position might be.

The growing menace in our country tonight, to personal safety, to life, to limb and property, in homes, in churches, on the playgrounds and places of business, particularly in our great cities, is the mounting concern or should be of every thoughtful citizen in the United States. Security from domestic violence, no less than from foreign aggression, is the most elementary and fundamental purpose of any government, and a government that cannot fulfill this purpose is one that cannot long command the loyalty of its citizens.

History shows us, demonstrates that nothing, nothing prepares the way for tyranny more than the failure of public officials to keep the streets safe from bullies and marauders.

Now we Republicans see all this as more—much more—than

the result of mere political differences, or mere political mistakes. We see this as the result of a fundamentally and absolutely wrong view of man, his nature and his destiny.

Those who seek to live your lives for you, to take your liberty in return for relieving you of yours; those who elevate the state and downgrade the citizen, must see ultimately a world in which earthly power can be substituted for Divine Will. And this nation was founded upon the rejection of that notion and upon the acceptance of God as the author of freedom.

Now those who seek absolute power, even though they seek it to do what they regard as good, are simply demanding the right to enforce their own version of heaven on earth, and let me remind you, they are the very ones who always create the most hellish tyranny.

Absolute power does corrupt, and those who seek it must be suspect and must be opposed. Their mistaken course stems from false notions, ladies and gentlemen, of equality. Equality, rightly understood as our founding fathers understood it, leads to liberty and to the emancipation of creative differences; wrongly understood, as it has been so tragically in our time, it leads first to conformity and then to despotism.

Fellow Republicans, it is the cause of Republicanism to resist concentrations of power, private or public, which enforce such conformity and inflict such despotism.

It is the cause of Republicanism to insure that power remains in the hands of the people—and, so help us God, that is exactly what a Republican President will do with the help of a Republican Congress.

It is further the cause of Republicanism to restore a clear understanding of the tyranny of man over man in the world at large. It is our cause to dispel the foggy thinking which avoids hard decisions in the delusion that a world of conflict will somehow resolve itself into a world of harmony, if we just don't rock the boat or irritate the forces of aggression—and this is hogwash.

It is further, the cause of Republicanism to remind ourselves, and the world, that only the strong can remain free; that only the strong can keep the peace.

Now I needn't remind you, or my fellow Americans regardless of party, that Republicans have shouldered this hard responsibility and marched in this cause before. It was Republican leadership under Dwight Eisenhower that kept the peace, and passed along to this Administration the mightiest arsenal for defense the world has ever known.

And I needn't remind you that it was the strength and the believable will of the Eisenhower years that kept the peace by using our strength, by using it in the Formosa Strait, and in Lebanon, and by showing it courageously at all times.

It was during those Republican years that the thrust of Communist imperialism was blunted. It was during those years of Republican leadership that this world moved closer not to war but closer to peace than at any other time in the last three decades.

And I needn't remind you, but I will, that it's been during Democratic years that our strength to deter war has been stilled and even gone into a planned decline. It has been during Democratic years that we have weakly stumbled into conflicts, timidly refusing to draw our own lines against aggression, deceitfully refusing to tell even our own people of our full participation and tragically letting our finest men die on battlefields unmarked by purpose, unmarked by pride of the prospect of victory.

Yesterday it was Korea; tonight it is Vietnam. Make no bones of this. Don't try to sweep this under the rug. We are at war in Vietnam. And yet the President, who is the Commander in Chief of our forces, refuses to say, refuses to say, mind you, whether or not the objective over there is victory, and his Secretary of Defense continues to mislead and misinform the American people and enough of it has gone by.

And I needn't remind you, but I will, it has been during Democratic years that a billion persons were cast into communist captivity and their fate cynically sealed.

Today—today in our beloved country we have an Administration which seems eager to deal with Communism in every coin known—from gold to wheat; from consulates to confidence, and even human freedom itself.

Now the Republican cause demands that we brand Communism as the principal disturber of peace in the world today. Indeed, we should brand it as the only significant disturber of the peace. And we must make clear that until its goals of conquest are absolutely renounced, and its relations with all nations tempered, Communism and the governments it now controls are enemies of every man on earth who is or wants to be free.

Now, we here in America can keep the peace only if we remain vigilant, and only if we remain strong. Only if we keep our eyes open and keep our guard up can we prevent war.

And I want to make this abundantly clear—I don't intend to let peace or freedom be torn from our grasp because of lack of strength, or lack of will—and that I promise you Americans.

I believe that we must look beyond the defense of freedom today to its extension tomorrow. I believe that the Communism which boasts it will bury us will instead give way to the forces of freedom. And I can see in the distant and yet recognizable future the outlines of a world worthy of our dedication, our every risk, our every effort, our every sacrifice along the way. Yes, a world that will redeem the suffering of those who will be liberated from tyranny.

I can see, and I suggest that all thoughtful men must contemplate, the flowering of an Atlantic civilization, the whole world of Europe reunified and free, trading openly across its borders, communicating openly across the world.

This is a goal far, far more meaningful than a moon shot.

It's a truly inspiring goal for all free men to set for themselves during the latter half of the twentieth century. I can see and all free men must thrill to the events of this Atlantic civilization joined by a straight ocean highway to the United States. What a destiny! What a destiny can be ours to stand as a great central pillar linking Europe, the Americas and the venerable and vital peoples and cultures of the Pacific.

I can see a day when all the Americas—North and South—will be linked in a mighty system—a system in which the errors and misunderstandings of the past will be submerged one by one in a rising tide of prosperity and interdependence.

We know that the misunderstandings of centuries are not to be wiped away in a day or wiped away in an hour. But we pledge, we pledge, that human sympathy—what our neighbors to the South call an attitude of sympático—no less than enlightened self-interest will be our guide.

And I can see this Atlantic civilization galvanizing and guiding emergent nations everywhere. Now I know this freedom was achieved through centuries by unremitting efforts by brave and wise men. And I know that the road to freedom is a long and a challenging road, and I know also that some men may walk away from it, that some men resist challenge, accepting the false security of governmental paternalism.

And I pledge that the America I envision in the years ahead will extend its hand in help in teaching and in cultivation so that all new nations will be at least encouraged to go our way; so that they will not wander down the dark alleys of tyranny or to the deadened streets of collectivism.

My fellow Republicans, we do no man a service by hiding freedom's light under a bushel of mistaken humility.

I seek an America proud of its past, proud of its ways, proud of its dreams and determined actively to proclaim them. But our examples to the world must, like charity, begin at home.

In our vision of a good and decent future, free and peaceful, there must be room, room for the liberation of the energy and the talent of the individual, otherwise our vision is blind at the outset.

We must assure a society here which while never abandoning the needy, or forsaking the helpless, nurtures incentives and opportunity for the creative and the productive.

We must know the whole good is the product of many single contributions. And I cherish the day when our children once again will restore as heroes the sort of men and women who, unafraid and undaunted, pursue the truth, strive to cure disease, subdue and make fruitful our natural environment, and produce the inventive engines of production, science and technology.

This nation, whose creative people have enhanced this entire span of history, should again thrive upon the greatness of all those things which we—we as individual citizens—can and should do.

During Republican years, this again will be a nation of men and women, of families proud of their role, jealous of their responsibilities, unlimited in their aspirations—a nation where all who can will be self-reliant.

We Republicans see in our constitutional form of government the great framework which assures the orderly but dynamic fulfillment of the whole man, and we see the whole man as the great reason for instituting orderly government in the first place.

We can see in private property and in economy based upon and fostering private property the one way to make government a durable ally of the whole man rather than his determined enemy.

We see in the sanctity of private property the only durable foundation for constitutional government in a free society.

And beyond that we see and cherish diversity of ways, diversity of thoughts, of motives, and accomplishments. We don't seek to live anyone's life for him. We only seek to secure his rights, guarantee him opportunity, guarantee him opportunity to strive with government performing only those needed and constitutionally sanctioned tasks which cannot otherwise be performed.

We, Republicans, seek a government that attends to its inherent responsibilities of maintaining a stable monetary and fiscal climate, encouraging a free and a competitive economy and enforcing law and order.

Thus do we seek inventiveness, diversity and creative difference within a stable order, for we Republicans define government's role where needed at many, many levels, preferably though the one closest to the people involved: our towns and our cities, then our counties, then our states, then our regional contacts and only then the national government.

That, let me remind you, is the land of liberty built by decentralized power. On it also we must have balance between the branches of government at every level.

Balance, diversity, creative difference—these are the elements of Republican equation. Republicans agree, Republicans agree heartily, to disagree on many, many of their applications. But we have never disagreed on the basic fundamental issues of why you and I are Republicans.

This is a party—this Republican party is a party for free men. Not for blind followers and not for conformists.

Back in 1858 Abraham Lincoln said this of the Republican party, and I quote him because he probably could have said it during the last week or so: "It was composed of strained, discordant, and even hostile elements." End of quote.

Yet all of these elements agreed on one paramount objective: to arrest the progress of slavery, and place it in the course of ultimate extinction.

Today, as then, but more urgently and more broadly than then, the task of preserving and enlarging freedom at home and of safeguarding it from the forces of tyranny abroad is great enough to challenge all our resources and to require all our strength.

Anyone who joins us in all sincerity we welcome. Those, those who do not care for our cause, we don't expect to enter our ranks in any case. And let our Republicanism so focused and so dedicated not be made fuzzy and futile by unthinking and stupid labels.

I would remind you that extremism in the defense of liberty is no vice.

And let me remind you also that moderation in the pursuit of justice is no virtue!

By the beauty of the very system, we Republicans are pledged to restore and revitalize, the beauty of this Federal system of ours is in its reconciliation of diversity with unity. We must not see malice in honest differences of opinion, and no matter how great, so long as they are not inconsistent with the pledges we have given to each other in and through our Constitution.

Our Republican cause is not to level out the world or make its people conform in computer-regimented sameness. Our Republican cause is to free our people and light the way for liberty throughout the world. Ours is a very human cause for very humane goals. This party, its good people, and its unquestionable devotion to freedom will not fulfill the purposes of this campaign which we launch here now until our cause has won the day, inspired the world, and shown the way to a tomorrow worthy of all our yesteryears.

I repeat, I accept your nomination with humbleness, with pride
and you and I are going to fight for the goodness of our land.
Thank you.

26 / LYNDON JOHNSON AND THE

GREAT SOCIETY

*In his State of the Union message to Congress,
January 4, 1965, President Johnson outlined his
Great Society program.*

World affairs will continue to call upon our energy and our
courage.

But today we can turn increased attention to the character of
American life.

We are in the midst of the greatest upward surge of economic
well-being in the history of any nation.

Our flourishing progress has been marked by price stability
that is unequaled in the world. Our balance-of-payments deficit
has declined and the soundness of our dollar is unquestioned.
I pledge to keep it that way. And I urge business and labor to
cooperate to that end.

We worked for two centuries to climb this peak of prosperity.
But we are only at the beginning of the road to the Great Society.
Ahead now is a summit where freedom from the wants of the body
can help fulfill the needs of the spirit.

We built this Nation to serve its people.

We want to grow and build and create, but we want progress
to be the servant and not the master of man.

We do not intend to live—in the midst of abundance—isolated
from neighbors and nature, confined by blighted cities and bleak

SOURCE: *Congressional Record,* 89th Cong., 1st sess. (1965), pp. 29–31.

suburbs, stunted by a poverty of learning and an emptiness of leisure.

The great society asks not how much, but how good; not only how to create wealth, but how to use it; not only how fast we are going, but where we are headed.

It proposes as the first test for a nation: the quality of its people.

This kind of society will not flower spontaneously from swelling riches and surging power.

It will not be the gift of government or the creation of Presidents.

It will require of every American, for many generations, both faith in the destination and the fortitude to make the journey.

And like freedom itself, it will always be challenge and not fulfillment.

And tonight we accept that challenge.

A National Agenda

I propose that we begin a program in education to insure every American child the fullest development of his mind and skills.

I propose that we begin a massive attack on crippling and killing diseases.

I propose that we launch a national effort to make the American city a better and a more stimulating place to live.

I propose that we increase the beauty of America and end the poisoning of our rivers and the air that we breathe.

I propose that we carry out a new program to develop regions of our country that are now suffering from distress and depression.

I propose that we make new efforts to control and prevent crime and delinquency.

I propose that we eliminate every remaining obstacle to the right and the opportunity to vote.

I propose that we honor and support the achievements of thought and the creations of art.

I propose that we make an all-out campaign against waste and inefficiency.

The Task

Our basic task is threefold—to keep our economy growing, to open for all Americans the opportunity that is now enjoyed by most Americans, and to improve the quality of life for all.

In the next six weeks I will submit special messages with detailed proposals for national action in each of these areas.

Tonight I would like just briefly to explain some of my major recommendations in the three main areas of national need.

A Growing Economy

BASIC POLICIES.   First, we must keep our Nation prosperous. We seek full employment opportunity for every American citizen. I will present a budget designed to move the economy forward. More money will be left in the hands of the consumer by a substantial cut in excise taxes. We will continue along the path toward a balanced budget in a balanced economy.

I confidently predict tonight—what every economic sign now tells us—the continued flourishing of the American economy.

But we must remember that fear of a recession can contribute to the fact of a recession. The knowledge that our Government will, and can, move swiftly will strengthen the confidence of investors and business.

Congress can reinforce this confidence by insuring that its procedures permit rapid action on temporary income tax cuts. And special funds for job-creating public programs should be made available for immediate use if recession threatens.

Our continued prosperity demands continued price stability. Business, labor and the consumer all have a high stake in keeping wages and prices within the framework of the guideposts that have already served the Nation so well.

Finding new markets abroad for our goods depends on the initiative of American business. But we stand ready—with credit and other help—to assist the flow of trade which will benefit the entire Nation.

ON THE FARMS.   Our economy owes much to the efficiency of our farmers. We must continue to assure them the opportunity to earn a fair reward. I have instructed the Secretary of Agriculture to lead a major effort to find new approaches to reduce the heavy cost of our farm programs and to direct more of our effort to the small farmer who needs the help the most.

INCREASED PROSPERITY. We can help insure continued prosperity through:

A regional recovery program to assist development of stricken areas left behind by our national progress;

Further efforts to provide our workers with the skills demanded by modern technology, for the laboring man is an indispensable force in the American system;

Extension of the minimum wage to more than 2 million unprotected workers;

The improvement and the modernization of the unemployment compensation system;

And, as pledged in our 1960 and 1964 Democratic platforms, I will propose to Congress changes in the Taft-Hartley Act, including section 14-B. I will do so hoping to reduce the conflicts that for several years have divided Americans in various States of our Union.

In a country that spans a continent modern transportation is vital to continued growth.

TRANSPORTATION FOR GROWTH. I will recommend heavier reliance on competition in transportation and a new policy for our merchant marine.

I will ask for funds to study high-speed rail transportation between urban centers. We will begin with test projects between Washington and Boston. On high-speed trains, passengers could travel this distance in less than four hours.

Opportunity for All

Second, we must open opportunity to all our people.

Most Americans enjoy a good life. But far too many are still trapped in poverty and idleness and fear.

Let a just nation throw open to them the city of promise:

To the elderly, by providing hospital care under social security and by raising benefit payments to those struggling to maintain the dignity of their later years;

To the poor and the unfortunate, through doubling the war against poverty this year;

To Negro Americans, through enforcement of the civil rights law and elimination of barriers to the right to vote;

To those in other lands that are seeking the promise of America, through an immigration law based on the work a man can do and not where he was born or how he spells his name.

To Enrich the Life of All

Our third goal is to improve the quality of American life.

THROUGH EDUCATION. We begin with learning.

Every child must have the best education that this Nation can provide.

Thomas Jefferson said that no nation can be both ignorant and free. Today no nation can be both ignorant and great.

In addition to our existing programs, I will recommend a new program for schools and students with a first-year authorization of 1 billion 500 million dollars.

It will help at every stage along the road to learning.

For the preschool years we will help needy children become aware of the excitement of learning.

For the primary and secondary school years we will aid public schools serving low income families and assist students in both public and private schools.

For the college years we will provide scholarships to high school students of the greatest promise and the greatest need and we will guarantee low interest loans to students continuing their college studies.

New laboratories and centers will help our schools lift their standards of excellence and explore new methods of teaching. These centers will provide special training for those who need and those who deserve special treatment.

THROUGH BETTER HEALTH. Greatness requires not only an educated people but a healthy people.

Our goal is to match the achievements of our medicine to the afflictions of our people.

We already carry on a large program in this country for research and health.

In addition, regional medical centers can provide the most advanced diagnosis and treatment for heart disease and cancer and stroke and other major diseases.

New support for medical and dental education will provide the trained people to apply our knowledge.

Community centers can help the mentally ill and improve health care for school-age children from poor families, including services for the mentally retarded.

THROUGH IMPROVING THE WORLD WE LIVE IN: THE CITY. An educated and healthy people require surroundings in harmony with their hopes.

In our urban areas the central problem today is to protect and restore man's satisfaction in belonging to a community where he can find security and significance.

The first step is to break old patterns—to begin to think, and work and plan for the development of entire metropolitan areas. We will take this step with new programs of help for the basic community facilities and for neighborhood centers of health and recreation.

New and existing programs will be open to those cities which work together to develop unified long-range policies for metropolitan areas.

We must also make some very important changes in our housing programs if we are to pursue these same basic goals.

So a Department of Housing and Urban Development will be needed to spearhead this effort in our cities.

Every citizen has the right to feel secure in his home and on the streets of his community.

To help control crime, we will recommend programs:

To train local law enforcement officers;

To put the best techniques of modern science at their disposal;

To discover the causes of crime and better ways to prevent it.

I will soon assemble a panel of outstanding experts of this Nation to search out answers to the national problem of crime and delinquency, and I welcome the recommendations and the constructive efforts of the Congress.

THE BEAUTY OF AMERICA. For over three centuries the beauty of America has sustained our spirit and has enlarged our vision.

We must act now to protect this heritage. In a fruitful new partnership with the States and cities the next decade should be a conservation milestone. We must make a massive effort to save the countryside and to establish—as a green legacy for tomorrow—more large and small parks, more seashores and open spaces than have been created during any other period in our national history.

A new and substantial effort must be made to landscape highways and provide places of relaxation and recreation wherever our roads run.

Within our cities imaginative programs are needed to landscape streets and to transform open areas into places of beauty and recreation.

We will seek legal power to prevent pollution of our air and water before it happens. We will step up our effort to control harmful wastes, giving first priority to the cleanup of our most contaminated rivers. We will increase research to learn much more about the control of pollution.

We hope to make the Potomac a model of beauty here in the Capital—and preserve unspoiled stretches of some of our waterways with a wild rivers bill.

More ideas for a beautiful America will emerge from a White House Conference on Natural Beauty which I will soon call.

ARTS AND SCIENCE. We must also recognize and encourage those who can be pathfinders for the Nation's imagination and understanding.

To help promote and honor creative achievements, I will propose a National Foundation on the Arts.

To develop knowledge which will enrich our lives and insure our progress, I will recommend programs to encourage basic science, particularly in the universities—and to bring closer the day when the oceans will supply our growing need for fresh water.

The Government

For government to serve these goals it must be moderate in structure, efficient in action, and ready for any emergency.

I am busy currently reviewing the structure of the entire executive branch of this Government. I hope to reshape and to reorganize it to meet more effectively the tasks of the 20th century.

Wherever waste is found, I will eliminate it.

Last year we saved almost $3.5 billion by eliminating waste in the National Government.

And I intend to do better this year.

Very soon I will report to you on our progress and on new economies that your Government plans to make.

Even the best of government is subject to the worst of hazards.

I will propose laws to insure the necessary continuity of leadership should the President become disabled or die.

In addition, I will propose reforms in the electoral college—leaving undisturbed the vote by States—but making sure that no elector can substitute his will for that of the people.

Last year, in a sad moment, I came here and I spoke to you after thirty-three years of public service—practically all of them here on this Hill.

This year I speak after one year as President of the United States.

Many of you in this Chamber are among my oldest friends. We have shared many happy moments and many hours of work, and we have watched many Presidents together. Yet only in the White House can you finally know the full weight of this Office.

The greatest burden is not running the huge operations of government—or meeting daily troubles, large and small—or even working with the Congress.

A President's hardest task is not to do what is right, but to know what is right.

Yet the Presidency brings no special gift of prophecy or foresight. You take an oath—you step into an office—and you must then help guide a great democracy.

The answer was waiting for me in the land where I was born.

It was once barren land. The angular hills were covered with scrub cedar and a few large liveoaks. Little would grow in that harsh caliche soil of my country. And each spring the Pedernales River would flood our valley.

But men came and they worked and they endured and they built.

And tonight that country is abundant—abundant with fruit,

and cattle, and goats, and sheep. And there are pleasant homes, and lakes, and the floods are gone.

Why did men come to that once forbidding land?

They were restless, of course, and had to be moving on. But there was more than that. There was a dream—a dream of a place where a freeman could build for himself, and raise his children to a better life—a dream of a continent to be conquered, a world to be won, a nation to be made.

Remembering this, I knew the answer.

A President does not shape a new and personal vision of America.

He collects it from the scattered hopes of the American past.

It existed when the first settlers saw the coast of a new world, and when the first pioneers moved westward.

It has guided us every step of the way.

It sustains every President. But it is also your inheritance and it belongs equally to all the people that we all serve.

It must be interpreted anew by each generation for its own needs; as I have tried, in part, to do tonight.

It shall lead us as we enter this third century of the search for "a more perfect Union."

This, then, is the state of the Union: Free, and restless, growing and full of hope.

So it was in the beginning.

So it shall always be, while God is willing, and we are strong enough to keep the faith.

27 / MORE THAN LEGAL EQUALITY IS REQUIRED

In his speech at Howard University, June 4, 1965,
President Johnson called for massive governmental
assistance to enable the Negro to overcome the handicaps
imposed by slavery and racial discrimination.

. . . Our earth is the home of revolution. In every corner of every continent men charged with hope contend with ancient ways in the pursuit of justice. They reach for the newest of weapons to realize the oldest of dreams, that each may walk in freedom and pride, stretching his talents, enjoying the fruits of the earth.

Our enemies may occasionally seize the day of change, but it is the banner of our revolution they take. And our own future is linked to this process of swift and turbulent change in many lands in the world. But nothing in any country touches us more profoundly, and nothing is more freighted with meaning for our own destiny than the revolution of the Negro American.

In far too many ways American Negroes have been another nation: deprived of freedom, crippled by hatred, the doors of opportunity closed to hope.

In our time change has come to this Nation, too. The American Negro, acting with impressive restraint, has peacefully protested and marched, entered the courtrooms and the seats of government, demanding a justice that has long been denied. The voice of the Negro was the call to action. But it is a tribute to

SOURCE: *Public Papers of the Presidents of the United States: Lyndon B. Johnson, 1965* (Washington: Government Printing Office, 1966), II, 635–640.

America that, once aroused, the courts and the Congress, the President and most of the people, have been the allies of progress.

LEGAL PROTECTION FOR HUMAN RIGHTS

Thus we have seen the high court of the country declare that discrimination based on race was repugnant to the Constitution, and therefore void. We have seen in 1957, and 1960, and again in 1964, the first civil rights legislation in this Nation in almost an entire century.

As majority leader of the United States Senate, I helped to guide two of these bills through the Senate. And, as your President, I was proud to sign the third. And now very soon we will have the fourth—a new law guaranteeing every American the right to vote.

No act of my entire administration will give me greater satisfaction than the day when my signature makes this bill, too, the law of this land.

The voting rights bill will be the latest, and among the most important, in a long series of victories. But this victory—as Winston Churchill said of another triumph for freedom—"is not the end. It is not even the beginning of the end. But it is, perhaps, the end of the beginning."

That beginning is freedom; and the barriers to that freedom are tumbling down. Freedom is the right to share, share fully and equally, in American society—to vote, to hold a job, to enter a public place, to go to school. It is the right to be treated in every part of our national life as a person equal in dignity and promise to all others.

FREEDOM IS NOT ENOUGH

But freedom is not enough. You do not wipe away the scars of centuries by saying: Now you are free to go where you want, and do as you desire, and choose the leaders you please.

You do not take a person who, for years, has been hobbled by chains and liberate him, bring him up to the starting line of a race and then say, "you are free to compete with all the others," and still justly believe that you have been completely fair.

Thus it is not enough just to open the gates of opportunity. All our citizens must have the ability to walk through those gates.

This is the next and the more profound stage of the battle for civil rights. We seek not just freedom but opportunity. We seek not just legal equity but human ability, not just equality as a right and a theory but equality as a fact and equality as a result.

For the task is to give 20 million Negroes the same chance as every other American to learn and grow, to work and share in society, to develop their abilities—physical, mental and spiritual, and to pursue their individual happiness.

To this end equal opportunity is essential, but not enough, not enough. Men and women of all races are born with the same range of abilities. But ability is not just the product of birth. Ability is stretched or stunted by the family that you live with, and the neighborhood you live in—by the school you go to and the poverty or the richness of your surroundings. It is the product of a hundred unseen forces playing upon the little infant, the child, and finally the man.

Progress for Some

This graduating class at Howard University is witness to the indomitable determination of the Negro American to win his way in American life.

The number of Negroes in schools of higher learning has almost doubled in fifteen years. The number of nonwhite professional workers has more than doubled in ten years. The median income of Negro college women tonight exceeds that of white college women. And there are also the enormous accomplishments of distinguished individual Negroes—many of them graduates of this institution, and one of them the first lady ambassador in the history of the United States.

These are proud and impressive achievements. But they tell only the story of a growing middle-class minority, steadily narrowing the gap between them and their white counterparts.

A WIDENING GULF

But for the great majority of Negro Americans—the poor, the unemployed, the uprooted, and the dispossessed—there is a much grimmer story. They still, as we meet here tonight, are another nation. Despite the court orders and the laws, despite the legislative victories and the speeches, for them the walls are rising and the gulf is widening.

Here are some of the facts of this American failure.

Thirty-five years ago the rate of unemployment for Negroes and whites was about the same. Tonight the Negro rate is twice as high.

In 1948, the 8 percent unemployment rate for Negro teenage boys was actually less than that of whites. By last year that rate had grown to 23 percent, as against 13 percent for whites unemployed.

Between 1949 and 1959, the income of Negro men relative to white men declined in every section of this country. From 1952 to 1963, the median income of Negro families compared to white actually dropped from 57 percent to 53 percent.

In the years 1955 through 1957, 22 percent of experienced Negro workers were out of work at some time during the year. In 1961 through 1963, that proportion had soared to 29 percent.

Since 1947, the number of white families living in poverty has decreased 27 percent while the number of poorer nonwhite families decreased only 3 percent.

The infant mortality of nonwhites in 1940 was 70 percent greater than whites. Twenty-two years later it was 90 percent greater.

Moreover, the isolation of Negro from white communities is increasing, rather than decreasing as Negroes crowd into the central cities and become a city within a city.

Of course Negro Americans as well as white Americans have shared in our rising national abundance. But the harsh fact of the matter is that in the battle for true equality too many—far too many—are losing ground every day.

THE CAUSES OF INEQUALITY

We are not completely sure why this is. We know the causes are complex and subtle. But we do know the two broad basic reasons. And we do know that we have to act.

First, Negroes are trapped—as many whites are trapped—in inherited, gateless poverty. They lack training and skills. They are shut in, in slums, without decent medical care. Private and public poverty combine to cripple their capacities.

We are trying to attack these evils through our poverty program, through our education program, through our medical care and our other health programs, and a dozen more of the Great Society programs that are aimed at the root causes of this poverty.

We will increase, and we will accelerate, and we will broaden this attack in years to come until this most enduring of foes finally yields to our unyielding will.

But there is a second cause—much more difficult to explain, more deeply grounded, more desperate in its force. It is the devastating heritage of long years of slavery; and a century of oppression, hatred, and injustice.

SPECIAL NATURE OF NEGRO POVERTY

For Negro poverty is not white poverty. Many of its causes and many of its cures are the same. But there are differences—deep, corrosive, obstinate differences—radiating painful roots into the community, and into the family, and the nature of the individual.

These differences are not racial differences. They are solely and simply the consequence of ancient brutality, past injustice, and present prejudice. They are anguishing to observe. For the Negro they are a constant reminder of oppression. For the white they are a constant reminder of guilt. But they must be faced and they must be dealt with and they must be overcome, if we are ever to reach the time when the only difference between Negroes and whites is the color of their skin.

Nor can we find a complete answer in the experience of other American minorities. They made a valiant and a largely successful effort to emerge from poverty and prejudice.

The Negro, like these others, will have to rely mostly upon his own efforts. But he just can not do it alone. For they did not have the heritage of centuries to overcome, and they did not have a cultural tradition which had been twisted and battered by endless years of hatred and hopelessness, nor were they excluded—these others—because of race or color—a feeling whose dark intensity is matched by no other prejudice in our society.

Nor can these differences be understood as isolated infirmities. They are a seamless web. They cause each other. They result from each other. They reinforce each other.

Much of the Negro community is buried under a blanket of history and circumstance. It is not a lasting solution to lift just one corner of that blanket. We must stand on all sides and we must raise the entire cover if we are to liberate our fellow citizens.

The Roots of Injustice

One of the differences is the increased concentration of Negroes in our cities. More than 73 percent of all Negroes live in urban areas compared with less than 70 percent of the whites. Most of these Negroes live in slums. Most of these Negroes live together—a separated people.

Men are shaped by their world. When it is a world of decay, ringed by an invisible wall, when escape is arduous and uncertain, and the saving pressures of a more hopeful society are unknown, it can cripple the youth and it can desolate the men.

There is also the burden that a dark skin can add to the search for a productive place in our society. Unemployment strikes most swiftly and broadly at the Negro, and this burden erodes hope. Blighted hope breeds despair. Despair brings indifferences to the learning which offers a way out. And despair, coupled with indifferences, is often the source of destructive rebellion against the fabric of society.

There is also the lacerating hurt of early collision with white hatred or prejudice, distaste or condescension. Other groups have felt similar intolerance. But success and achievement could wipe it away. They do not change the color of a man's skin. I have seen this uncomprehending pain in the eyes of the little, young Mexican-American schoolchildren that I taught many years ago. But it can be overcome. But, for many, the wounds are always open.

FAMILY BREAKDOWN

Perhaps most important—its influence radiating to every part of life—is the breakdown of the Negro family structure. For this, most of all, white America must accept responsibility. It flows from centuries of oppression and persecution of the Negro man. It flows from the long years of degradation and discrimination, which have attacked his dignity and assaulted his ability to produce for his family.

This, too, is not pleasant to look upon. But it must be faced by those whose serious intent is to improve the life of all Americans.

Only a minority—less than half—of all Negro children reach the age of eighteen having lived all their lives with both of their parents. At this moment, tonight, little less than two-thirds are at home with both of their parents. Probably a majority of all Negro children receive federally-aided public assistance sometime during their childhood.

The family is the cornerstone of our society. More than any other force it shapes the attitude, the hopes, the ambitions, and the values of the child. And when the family collapses it is the children that are usually damaged. When it happens on a massive scale the community itself is crippled.

So, unless we work to strengthen the family, to create conditions under which most parents will stay together—all the rest: schools, and playgrounds, and public assistance and private concern, will never be enough to cut completely the circle of despair and deprivation.

To Fulfill These Rights

There is no single easy answer to all of these problems.

Jobs are part of the answer. They bring the income which permits a man to provide for his family.

Decent homes in decent surroundings and a chance to learn—an equal chance to learn—are part of the answer.

Welfare and social programs better designed to hold families together are part of the answer.

Care for the sick is part of the answer.

An understanding heart by all Americans is another big part of the answer.

And to all of these fronts—and a dozen more—I will dedicate the expanding efforts of the Johnson administration.

But there are other answers that are still to be found. Nor do we fully understand even all of the problems. Therefore, I want to announce tonight that this fall I intend to call a White House conference of scholars, and experts, and outstanding Negro leaders—men of both races—and officials of Government at every level.

This White House conference's theme and title will be "To Fulfill These Rights."

Its object will be to help the American Negro fulfill the rights which, after the long time of injustice, he is finally about to secure.

To move beyond opportunity to achievement.

To shatter forever not only the barriers of law and public practice, but the walls which bound the condition of many by the color of his skin.

To dissolve, as best we can, the antique enmities of the heart which diminish the holder, divide the great democracy, and do wrong—great wrong—to the children of God.

And I pledge you tonight that this will be a chief goal of my administration, and of my program next year, and in the years to come. And I hope, and I pray, and I believe, it will be a part of the program of all America.

WHAT IS JUSTICE

For what is justice?

It is to fulfill the fair expectations of man.

Thus, American justice is a very special thing. For, from the first, this has been a land of towering expectations. It was to be a nation where each man could be ruled by the common consent of all—enshrined in law, given life by institutions, guided by men themselves subject to its rule. And all—all of every station and origin—would be touched equally in obligation and in liberty.

Beyond the law lay the land. It was a rich land, glowing with more abundant promise than man had ever seen. Here, unlike any place yet known, all were to share the harvest.

And beyond this was the dignity of man. Each could become whatever his qualities of mind and spirit would permit—to strive, to seek, and, if he could, to find his happiness.

This is American justice. We have pursued it faithfully to the edge of our imperfections, and we have failed to find it for the American Negro.

So, it is the glorious opportunity of this generation to end the one huge wrong of the American Nation and, in so doing, to find America for ourselves, with the same immense thrill of discovery which gripped those who first began to realize that here, at last, was a home for freedom.

All it will take is for all of us to understand what this country is and what this country must become.

The Scripture promises: "I shall light a candle of understanding in thine heart, which shall not be put out."

Together, and with millions more, we can light that candle of understanding in the heart of all America.

And once lit, it will never again be put out.

28 / THE PROBLEM BEFORE US

Urban affairs expert Daniel P. Moynihan, one of the authors of President Johnson's Howard University speech, examines the crisis facing the United States in the years ahead in this article in The New Leader.

President Johnson is said to be fond of relating the experience of an out-of-work school teacher who applied for a position in a small town on the Texas plains at the very depths of the depression. After a series of questions, one puckered old rancher on the school board looked at the applicant and asked, "Do you teach that the world is round or flat?" Finding no clues in the faces of the other board members, the teacher swallowed hard and allowed he could teach it either way.

That is the position of just about anyone who would assay the state of the American republic at this moment from that middling vantage point known generally as liberalism. Two views are possible: On the one hand, it may be argued that the nation is entering a period of political instability from which it will not emerge intact: on the other, that we have entered a troubled time and will not only survive, but will emerge from it wiser and having demonstrated anew the deep sources of stability in American life.

I cannot imagine what would constitute irrefutable evidence for either stand and I assume that persons adopt one or the other according to their personal taste and condition. The apocalyptic view has many supporters, of course, most notably those of the newly emergent Left who foresee a period of Right-wing oppres-

SOURCE: Daniel P. Moynihan, "The Politics of Stability," *The New Leader*, L, 20 (October 9, 1967), 6–10. Copyright The American Labor Conference on International Affairs, Inc. Reprinted by permission of Mr. Daniel P. Moynihan and *The New Leader*.

sion and excess, followed by the triumph of a new ideology—a conviction that will seem absurd to anyone who has ever visited East Berlin. The more sanguine view commends itself to those who would like to believe it true. This includes, almost without exception, any liberal who has shared considerably in the "rewards" of American life and who can look forward to continued sharing on, if anything, more favorable terms.

The alternatives, then, are to agree with Andrew Kopkind that this past summer the war abroad and the revolution at home contrived to "murder liberalism in its official robes" (with few mourners), or to conclude that although we are in a lot of trouble, we can think and work (and pray) our way out of it. It is worth stressing that no one whose views we have learned to trust over the years would offer us a happier option than the latter, which means that if we do not think well enough, or work hard enough, or if our prayers are not answered, we can bring this republic to ruin.

Certainly things have not turned out as we had every reason to think they would. Walter Lippmann, with merciless clarity, has argued that the unexampled mandate of the 1964 election was "to be quiet and uninvolved abroad and to repair, reform and reconstruct at home." Fate took another direction, and has exacted a double price: not only troubles abroad, but disasters at home because of—or seemingly because of—the troubles abroad. Tom Wicker has stated the matter plainly, as is his failing. "The war," he wrote at the end of last August, "has blunted and all but destroyed the hopeful beginnings of the Great Society. It has produced the gravest American political disunity in a century, and it has aggravated the profound discontent with America of the postwar generations."

The violence abroad and the violence at home—regardless of political persuasion, all agree that these are the problems, that they are somehow interconnected, and that in combination they have the potential for polarizing, then fracturing, American society. But the situation is especially embarrassing for American liberals, because it is largely they who have been in office and presided over the onset both of the war in Vietnam and the violence in American cities. Neither may be our fault, yet in a world not overmuch given to nice distinctions in such matters, they most surely must be judged our doing.

The Vietnam war was thought up and is being managed by the men John F. Kennedy brought to Washington to conduct American foreign and defense policy. They are persons of immutable conviction on almost all matters we would consider central to liberal belief, as well as men of personal honor and the highest intellectual attainment. Other liberals also helped to persuade the American public that it was entirely right to be setting out on the course which has led us to the present point of being waist deep in the Big Muddy. It is this knowledge, this complicity if you will, that requires many of us to practice restraint where others may exercise all their powers of invective and contempt. The plain fact is that if these men got us into the current predicament, who are *we* to say we would have done better?

This is more the case with respect to the violence at home. The summer of 1967 came in the aftermath of one of the most extraordinary periods of liberal legislation, liberal electoral victories, and the liberal dominance of the media of public opinion that we have ever experienced. The period was, moreover, accompanied by the greatest economic expansion in human history. And to top it all, some of the worst violence occurred in Detroit, a city with one of the most liberal and successful administrations in the nation; a city in which the social and economic position of the Negro was generally agreed to be far and away the best in the nation. Who are we, then, to be pointing fingers?

The question is addressed as much to the future as to the past, for the probabilities are that the present situation will persist for some time. . . .

What, as someone once said, is to be done? I offer three propositions.

1—Liberals must see more clearly that their essential interest is in the stability of the social order; and given the present threats to that stability, they must seek out and make much more effective alliances with political conservatives who share their interest and recognize that unyielding rigidity is just as great a threat to continuity of the social order as an anarchic desire for change.

For too long we have been prisoners of the rhetoric that Republicans do not know or care about the social problems of the nation. This is not only a falsehood, but as any New York Democrat can testify, it is seen by the electorate to be a falsehood. In New York City two years ago, Mayor Lindsay was elected because he was the most liberal of the three candidates. Last year, Governor Rockefeller was re-elected for precisely the same reason. The hooting at the callous indifference of Republicans toward human needs recently reached considerable levels in the rumpus over the rat bill. I don't doubt they deserved what they got in that uproar. The argument can nonetheless be made that we would have more to show for it all if somewhere along the line the Democrats had taken at face value the statement of Congressman Melvin R. Laird (R.-Wis.) that he was in favor of "massive" Federal aid to city governments, but not through the techniques of proliferating grant-in-aid programs which he and many like him thought to be an ineffective form of administration.

Interestingly, in the area of foreign affairs the idea that Republican Congressmen and Senators are supporters of a moderate course is more readily accepted. It is time the idea became familiar in domestic matters. It is pleasant to hear the New Left declare that the white liberal is the true enemy because he keeps the present system going by limiting its excesses, yet the truth is that the informed conservatives deserve the greatest credit for performing this function—the Robert Tafts of the nation—and at the present juncture they are needed.

2—Liberals must divest themselves of the notion that the nation—and especially the cities of the nation—can be run from agencies in Washington.

Potomac fever became a liberal disease under the New Deal and it has turned out not only to be catching but congenital having somehow worked into the gene structure itself. The syndrome derives from one correct fact that is irrelevant and two theories that are wrong.

It is certainly a fact that strolling across Lafayette Park to endorse or to veto a public works program is much more agreeable than having to go through the misery of persuading 50 state

Legislatures. But this has to do with the personal comfort of middle-aged liberals, not with the quality of government action, and in a time of some trouble comfort cannot be the sole consideration.

The first theory is that the national government and national politics are the primary sources of liberal social innovation, particularly with respect to problems of urbanization and industrialization. I do not believe history will support this notion, for the cities and to a lesser extent the state governments have been the source of the preponderance of social programs in the 20th century—mostly the cities and states in the North, of course. Probably the most important reason for this is that until recently these were the areas where such problems first appeared, and where the wealth and intellect—and political will—existed to experiment with solutions.

There is another reason which we tend to be reluctant to talk about, but whose discussion is perhaps admissible in a time of trouble. In the spectrum of regional politics, the South has for a century been the most social and politically conservative part of the nation. In the spectrum of American religious groups, American Protestants have fairly consistently been more conservative than American Catholics, and Catholics in turn more so than American Jews. It happens that Washington is, for practical purposes, a Southern Protestant city which combines both these pervasive conservative tendencies—or at least has done so in the past. In an odd combination of historical events, the cities of the North have been dominated by Catholic votes and Jewish intellect, and the result very simply has been a much greater level of liberal political innovation. If this potential has not been much in evidence of late, it is mostly, I believe, because we have allowed state and local governments to get into such fiscal straits that they have no resources left for innovation. But the impulse and potential remain there rather than in Washington.

The second theory I have labelled false is that you can run the nation from Washington. I don't believe you can, at least not with respect to the kind of social change liberals generally seek to bring about. In the field of legislating social attitudes and practices, it is pretty clear that the old-time Tories had a point when they said you can't change human nature—for good or for ill—with a bill-signing ceremony in the Rose Garden. I would note that twenty years ago the Taft-Hartley Act outlawed the closed shop, and that today the closed shop is probably more completely in effect in our building trade unions than ever in history.

The record of social innovation through various public programs is equally unreassuring, largely because the American system of public administration has turned out not to be very good at that sort of thing. Richard Rovere recently noted that "the new Federal agencies set up to deal with the distress of the cities—the Office of Economic Opportunity, the Department of Housing and Urban Development, and the Department of Transportation—have turned in generally disappointing performances." Not because of their leadership, which has often been brilliant, but because of the resources available, and particularly the bureaucracy available. Rovere continues: "In the new agencies, for example, almost everyone feels that there is no greater hindrance to the war on poverty and no greater force for the perpetuation of slums than the public-welfare system administered by, and providing a *raison d'être* for, a huge, entrenched, and complacent sub-bureaucracy in H.E.W." Think of the dreams that had to die before that sentence could be written! But it happens to be true.

"How one wishes," Nathan Glazer writes in a forthcoming article, "for the open field of the New Deal, which was not littered with the carcasses of half successful and hardly successful programs, each in the hands of a hardening bureaucracy." But the pattern persists: the bright idea, the new agency, the White House swearing in of the first agency head, the shaky beginning, the departure eighteen months later of the first head, replacement by his deputy, the gradual slipping out of sight, a Budget Bureau reorganization, a name change, a new head, this time from the civil service, and slowly obscurity covers all. Who among us today could state with certainty exactly what did become of the Area Redevelopment Administration, that early, shining creation of the New Frontier?

But the biggest problem of running the nation from Washington is that the real business of Washington in our age is pretty
much to run the world. That thought may not give any of us
great pleasure, but my impression is that it is a fact and we had
better learn to live with it. Martin Luther King, Jr., and many
other liberals, are no doubt correct in holding that the war in
Vietnam has stalemated government efforts on behalf of Negroes
at home, but they are wrong, I would think, in their proposed
solution: The government should get out of Vietnam. As far as I
can see, an American national government in this age will always
give priority to foreign affairs. A system has to be developed,
therefore, under which domestic programs go forward regardless
of what international crisis is preoccupying Washington at a
given moment. This, in effect, means decentralizing the initiative
and the resources for such programs.

3—Liberals must somehow overcome the curious condescension that takes the form of defending and explaining away anything, however outrageous, which Negroes, individually or collectively, might do.

Over the course of the summer it became clear that there are
two distinct, though related, groups in the Negro community.
One is the vast Negro underclass that has somehow grown up in
our Northern cities; a disorganized, angry, hurt group of persons
easily given to self-destructive violence. Alongside it is a group of
radical, nihilistic youth, not themselves members of this underclass, but identifying with it, able to communicate with it, and
determined to use it as an instrument of violent, apocalyptic con-
frontation with a white society they have decided is irredeemably
militaristic and racist. I do not believe we have yet realized the
depth and intensity of this second group's feelings, nor the extent
to which it has succeeded in politicizing the always existing tor-
ment of the urban masses—persuading them both of the inevita-
bility and the desirability of a nihilistic solution. All the signs
declare that the violence is not ended. Worse still, a new set of
signs tells us something that is painful, even hateful to have to
hear: We must prepare for the onset of terrorism. Indeed, it may
already have begun. How widespread and how successful remains

to be seen, but the probability is so great that ignoring it would be an act of irresponsibility or of cowardice.

For liberals, this poses a special problem that derives in a sense from our own decencies. Trying to be kind, trying to be helpful, we somehow have got into the habit of denying the realities of the life-circumstances of the lower class, and this has curiously paralyzed our ability to do anything to change these realities. Typically, we have blamed ourselves for the shortcomings of the poor —and left it at that. A terrifying example was the response in ultra-liberal quarters to the findings of James S. Coleman in his massive report on *Equality of Educational Opportunity.* Coleman, a distinguished social scientist, concluded that the disastrously low level of educational achievement on the part of most Negro youth was the result not nearly so much of the quality of their schools, as of their own family background and that of their classmates at school. With the hand of the Federal bureaucracy barely concealed, Coleman was labelled a racist by people who went on their way deploring conditions in slum schools and blaming Lyndon Johnson or John Lindsay; they were not disturbed by the thought that they might be wrong, or that the politics of stability might involve something more hardheaded than the untroubled indulgence of sado-masochistic fantasy.

The point is a simple one: There is nothing whatever to be done to change the minds of the Negro nihilists and their white associates, who have been so much in evidence of late. Their course is set. The only option for the nation is to deprive them of the Negro underclass which is the source of their present strength. This means facing up to some of the realities of life in that class that liberals have been notoriously unwilling to acknowledge, so much so that I would not be surprised if it developed that this fact itself was an element in the rage that roared through the streets of America this past summer.

The situation of the Negro masses today is startlingly like that of Yank, the quintessential, apolitical proletarian stoker in one of Eugene O'Neill's plays. Determined to make the world of the first-class passengers recognize his existence, he makes his way to Fifth Avenue and the 50s and begins jostling top-hatted gentlemen and insulting bejeweled, befurred ladies. He elicits only politeness, which actually is a refusal to acknowledge that he is what he knows himself to be. He is driven mad by "I beg your pardons," finally turns violent, and in the end is destroyed.

The time for confronting the realities of black and white has come in America. It will not be pretty. More is the reason that liberals, rather than avoiding or explaining away that reality, should be the ones to work hardest at moving the nation in sane directions. Such words come easy; the effort itself will go against most of our tendencies. But we would do well to remember similar times of crisis in the past when our failure to lead gave the direction of events to others whose purpose was more to destroy than to build. If the politics of stability are to come to anything, they must be translated into programs.

In foreign affairs, surely, this involves the recognition that getting out of Vietnam is not just a matter of summoning the will, but also of finding a way. It is time to acknowledge that the prestige and the credibility of the Armed Forces is involved and is entitled to consideration, as is the self-regard of the tens of thousands of American youths who perform honorably and well in those jungles because they were asked or told to do so by their government. The task of liberals is to make it politically worthwhile and possible for the administration to disengage. This requires that we continue to work within the party system, and to make clear that we do in fact love peace more than we love the Vietcong. It also requires us to be unrelenting in our exposure of what the war really is doing to the Vietnamese people, and of the future obligations which we incur with every day of its prolongation. In this respect, it seems to me that Senator Edward Kennedy's inquiry into civilian casualties is a model of informed and effective liberal action.

In domestic affairs, we have got to become a great deal more rigorous in the assessment not only of the reality of problems, but of the nature of proposed solutions. We have to pay attention to what it is we are good at, and to work from strength. In particular, we must attend to what the Federal government is good at. On examination, this becomes fairly clear. The Federal government is good at collecting revenues, and rather bad at disbursing services. Therefore, we should use the Federal fisc as an instrument for redistributing income between different levels of government, different regions and different classes. If state and local governments are to assume effective roles as innovative and creative agents, they simply must begin to receive a share of Federal revenues on a permanent, ongoing basis. Let us be frank: The original, determining opposition to this proposition in Washington has come from liberals, not conservatives, and we should be ashamed of ourselves.

At stake is not just the viability of municipal governments, but also the sense of urban populations controlling their own destinies. Fifty years of social reform has pretty well destroyed the bases of working class politics in this country. It is not at all funny to note that having broken the power of the bosses, destroyed their control over city jobs and cleaned up the police force to boot, we find the Federal government pouring millions into what Bayard Rustin has termed a "bedlam" of community action programs to overcome the sense of powerlessness among the urban poor, while private donations are sought to enable mayors to hire proletarians who could never pass civil service examinations, and the Justice Department laments the fact that organized crime rather than the police seems to control the streets. The next irony in the history of the Negro in America will be that having acquired a majority of the votes in a number of major American cities, he will find direction of city affairs has been transferred to Washington. Unless we start now to reverse that trend.

Finally, it is also reasonably clear that we must begin getting private business involved in domestic programs in a much more systematic, purposeful manner. Making money is one thing Americans are good at, and the corporation is their favorite device for doing so. What aerospace corporations have done for getting us to the moon, urban housing corporations can do for the slums. All that is necessary, one fears, is to let enough men make enough money out of doing so. It is encouraging to note how much ferment there seems to be in this direction at this time; hopefully, the liberal community will support the effort to involve private business rather than oppose it.

The politics of stability are not at first exciting. It is only when we come to see how very probably our national life is tied to them that they acquire a sudden interest.